Rational Expectations in Macroeconomics

Rational Expectations in Macroeconomics

An Introduction to Theory and Evidence

C. L. F. Attfield, D. Demery
and N. W. Duck

Basil Blackwell

© Clifford Attfield, David Demery, Nigel Duck, 1985

First published, 1985
Basil Blackwell Ltd.
108 Cowley Road, Oxford OX4 1JF, UK.

Basil Blackwell Inc.
432 Park Avenue South, Suite 1505,
New York, NY 10016, USA

British Library Cataloguing in Publication Data
Attfield, C.L.F.
  Rational expectations in macroeconomics: an introduction to theory and evidence.
  1. Rational expectations (Economic theory)——
  Mathematical models   2. Macroeconomics
  I. Title   II. Demery, David   III. Duck, N.W.
  339.3'01   HB199

ISBN 0-631-13663-X
ISBN 0-631-13964-8 Pbk

Typeset by Katerprint Co. Ltd, Oxford
Printed in Great Britain by TJ Press, Padstow

To our parents

Contents

List of Tables and Figures

FIGURES

Preface

In the last 10 years, much of the research and debate in macroeconomics has been dominated by one particular hypothesis. It is a hypothesis about the way in which people in the economy form their expectations of economic variables. The theory is called the rational expectations hypothesis. The first aim of this book is to explain what this hypothesis is. The second aim is to convey some idea of its importance in macroeconomics – in particular what it implies about how the macroeconomy works and what it implies for policies to achieve macroeconomic objectives. The third aim of the book is to explain how the rational expectations hypothesis can be tested using macroeconomic data. And the fourth aim is to give some indication of what has been learnt about the relevance of the hypothesis from the tests that have been carried out.

The book is primarily intended for students who have studied macroeconomics for at least a year and who, therefore, have some idea of the importance of expectations within macroeconomics, but who have not yet studied in any depth the rational expectations hypothesis. The book, therefore, is very much an introduction to the topic; we have not set out to explain all the implications of the rational expectations hypothesis for macroeconomics (even were that possible). To attempt to do so would involve the introduction of material which is technically very demanding, much of which is covered in other books, notably Begg (1982) and Minford and Peel (1983).

Because the book is an introduction, we shall assume only average mathematical skills and where possible use verbal and diagrammatic techniques rather than mathematics to explain points. This, however is not always possible, for the rational expectations hypothesis leads inevitably at times to complications which can only efficiently be dealt with mathematically. This is particularly true in the discussion of the econometric issues raised in testing the rational expectations hypothesis. But even here the mathematics employed rarely requires knowledge of more than simple algebra.

The book is organized as follows. In chapter 1 we illustrate the pervasive importance of expectations in macroeconomics. In chapter 2 we present a general statement of the rational expectations hypothesis which forms the basis of the rest of the book. We also consider some of the general criticisms that have been directed against the hypothesis. Chapter 3 incorporates rational expectations within a simple but widely used closed-economy macroeconomic model and thereby derives some of the most important and controversial results associated with the rational expectations hypothesis. In chapter 4 we examine some of the criticisms that have been made of the model presented in chapter 3. Chapter 5 extends the model developed in chapter 3 to deal with an open economy. In chapter 6 we outline some basic principles for the testing of the rational expectations hypothesis. Chapters 7, 8 and 9 examine some of the more important attempts that have been made to test for the validity of rational expectations within macroeconomics. In chapter 10 we summarize the book and present some conclusions.

During the preparation of this book, the authors were in receipt of a grant from the Leverhulme Trust for research into rational expectations and macroeconomics, which they gratefully acknowledge. They are particularly grateful to Willem Buiter, Angus Deaton, Giancarlo Marini and Caroline Joll for helpful discussions on many of the ideas expressed in this book. They also appreciated help from members of the Leverhulme Workshop in the University of Bristol, especially from John Beath, Paul Bowles, Martin Browning, Richard Dunn, Susan Harvey, Simon Musgrave, Martin Snell, David Webb, David Winter and Alan Winters. The authors are especially grateful to Pat Shaw for the speed and efficiency with which she processed the final text.

C.L.F. Attfield
D. Demery
N.W. Duck
University of Bristol 1984

1

Expectations in Macroeconomics

1.1   THE IMPORTANCE OF EXPECTATIONS IN MACROECONOMICS

It would be difficult to exaggerate the importance of the role expectations play throughout macroeconomics. Few if any of the individual macroeconomic relationships such as the consumption function or the demand for money function are likely to be entirely free from the influence of *expected* variables such as expected income or the expected interest rate. And when these individual relationships are combined to form a full macroeconomic model of the economy the general characteristics and policy implications of that model are likely to be heavily dependent upon precisely how expectations are formed. This book is primarily about one theory of how expectations are formed, the theory of rational expectations. We begin it by illustrating the pervasive importance of expectations in macroeconomics with the use of three examples: the simple Keynesian IS–LM model; the permanent-income hypothesis; and the natural-rate hypothesis.

(a) Expectations in the Keynesian IS–LM model

As a first illustration of the importance of expectations, consider the elementary Keynesian view of the economy expressed in conventional IS–LM terms. According to this view the IS curve is volatile: it is likely to shift by quite large amounts as firms change the amount of investment expenditure they wish to undertake. Such volatility in the IS curve would not be of great importance for the level of aggregate demand in the economy if the LM curve were very steep: it would merely lead to sharp changes in the rate of interest. But another important feature of the elementary Keynesian analysis is that the LM curve is not steep; quite the contrary, it is likely, at times anyway, to be horizontal. It follows then that sharp fluctuations in aggregate demand will occur as sharp shifts in the position of the IS curve interact with a near horizontal LM curve. Indeed this can be seen as the essential message of Keynes's *General Theory*: sharp fluctuations in aggregate demand can originate in the private sector and because they are likely to lead to sharp, undesirable fluctuations in the level of output and employment the government should vary its own expenditures to offset them.

But why do Keynesians believe that the IS curve is volatile and the LM curve horizontal? The general answer to both questions is the same: because of their beliefs about how expectations of certain variables are formed. The volatile IS curve arises in Keynes's view because firms' expectations about the future profitability of their investment projects are themselves highly volatile, or subject to what Keynes himself called 'animal spirits' as explained in the following quotation:

> Most . . . of our decisions to do something positive . . . can only be taken as a result of animal spirits – of a spontaneous urge to action rather than inaction and not as the outcome of a weighted average of quantitative benefits multiplied by quantitative probabilities. Enterprise only pretends to itself to be mainly actuated by the statements in its own prospectus, however candid and sincere. Only a little more than an expedition to the South Pole is it based on an exact calculation of benefits to come. Thus if animal spirits are dimmed and the spontaneous optimism falters . . . enterprise will fade and die – though fears of loss may have a basis no more reasonable than hopes of profit had before. (J. M. Keynes, 1936, pp. 161–62)

Thus a belief about expectations plays the key role in the volatility of the IS curve. Another belief about expectations plays the key role in determining the slope of the LM curve. This concerns expectations about the future interest rate. According to Keynes's view of the demand for money the typical individual holds a view or an expectation of what the future interest rate is likely to be. If the actual interest rate is below its expected value the individual is expecting the interest rate to rise and hence the price of bonds to fall. There will, for each individual, be some actual rate of interest so low that the expected losses from holding bonds just outweigh the interest earned on them. At this interest rate – sometimes called the critical rate of interest – the individual's demand for money becomes extremely responsive to a change in the rate of interest: if the interest rate falls below the critical rate the individual, fearing large capital losses on bond holdings, will wish to hold no bonds and her demand for money will increase sharply. On certain assumptions there will be some interest rate so low that the demand for money in the whole economy will likewise become very responsive to interest-rate changes. It is this extreme responsiveness of the demand for money to changes in the rate of interest – the so-called liquidity trap – which makes the LM curve horizontal and implies that sharp fluctuations in aggregate demand will occur in response to movements of the IS curve. If expectations about the future interest rate changed quickly in response to changes in the actual rate of interest these sharp fluctuations in aggregate demand might be short-lived and for policy purposes unimportant. But Keynes and his followers believed that expectations about the future rate of interest were very slow moving, indeed for most purposes it was assumed that the expected or normal interest rate was for each individual a constant. Thus the LM curve was horizontal at a more or less constant rate of interest.

Expectations therefore play a key dual role in the elementary Keynesian analysis: volatile expectations about the profitability of future investment projects are the source of sharp shifts in the IS curve; near constant expectations about the future rate of interest are part of the mechanism by which such shifts produce sharp movements in aggregate demand.

And of course the precise assumptions made in each case are crucial to the policy implications of the Keynesian model. If they were changed the policy implications could be quite different. For example, if expectations about the future profitability of investment projects were *constant* but expectations about the future level of interest rates highly sensitive to the *current* value of the interest rate, the IS curve might not be volatile and the LM curve not be flat at a constant rate of interest. As a result fluctuations in the private sector's spending plans would not be severe and government measures to offset them would not be so necessary. Thus a major policy implication of the *General Theory* would no longer follow.

(b) Expectations and the consumption function

One development in the post-Keynesian theory of the consumption function has been the concept of permanent income. We shall discuss this more fully in Chapter 9. The essential idea is that when deciding the level of their consumption expenditure people will take into account a fairly long-term view of their income prospects. Thus when deciding how much to spend in any month or year they will not consider merely their actual income in that month or year. Instead their consumption will be related to what is termed their permanent income. It is difficult to define the term permanent income precisely but it is clearly related to expectations about income prospects. Indeed its originator, Friedman (1957), describes the permanent component of income as 'analogous to the "expected" value of a probability distribution' (p. 21).

The actual value of consumption expenditure in any period – which is a key component of total spending in an economy – depends then on an expected variable, in this case expected or permanent income. So here too expectations play a crucial role: if a rise in actual income causes a rise in expected income consumption expenditure will rise, whereas if, when actual income rises, expected income remains unchanged then so will consumption expenditure. And this result has wider macroeconomic implications. If the government increases its own expenditure in an effort to stimulate the economy and if this causes a rise in actual income, there will, according to the Keynesian view of consumption, be further increases in spending because consumption expenditure rises as actual income rises. This is the basic idea behind Keynes's multiplier. But if consumption expenditure is determined by permanent or expected income, and if the rise in government expenditure leaves expected income unchanged then there may not be the type of multiplier process which Keynes predicted. So the method by which people form their expectations about their income may be important not only for the purposes of predicting consumption expenditure, but also for the ability of government policies to affect aggregate demand.

(c) Expectations and the natural rate hypothesis

As a final illustration of the importance of expectations consider the so-called natural rate of unemployment hypothesis as put forward by Friedman (1968). Again, we shall have more to say about this in later chapters but its central point can be made quite simply. Workers are interested not in the *nominal* value of their wage rate, W, but its *real* value – the quantity of goods it will buy – W/P where P is the general level of prices. But whilst workers will know the value of the nominal wage rate that they are receiving they cannot know for certain what the prices of all goods will be when they come to buy them. They will, therefore, have to form an *expectation* of what the general level of prices will be. If their nominal wage and their expectation of the general level of prices together make them think that their real wage is high they will supply more labour, whereas if their real wage looks to them to be low they will not. Imagine now an increase in aggregate spending which is tending to raise prices and is encouraging firms to raise the nominal wage rate they are offering to workers in order to attract more labour. If workers correctly foresee the rise in prices they will realize that the higher nominal wages they are being offered do not imply higher real wages and will therefore not supply any more labour – thus the rise in aggregate spending will have little or no effect on employment. But if workers do not foresee the rise in prices then the higher nominal wage offers will appear to them to imply higher real wages and they will therefore supply more labour. In this case the rise in aggregate spending will have stimulated employment.

The precise method by which workers form their expectations of future prices is therefore crucial to the influence of aggregate spending on employment. And since one way in which governments attempt to influence employment is by influencing aggregate spending it follows that the way in which workers form their expectations is important for the power of government policy to influence employment.

1.2 THE NEED FOR A THEORY OF EXPECTATIONS

The pervasive importance of expectations is at the same time a frustration and a challenge to macroeconomics. It is frustrating because so little data are available on expectations. Data are readily available on prices, interest rates, income, unemployment and many other series. But these are all *actual* or *ex post* variables. There are very few series on expected or *ex ante* variables such as the expected level of prices, the expected interest rate, expected income etc. And the reason is not hard to see: it would be an enormously costly business to ask everyone in an economy what they expected the interest rate to be in the future, or their income, or the level of prices. Of course modern methods of sampling employed by market research firms would render it unnecessary to ask *everyone* what their expectations are but it would still be costly to obtain even a single, continuous and accurate expectations series. What is more, even if the collection of such data were to begin now it would be several years before a sufficiently large amount of data became available. In the meantime the frustration would remain: expectations are theoretically important in macroeconomics but we are unable to test or measure their importance directly because we simply do not have data on expected variables. Even if such series are available there is an additional problem. Beliefs about the future are not easily interpretable. One individual, asked about his future price expectations, may have thought little about it if his own welfare does not depend on being right. Another, say a trade union official negotiating a wage bargain for his workers, may well have thought much more carefully. The expectations series may include both these individuals, weighting them equally. But for the purposes, say, of explaining the behaviour of wages the trade union official's expectation might be much more important. Thus the usefulness of the series on expectations might be severely limited. The general but not complete absence of direct measures of expectations, and the problems associated with them provide a challenge to economists: is it possible to devise a theory of how expectations are formed which is *general* in its applicability, which can be *tested* and which allows us to estimate macroeconomic relationships which include apparently unobservable expectations terms?

The theory of rational expectations can be seen as an attempt to provide such a general theory of expectations formation. We begin our explanation of that theory in the next chapter. As a prelude to that chapter we consider in the remainder of this chapter an important, earlier theory of expectation formation which has been frequently used in empirical work in macroeconomics. This is known as the *adaptive expectations hypothesis*. It has been used extensively to model expected inflation (see particularly Cagan, 1956), and permanent income (see Friedman, 1957), and many other expected variables.

1.3   THE ADAPTIVE EXPECTATIONS HYPOTHESIS

The essential idea of adaptive expectations is simple. Imagine you are forming an expectation about what the rate of inflation will be this year. And imagine that the inflation rate you were expecting for last year was 10 per cent. If last year the actual rate of inflation was 10 per cent it seems plausible that you will not change your expectation about the inflation rate for this year: you will expect 10 per cent for this year too. But if last year the inflation rate was higher than 10 per cent, at say 20 per cent, it seems likely that you will change your expectation of inflation for this year; more precisely it seems likely that you will raise it above 10 per cent but not necessarily all the way to 20 per cent. And if the inflation rate last year was below 10 per cent, at say 4 per cent, it seems likely that you will lower your expectation for this year to somewhere between 10 and 4 per cent. The exact amount by which you raise or lower your expectation is not easy to determine, but the general idea is clear enough. It is likely that people will change their expectations of any variable if there is a difference between what they were expecting it to be last period and what it actually was last period. Specifically, they will raise their expectation if the actual value last period was higher than they were expecting, and they will lower their expectation if the actual value last period was below what they were expecting. If their expectation last period turned out to be correct they will not change their expectation.

This idea that people will adapt or change their expectations in response to last period's error has a number of attractive features. First it implies that if, for example, the inflation rate rises from 5 to 20 per cent and remains there people's expectations of inflation will gradually rise (if they were initially expecting inflation less than 20 per cent), until they have 'homed in' on the new rate of 20 per cent. Similarly if actual inflation falls back again to 5 per cent and remains there then once again people's expectations will gradually fall until they have homed in on the new rate of

5 per cent. So the adaptive expectations hypothesis has this appealing feature that whilst people can be fooled temporarily by the type of changes in the inflation rate we have assumed, they will not be fooled in the longer run. It may, of course, take some time for people to adapt their expectations fully but eventually they will catch on.

In addition to its intuitive appeal the hypothesis is apparently fairly general: we could easily have substituted unemployment, or the interest rate, or the rate of growth of real income for the inflation rate in the previous paragraph and the hypothesis would be just as reasonable.

A third attractive feature of the hypothesis is that it allows us to relate expected unobservable variables to actual observed variables. To see this we must first put the adaptive expectations hypothesis into a simple algebraic form. Imagine that we want to use the concept of permanent or expected income, perhaps to test Friedman's permanent income hypothesis. Of course we do not have a direct measure of expected income, it is unobservable, but if the adaptive expectations hypothesis is correct then the following will be true:

$$Y_t^e - Y_{t-1}^e = \alpha(Y_{t-1} - Y_{t-1}^e) \qquad (1.1)$$

where Y_t^e = expected income in period t;
         Y_{t-1} = actual income in period $t-1$; and
         α = a positive fraction.

This equation can be simply re-written as

$$Y_t^e = \alpha Y_{t-1} + (1-\alpha)Y_{t-1}^e \qquad (1.2)$$

But if equation (1.2) is generally true then it must be true for last period as well, and the period before, and the period before that, and so on. Algebraically we can derive from equation (1.2) equations (1.3)–(1.5)

$$Y_{t-1}^e = \alpha Y_{t-2} + (1-\alpha)Y_{t-2}^e \qquad (1.3)$$

$$Y_{t-2}^e = \alpha Y_{t-3} + (1-\alpha)Y_{t-3}^e \qquad (1.4)$$

$$Y_{t-3}^e = \alpha Y_{t-4} + (1-\alpha)Y_{t-4}^e \qquad (1.5)$$

and so on ad infinitum.

Using equations (1.3)–(1.5) we can substitute for Y_{t-1}^e in equation (1.2) and obtain

$$Y_t^e = \alpha Y_{t-1} + \alpha(1-\alpha)Y_{t-2} + \alpha(1-\alpha)^2 Y_{t-3} + \alpha(1-\alpha)^3 Y_{t-4} + \ldots \qquad (1.6)$$

This links the unobservable variable – expected income – to the observable variables – actual income in all previous periods. Of course one remaining problem is that, taken literally, equation (1.6) implies that to measure expected income this period we need observations on actual income which go back to the beginning of our time period. But if 'α' is less than 1, as seems plausible, then actual income in any period has less effect on current expected income the further back in time that period is. In other words the most recent observations on actual income dominate the formation of expectations about future income. As a result if we link the unobservable expected income to the observable values of actual income in say only the last 5 years we will not be far wrong.

Offsetting these attractive features are a number of disadvantages. First of all it is not always going to be the case that if the actual value of a variable last period exceeded what you were expecting it to be you will raise your expectation of that variable in the coming period. For example, imagine that the government has announced that it intends to increase the money supply over the coming year by 10 per cent. At the beginning of the year you might reasonably expect that the money supply at the end of the first 6 months will be roughly 5 per cent higher than it was at the beginning of the year. But what if it turns out to be 10 per cent higher? Does this make you expect that in the next 6 months the rate of growth of the money supply will be higher than 5 per cent as the adaptive expectations hypothesis suggests? Or does it make you expect a rate of growth of 0 per cent so that over the year as a whole the money supply will have grown in line with the government's stated policy? It is not immediately obvious what you should expect. One certainly cannot rule out the second possibility *a priori*, and so the adaptive expectations hypothesis may be misleading.

A second disadvantage is this. Imagine an economy in which the inflation rate oscillates each period between 0 and 10 per cent. The adaptive expectations hypothesis implies that people will always expect something in between 0 and 10 per cent. But is this likely when the pattern of the inflation rate is so obvious? Why should people expect an inflation rate that never occurs and never expect the inflation rates that do occur?

A related disadvantage of the adaptive expectations hypothesis is that if the variable about which an expectation is being formed is continually rising (or continually falling) then the expectation will always be less than (or greater than) the actual variable. For example, start off with everyone expecting an inflation rate of 0 per cent and let the actual inflation rate be 0 per cent. And let people form expectations adaptively in accordance with the following:

$$\dot{P}_t^e = 0.5\dot{P}_{t-1} + 0.5\dot{P}_{t-1}^e \tag{1.7}$$

where $\dot{P}_t$ is the actual rate of inflation in period t, and $\dot{P}_t^e$ is the expected rate of inflation in period t.

Now let inflation start to rise at a rate of 1 per cent each year. So in year one inflation is 1 per cent; in year two 2 per cent; in year three 3 per cent and so on. In year one expected inflation is 0 per cent because last year expectations of 0 per cent were correct. In year two expectations of inflation will rise to half the difference between actual inflation in year one viz. 1 per cent, and what was expected for last year, viz. 0 per cent. So for year two expected inflation will be 0.5 per cent. For year three expectations of inflation will again be revised to 1.25 per cent; in year four to 2.125 per cent and so on. But each year the actual inflation rate is higher than expected. Is it sensible to assume that people will continue to form expectations in a way which leads them to underpredict the inflation rate every period? Won't they realize that their current method of forming expectations is leading to an obvious, systematic pattern in their fore-casting errors and won't they therefore change the method they are using to forecast the inflation rate? One way in which they might do this, suggested by Flemming (1976), is by 'shifting gear': they might begin to form expectations about the rate of change of inflation rather than the level of inflation. But if they do change the method by which they form expecta-tions, whether by shifting gear or not, the adaptive expectations hypothesis as formulated above is inadequate because it does not give any guide about when or under what conditions such a change in the method of expecta-tions formation will take place, nor about the precise form of the change.

A final criticism of the adaptive expectations hypothesis is that it assumes that typical economic agents limit themselves to a very narrow set of information when they are forming expectations: that is, the hypothesis assumes that people look only at the past values of the variable they are trying to forecast. Why should people do this? Why shouldn't they make use of a lot more information which is readily available and which may have a bearing on the future behaviour of a variable they are trying to predict? As an obvious example take the abandonment of fixed exchange rates in the early 1970's. In the case of the U.K. this move to a more flexible exchange rate regime was accompanied by a large stimulus to the economy in the form of higher government spending and an increased rate of monetary growth. The fixed exchange rate was abandoned explicitly because it was felt that pressures for the exchange rate to depreciate were bound to occur as a result of the sharp boost being given to aggregate demand and the government did not want these pressures to interfere with its aggregate demand policies. In these circumstances it would surely have been foolish to base an expectation of the future course of the exchange rate on past values of the exchange rate alone. People were practically being told that the exchange rate was going to depreciate. Why should they not use that freely available information in forming their expectations about the exchange rate?

This is a particularly dramatic example of a general point. Often, indeed almost always, the information available to people forming expectations about a variable is wider than merely the past values of that variable. At the very least the adaptive expectations hypothesis ought to explain why people might not use that information. All these criticisms imply that the adaptive expectations hypothesis is deficient: it is not an adequate general theory of how expectations are formed. It can be best be regarded as a useful, for some purposes a very useful, empirical approximation.

SUGGESTIONS FOR FURTHER READING

For a general discussion of uncertainty in economics see Shackle (1958). Keynes (1936, Ch. 12) contains an interesting discussion of the formation of expectations with particular reference to expectations about the prospective yields of a capital-asset. Muth (1960) and Walters (1971) are early attempts to apply something like the rational expectations hypothesis to a macroeconomic model.

2

The Theory of Rational Expectations

This chapter provides the foundations for the rest of the book. It explains the theory of rational expectations and examines some of the criticisms of it. In this chapter both the explanation of the theory and the examination of the criticisms are general in nature. This is to emphasize the general applicability of the theory: it is not a theory which *just* applies to expectations about, say, inflation, or income; it is intended as a theory of how expectations of a wide range of economic variables are formed. In later chapters we shall use the theory in specific contexts and thereby derive some more precise results, but here we just establish the basic ideas behind rational expectations. The first, and fundamental one is that many economic variables should be seen as being determined by *processes*. The process determining a variable can be seen as limiting the potential values of that variable and in doing so it provides a basis for a rational expectation. It is this fundamental idea that we now explain.

2.1 VARIABLES AS THE OUTCOME OF PROCESSES

Imagine that you are trying to forecast the behaviour of a variable Y and all you have to go on are the past values or 'history' of Y. And imagine that Y's history can be depicted in the bold line labelled Y in figure 2.1. At the beginning of the current period (t), you are trying to forecast the value of Y over the next five periods. Consider the figure and work out what you would forecast.

Clearly the value of Y has fluctuated between 10 and 20 and so it would be strange if you forecast a value for Y which was greater than 20 or less than 10. Why should such values occur if they have never occurred before? You cannot know for certain that they will not occur but you have no real reason for believing that they are about to. So, at the very least we would expect most people to guess five values of Y which lie between 10 and 20.

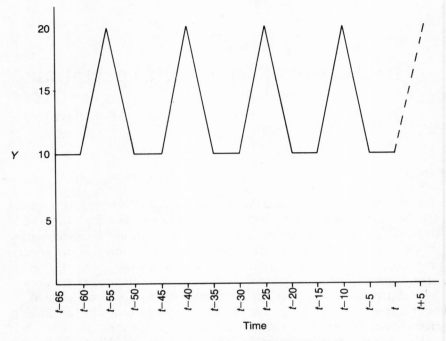

FIGURE 2.1   The behaviour of Y through time.

But we can go further than that, for it is clear from figure 2.1 that up to now Y has followed an obvious and simple pattern. For five periods it takes on a value of 10. For the next five periods it steadily increases by two units per period; and for the five periods after that it steadily decreases by two units per period. It is then constant at 10 for five periods and the process is repeated. Because there appears to be a process governing the behaviour of Y, and because it is possible to see what that process is, it seems natural to use one's knowledge of that process to forecast the next five values of Y. In which case one would make the predictions shown as the dotted line in figure 2.1. If the process governing the behaviour of Y does not change then the actual value of Y will equal the prediction or expectation of Y.

This example is, of course, very simple but it does illustrate a fundamentally important idea. If variables are determined by systematic *processes* – if there are patterns to a variable's behaviour – then if you can find out what these patterns are, it will be a great advantage to you when attempting to forecast the behaviour of the variable concerned. The processes and links will in general be more complex than the very simple process illustrated in figure 2.1 but even when they are, it will nevertheless still be true that if the process determining a variable can be identified, expectations about the variable will be more accurately formed. To illustrate this point we draw in figure 2.2 the 'history' of a variable X up to the beginning of period t, and we label the line X. What would you predict for the next five values of X?

This case is clearly more difficult since the pattern or process is harder to identify. X appears never to rise above 20 or fall below 10; it is often constant at 10; and when disturbed from this value it rises by two units for five periods and then falls by two units for five periods. But it is not easy to predict exactly when X is about to be disturbed. So on the basis of its 'history', X is more difficult to predict than Y. But what if there is a plausible economic theory which says that the value of X in any period is determined by the value of another variable Z in the previous period? In figure 2.2. we plot the 'history' of this other variable Z in the line labelled Z. And it is clear from this line that the behaviour of Z provides the key to the pattern or process determining the behaviour of X.

The variable Z is usually constant at 5, but occasionally it rises to 7.5 for one period and then drops back again. Whenever Z rises above 5 the value of X next period is disturbed from its 'usual' value of 10 and behaves in the way described in the previous paragraph. So the timing of the disturbance to X is now predictable. If Z in the previous period was 7.5 it will trigger a

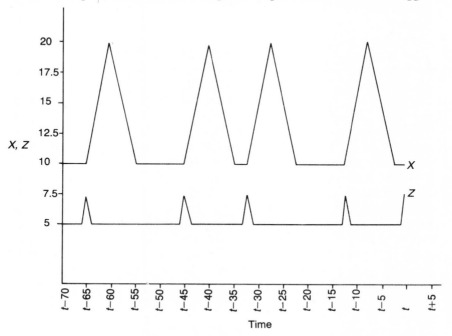

FIGURE 2.2   The behaviour of X and Z through time.

drawn out disturbance in X beginning in the current period. Since in the period immediately before the current period, Z did rise above its 'usual' value it would be sensible to predict that a drawn out disturbance in X was about to occur. Any other prediction would imply either a failure to use all the information available about the process determining X or the use of 'false' information, for example that the process governing the behaviour of X has suddenly changed.

This example takes one stage further the fundamental idea about variables being determined by identifiable processes. In the first illustration the process determining Y was very simple and involved no variable other than Y. In this second example another variable is involved in the process. But the fundamental result is the same and can be stated quite generally: if the process determining a variable can be identified then the prediction of the variable's future value can be improved. This will be true whether the process is very simple as in the case illustrated in figure 2.1, or more complex, as in the case shown in figure 2.2.

An implication of this general result is that predictions of any variable will be improved as more information relating to the process determining the variable is used in forming the prediction. Therefore a sensible forecaster will always use the available information on the relevant process when making a forecast of any variable. A forecaster who does not use the available information on the process is acting inefficiently, his forecast errors will be unnecessarily large.

The inefficiency of forecasts which do not use all the available information relating to the process determining the variable concerned has already been illustrated in Chapter 1. There we described three cases where adaptive expectations were inefficient. In the first, inflation oscillated each period between 0 and 10 per cent; in the second, inflation increased each period by 1 per cent; and in the third, drawn from the actual behaviour of the British Government in the 1970s, the previously fixed exchange rate was to be depreciated as a result of expansionary monetary and fiscal policy. In all three cases expectations about the relevant variable would be more accurate if the process determining the variable concerned were identified and used as the basis for prediction. The patterns or processes in the first two illustrations are very simple. Once identified they allow forecasters to make perfectly accurate predictions. In the third case the process is much more vague, but clearly forecasts of the future value of the exchange rate which take account of the available information on the government's aggregate demand policies will be more accurate than those that do not.

2.2 PROCESSES AND RATIONAL FORECASTS

It is on the basis of these considerations that the theory of rational expectations argues the following. Sensible people will use all the available information relating to the process determining a variable when forming their forecast or expectation of that variable. In economics it is usual to assume that people act sensibly or rationally. Therefore, when modelling how people form their expectations about any variable, economists should assume that expectations are formed on the basis of all the available information relating to the true or actual process governing the behaviour of the variable.

The central idea of the rational expectations hypothesis can be stated formally as follows. Imagine an economic variable, Y, whose value in any period t is *actually* determined by its own lagged values and by lagged values of other variables X and Z in accordance with the following process:

$$Y_t = \alpha_0 + \alpha_1 Y_{t-1} + \alpha_2 X_{t-1} + \alpha_3 Z_{t-1} \tag{2.1}$$

where X, Y, and Z are all variables and α_0, α_1 etc. are constant coefficients.

It is worth emphasizing that this equation is merely an algebraic representation of a *process*, though apparently a more complex one than those shown in figures 2.1 and 2.2. It is also at this stage a very general representation: we have not said precisely what X, Y, and Z represent, nor what the precise values of the α coefficients are. The reason for this generality is that the rational expectations hypothesis is a general hypothesis about expectations formation: it is not meant to apply solely to expectations of inflation, or expectations of income or expectations of anything else. It is put forward as having *general* applicability to a wide range of expectations about economic phenomenon. In fact the hypothesis of rational expectations was originally applied to the problem of forecasting the future price of a good which took time to produce. Its originator was John Muth (1961).

Imagine now that the process described in equation (2.1) has repeated itself sufficiently often for those forming an expectation about Y to be aware of its nature. (Just as when asked to guess the next values of Y in figure 2.1 you were shown a sufficiently long 'history' of Y to be able to identify the process determining Y.) This means that they know which variables are affecting Y, i.e. its own lagged values and the lagged values of X and Z as shown in equation (2.1). It also means that they know the actual values of the coefficients, the αs, because these determine or are part of the process determining Y.

Consider a person at the end of period $t-1$, who is trying to form an expectation about the value Y is going to take in period t. She knows that the process determining Y is given by equation (2.1): knowledge of this process is therefore said to be part of her *information set* at the end of period $t-1$. If, as we shall assume, by the end of period $t-1$ she also knows the value of all the lagged values of Y, X and Z, i.e. all the variables on the right-hand side of equation (2.1), these too are part of her information set at the end of period $t-1$. If she is rational her expectation of what Y is going to be in period t, the expectation being formed on the basis of her information set at the end of period $t-1$, will be formed in line with the process determining Y as follows:

$$E_{t-1}Y_t = \alpha_0 + \alpha_1 Y_{t-1} + \alpha_2 X_{t-1} + \alpha_3 Z_{t-1} \qquad (2.2)$$

where $E_{t-1}Y_t$ is the expectation of Y_t formed on the basis of the information available at the end of period $t-1$.

More formally, $E_{t-1}Y_t$ is equal to $E(Y_t|I_{t-1})$ where E is the mathematical expectations operator and I_{t-1} is the set of information available at period $t-1$. The rational expectation of Y_t formed at period $t-1$ is the mathematical expectation of Y_t *conditional on the available information*. In the remainder of this book E_i is the rational expectations operator for expectations formed on the basis of information dated period i.

It is an obvious implication of equation (2.2) that if Y does indeed continue to follow the process shown in equation (2.1) then this person's expectation will be perfectly accurate. To put that another and, for what follows, more helpful way, the person's *forecasting* or *expectational error* is zero. The expectational error is defined as the difference between the actual value a variable takes and the value the person was expecting it to take.

This result, that the expectational error will be zero every period, is not a general result. It is not generally the case that the rational expectations hypothesis implies forecasters and expectations are always right. We have obtained that result in this case because we have assumed something very special about the process determining Y. We have assumed that it is *deterministic*. Most economic processes are not thought of as deterministic but *stochastic*. This means that they include an inherently unpredictable element. The usual rationalization of this is that economics is about the behaviour of human beings and there is a basic and unpredictable element of randomness in human responses. The way to incorporate this element of randomness in any process such as that shown in equation (2.1) is to add to it a random variable term. This we do in equation (2.3).

$$Y_t = \alpha_0 + \alpha_1 Y_{t-1} + \alpha_2 X_{t-1} + \alpha_3 Z_{t-1} + u_t. \qquad (2.3)$$

Here the term u_t is a random variable which may be positive or negative. Since this variable is seen as the net result of many random factors affecting human behaviour, many pulling in opposite directions it is natural to think of small values of u occurring more frequently than large values. In fact it is usual to think of u as a variable with a probability distribution centered at zero and having a constant and finite variance (σ_u^2).

The really important feature of u is that its value in period t is unknown at the end of period $t-1$. Its value only becomes known at the end of period t, it is not part of the information set at period $t-1$. But it is clear from equation (2.3) that a rational forecaster who is using the process which actually determines Y to forecast at the end of period $t-1$ the value of Y in the current period has to form some expectation of the value u is going to take in period t. That is, the rational expectation of Y in period t based on the information set at the end of period $t-1$ must be formed in accordance with equation (2.3) as:

$$E_{t-1}Y_t = \alpha_0 + \alpha_1 Y_{t-1} + \alpha_2 X_{t-1} + \alpha_3 Z_{t-1} + E_{t-1}u_t \qquad (2.4)$$

where $E_{t-1}u_t$ is the expectation of u_t formed on the basis of all the information available at the end of the period $t-1$.

To be consistent, the rational expectations hypothesis must assume that the expectation formed by the rational person of this period's value of u is made on the basis of the process determining u given the available information at period $t-1$. If, as we shall assume, the process determining u is such that u is a random term with a *mean* of zero whose value cannot be predicted on the basis of any information available in period $t-1$, it follows that the best guess a rational agent can make of the current value of u is that it will equal its *mean* value. In other words the rational expectation of u in period t, based on the information set available in period $t-1$, is that u will equal zero. Formally,

$$E_{t-1}u_t = 0. \qquad (2.5)$$

It follows from this that the rational expectation of Y in period t, based on the information available at period $t-1$, can be written as follows:

$$E_{t-1}Y_t = \alpha_0 + \alpha_1 Y_{t-1} + \alpha_2 X_{t-1} + \alpha_3 Z_{t-1}. \qquad (2.6)$$

If the actual value of Y is determined in accordance with equation (2.3), it follows that the expectational error will be given by equation (2.7).

$$Y_t - E_{t-1}Y_t = u_t. \qquad (2.7)$$

2.3   THE GENERAL CHARACTERISTICS OF RATIONAL EXPECTATIONS

Equations (2.1) – (2.7) are of fundamental importance to the rest of this book, so it is worth repeating what they imply. Equation (2.3) shows that the variable Y is determined by a particular process as described by the right-hand side of that equation. If people who are trying to form an expectation about Y have knowledge of that process it will make sense for them to form their expectation of Y using that knowledge. If at the end of period $t-1$ they know the value of Y_{t-1}, X_{t-1} and Z_{t-1} their expectation of Y for period t will be given by equation (2.6). It follows that if the process determining Y remains unchanged, their forecast or expectational error will be the random component of Y, that is u. A number of important implications follow from the fact that if the process determining Y is understood the error of a rational expectation of Y is the same as the random component of the process determining Y. They are as follows, (a) the mean or average error is zero, (b) there will be no discernible pattern to the expectational error, (c) the rational expectation is in general the most accurate expectation it is possible to form. We discuss each of these characteristics in turn.

(a) The errors of rational expectations are on average zero

It is clear from equation (2.7) that once the process determining Y is allowed to be stochastic, i.e. to include the random component, u, the rational expectation of Y will not always be perfectly accurate. For the random component u is inherently unpredictable. Its value only becomes known after it has occurred, it cannot be accurately guessed beforehand. So even if the process determining Y is known and even if the values of Y_{t-1}, X_{t-1} and Z_{t-1} are known in time to predict Y_t, the value of u_t would not be known. The best the rational forecaster could do is expect the mean or average value of u. But the mean value of u is assumed to be zero. (In fact the mean value of u is really *defined* to be zero. For if the average value of u was not zero but say 5 then the constant term on the right-hand side of equation (2.7) would be defined to be 5 units higher and the random error term redefined as the old one minus 5 so that its mean value was zero.) It follows that the error made each period by the rational forecaster will equal the actual value of u in that period. Sometimes the error will be positive, sometimes negative, sometimes zero. But on average or over a large number of periods the negative errors will cancel out with the positive ones, leaving an average error of zero.

So once the process determining Y is allowed to be stochastic, rational expectations no longer have the implausible characteristic of being perfectly accurate each period. Instead they have the 'softer' feature of being correct *on average*. This is quite consistent with large or even very large errors in any individual period. The size of the expectational error depends upon the size of the unpredictable component of the process itself. If the absolute value of u (remember u can be positive or negative) tends to be large then so will the error of a rational forecast, but that will be because Y is inherently difficult to predict not because of an unintelligent forecasting method. And since u can be large and negative as well as large and positive the mean value of u and hence the average expectational error will still be zero.

(b) The errors of rational expectations exhibit no pattern

In discussing the theory of adaptive expectations we argued that if the variable being forecast was always rising, an adaptive expectation of it would always be below the actual value of the variable. There would, in other words, always be a positive error. The method by which expectations are made is hardly likely to remain unchanged in the face of such an obvious pattern to mistakes. But the adaptive expectations hypothesis does not indicate when the method of forecasting will change or how. It thus admits the possibility of a pattern to forecasting errors but is silent about the likely response to the recognition of such a pattern.

The theory of rational expectations is less vulnerable to this criticism in that it rules out any pattern in forecasting errors and is more precise about when the method of forming expectations will change. For if expectations are rationally formed, the forecasting or expectational error will equal the random element in the process determining the variable being forecast. And by assumption this random element itself exhibits no pattern: it cannot be predicted on the basis of any information available at the time the forecast is being made. Since the random element, u, exhibits no pattern then neither does the forecasting error if expectations are rational. But what if the random element u *does* exhibit a pattern? What if, for example, the current value of u is linked to the previous period's value of u in the following way:

$$u_t = \beta_1 u_{t-1} + \varepsilon_t. \tag{2.8}$$

where ε_t is a random error with zero mean which cannot be predicted on the basis of any information available at the end of period $t-1$ and β_1 is a fraction.

The answer given by the rational expectations hypothesis is simply this. If u is being determined by the process described in equation (2.8) then rational people will form their expectation of the current period's value of u in accordance with that process. And since the value of u in the previous period, $t-1$, will be part of the available information at end of period $t-1$, it follows that the forecast of u will diverge from the actual value of u by the unknown, unpredictable element ε_t. This latter element of course exhibits no pattern and has a mean value of zero. Thus even if u did exhibit a pattern the rational forecast of Y would on average still be correct and the forecasting error would exhibit no pattern. As for the timing of a change in the method of forming expectations the rational expectations hypothesis suggests that so long as the process determining a variable does not change neither will the method of forming expectations. But if the actual process determining a variable is known to have changed then the method by which expectations are formed will change in line with it.

(c) Rational expectations are the most accurate expectations

Forecasts of a variable Y made using all the available information on the *true* process determining Y are bound to be at least as accurate and usually more accurate than forecasts of Y made on some other basis. By the term 'more accurate' we do not mean that in every particular instance the rational expectation will be closer to the actual value of Y than a non-rational expectation. It is perfectly possible to form an expectation stupidly and by chance be right. It would be a fluke, but flukes can happen. However, by their very nature they do not occur regularly. More often than not, the rational expectation, the expectation formed in accordance with the process actually determining the variable, will be a more accurate expectation than one formed on another basis. To put this point another way, however expectations are formed the unpredictable part of Y cannot regularly be predicted. So any method of expectations formation will be inaccurate to a degree determined by the likely range of values that u can take. But it is possible to be even more inaccurate by forecasting without reference or with only partial reference to the process determining the variable. Thus there is no scope to be more accurate than the rational expectations method, but there is plenty of scope to be less.

This point can be expressed formally as follows. The unpredictability of the variable Y arises because of the presence of the random element u. This latter variable has a mean of zero but in any period can take on a positive or negative value. However, there are certain limits to the possible values of u, that is u can be seen as having a finite variance, σ_u^2. From this variance we can tell how likely it is that any given value of u will occur. If the variance of u is very high then very high (absolute) values of u are quite likely to occur. If the variance of u is very low then only low (absolute) values of u are likely to occur. The variance of u can therefore be seen as measuring the inherent unpredictability of Y. The higher the variance of u the more unpredictable Y is, and so the more inaccurate any forecast of Y is likely to be. In the limit, if the variance of u is zero Y is perfectly predictable: u is always zero, it never varies and so we are back to the case illustrated in equations (2.1) and (2.2). At the opposite extreme if the variance of u is infinite then Y is a perfectly unpredictable variable: its value could be anything between plus and minus infinity. In general we shall be dealing with the more plausible case where u has a non-zero but finite variance.

The actual size of the variance of u sets an upper limit on the accuracy of any method of forecasting Y. But if expectations are formed rationally the expectational error in any period is identified as the random element u in that period. The likely range of the forecasting errors is therefore the same as the likely range of the unpredictable component of the process determining Y. In this case then the upper limit of accuracy is reached. With any other method of forecasting the level of accuracy over any significant length of time can only be lower, it cannot be higher. In this formal sense then rational expectations are the most efficient method of forecasting: the variance of the forecasting errors will be lower under rational expectations than under any other method of forecasting or forming expectations.

2.4 GENERAL CRITICISMS OF THE THEORY OF RATIONAL EXPECTATIONS

Now that we have stated what a rational expectation is – one formed using all the available information relating to the actual process determining a variable – and now that we have examined the main characteristics of the forecasting errors from rationally formed expectations – a mean of zero, no pattern to them, and the lowest variance of any forecasting method – we turn to some criticisms of the rational expectations hypothesis *per se*. In subsequent chapters we discuss the implications of the rational expectations hypothesis for macroeconomics and the criticism directed against it in that context.

The main criticisms of the rational expectations hypothesis *per se* can be grouped under four headings, (a) the plausibility of rationality itself, (b) the assumptions it makes about the availability of information, (c) the limits to its applicability, and (d) the scope for testing it.

(a) The plausibility of rationality

One criticism of the rational expectation hypothesis takes the following form. Is it really at all plausible to assume that when forming expectations the typical individual is sufficiently sensible to use all the available information about the process determining a variable? Is it not rather the case that in reality people are often very ignorant about economic matters? How many people, for example, would be able to give a reasonably precise definition of what the money supply is, let alone tell you at what rate it has been growing? Yet information on the growth of the money supply is fairly easy to come by and many economists believe that the rate of growth of the money supply plays a key role in the process by which the rate of inflation is determined. So if people are forming rational expectations about the rate of inflation they ought to know what the money supply is and how it has been growing. Essentially this criticism is that a major assumption behind rational expectations is wholly implausible.

There are a number of responses that can be made to this criticism. First of all the idea that the typical individual is capable of making the best of the opportunities open to him is a common one in economics. For example in demand theory it is assumed that the typical person chooses to consume goods at a point given by the tangency of an indifference curve and a budget constraint. The mathematics behind this choice strategy is highly sophisticated and for the vast majority of people completely unintelligible. Yet it is assumed that people act as if they understand it. Similarly firms are assumed to act as if they understood the complicated mathematics behind the requirement that they select that level of output at which marginal cost equals marginal revenue.

No-one believes that the typical consumer or firm really could explain the mathematical complexities involved in making the best of the opportunities open to them. But the important questions are how good are the theories which assume that consumers and firms act as if they do understand these complexities at predicting the data on what consumers buy and what output levels firms decide on? If the result of assuming that firms and consumers act as if they do understand these complexities, are theories which make accurate predictions then the assumption of mathematical awareness is thereby shown to be a useful one.

The idea that people make the best of the opportunities open to them when forming expectations can be justified along the same lines. In other words the ultimate test of the usefulness of the assumption that people act rationally when forming their expectations is the accuracy of the predictions made by the theory of rational expectations. However, it may be felt unwise to consider such tests of rationality in expectations formation without first providing some arguments for the intuitive plausibility of the assumption. One such argument is that in many instances the typical *individual* does not have to form an expectation on his own: other people will do it for him. These other people may be firms who specialize in or provide the service of making economic forecasts; they may be trade unions who negotiate wage claims for their members; or they may be government bodies who make their forecasts public. All of these will have an incentive to provide the best forecasts they can of any variable and as we have seen this implies an incentive to form expectations rationally. On this argument then the fact that the typical *individual* cannot define the money supply is irrelevant: he obtains forecasts from people who can, and is, if you like, rational at one remove. A second argument in favour of the intuitive plausibility of the assumption of rationality is that irrational expectations can lead to overprediction or underprediction. It is not at all clear that irrationality should consistently lead to one or the other. Some individuals might irrationally overpredict and others irrationally underpredict. This is quite consistent with expectations on average being rational.

A more subtle criticism of the role of rationality in the rational expectations hypothesis is this. Usually in economic theory rationality implies that the typical person weighs up the costs and benefits of any activity and carries out that activity up to the point where the marginal costs of it equal the marginal benefits. So, for example, a firm increases its level of output up to the point where the marginal revenue gained from producing and selling an additional unit of output is equal to the marginal cost of so doing. When applied to expectations formation this principle implies that forecasters should weigh up the marginal costs of acquiring more information about the process determining a variable and the marginal benefits of making more accurate forecasts. When the two are equal forecasters should not attempt to acquire any more information to improve their forecasts, it is not worth it. But the point at which the marginal costs and marginal benefits are equal does not necessarily correspond to the point at which the forecasting error is equal to the purely random component of the determining process. It may be that knowledge about some determining variable could be obtained and extra accuracy thereby achieved but only at a price which it is not worth paying. In which case the forecasting error will tend to be absolutely greater than the random element in the determining process.

This criticism is a valid one but for most purposes not one of great significance. The reason for this is that forecasting errors themselves are observed at no cost. For example any error in your forecast about the level of prices is observed as a costless side effect of shopping. In other words the marginal cost of information about one's forecasting errors is negligible. It must therefore be worthwhile to exploit this information fully, until its marginal benefit is zero. Two implications of this are that the average error of expectations will be zero and the errors themselves will exhibit no pattern. For if either of these is not the case the information on past errors is not being fully exploited. Hence two of the characteristics of rational expectations would remain even where expectations are formed after a weighing up of the costs and benefits of acquiring information. All that would be different is that expectations would be less efficient than they could be if all the available information was used. But they would still be more accurate than expectations formed by any other method.

(b) The availability of information

In outlining the theory of rational expectations we assumed that the process determining Y is known and that the values of the variables in that process are known at the end of period $t-1$. But what if the process determining Y contains variables whose values are not known at the end of period $t-1$? How will a rational agent forecast the value of Y in period t then? And how exactly do people learn the nature of the process determining Y?

The first of these questions has a straightforward answer. If, at the end of period $t-1$ the rational agent does not know the true value of X in period $t-1$ and if the value of X in period $t-1$ determines the value of Y in period t then in order to form a rational expectation of Y in this period the agent will have to form an expectation of the value of X in period $t-1$. And of course this expectation of the value X took in period $t-1$ will be a rational one, it will use all the information on the process determining X that is available when the expectation is being made.

For example, let the process determining Y be as shown in equation (2.9).

$$Y_t = \alpha_0 + \alpha_1 Y_{t-1} + \alpha_2 X_{t-1} + \alpha_3 Z_{t-1} + u_t. \tag{2.9}$$

where the notation is as before.

But let the value of X_{t-1} be unknown at the end of period $t-1$; it may be a variable like industrial production which is difficult to calculate and takes time to be published. And let the process determining X in any period t be as shown in equation (2.10).

$$X_t = \beta_0 + \beta_1 V_{t-1} + \beta_2 W_{t-1} + \varepsilon_t. \tag{2.10}$$

where V and W are other variables; the βs are coefficients; and ε is a random error term with mean zero.

If the process determining X is known and if at the end of period $t-1$ the forecaster knows the value of all the variables which influenced X in period $t-1$ except the random term, ε_t, then the rational forecast of the unknown value of X in period $t-1$ will be as shown in equation (2.11).

$$E_{t-1} X_{t-1} = \beta_0 + \beta_1 V_{t-2} + \beta_2 W_{t-2}. \tag{2.11}$$

This expectation of the value of X in period $t-1$ will be used in place of the actual value of X in period $t-1$ in the forecast of the value Y for period t. Thus if the value of X in period $t-1$ is unknown the rational expectation of Y in period t using all the information available at the end of period $t-1$ will be as shown in equation (2.12).

$$E_{t-1} Y_t = \alpha_0 + \alpha_1 Y_{t-1} + \alpha_2[\beta_0 + \beta_1 V_{t-2} + \beta_2 W_{t-2}] + \alpha_3 Z_{t-1}. \tag{2.12}$$

The forecasting error will therefore be given by equation (2.13) as:

$$Y_t - E_{t-1} Y_t = u_t + \alpha_2 \varepsilon_{t-1}. \tag{2.13}$$

Since both u_t and ε_t are random errors with means of zero, and neither can be even partly predicted on the basis of any information available at the end of period $t-1$, it follows that the forecasting error has a mean of zero and cannot be predicted on the basis of any information available at the end of period $t-1$. Furthermore if the actual value taken by X in period $t-1$ is for whatever reason unknown at the end of period $t-1$ the forecast of Y shown in equation (2.12) and identified as the rational forecast or expectation will in general be the most accurate forecast. No other forecasting method will reach this upper limit of accuracy imposed by the random element in the process determining Y and the random element in the process determining X in period $t-1$.

So the question, What are the implications for rational expectations if the process determining Y contains a variable whose value is unknown at the time the forecast is to be made?, is a relatively easy one to answer. Much more difficult is the question of how people become aware of the process determining a variable. How do they know which variables are important influences on Y, and how do they know the actual size of the coefficients in the process determining Y, i.e. the values of the αs in equation (2.9)?

The usual answer is in line with the approach to rational expectations adopted at the beginning of this chapter. The rational expectations hypothesis is seen as applying to processes which recur and are therefore at least capable of being identified. And of course there is an incentive to improve the accuracy of one's forecasts by discovering the process determining a variable. But the fact that there is an incentive to improve accuracy does not guarantee that the process determining a variable will be discovered. After all, there is an incentive to forecast inflation accurately but still quite fierce disagreement amongst professional economists about what the actual process determining inflation is.

This point is a serious one but there are a number of arguments that can be put forward in favour of retaining the assumption that rational forecasters know the process determining a variable. First, as more evidence becomes available about the process, the process should become more rather than less precisely known. Knowledge of the process is therefore likely to be growing, and the assumption that people know the process is therefore becoming more true rather than less true. This argument illustrates an important feature of the rational expectations hypothesis. Rational expectations are an *equilibrium* concept: models of any economic variable in which expectations play a part but which do not assume rational expectations cannot be full equilibrium models. For if more information is becoming available about the process determining the variable and if this is leading to changes in the method by which expectations are formed then clearly the method of expectations formation is not 'at rest', and so the model itself is not in full long-run equilibrium. The assumption of rational expectations can in this sense be seen as helping to define the full equilibrium.

A second, related argument is that the imposition of any other assumption is likely to be just as arbitrary as the assumption of knowledge of the process. What determines which part of the process is known and which part is not? At the very least some reason ought to be given for believing that the process is not known, and some justification given for imposing a particular non-rational method of expectations formation. This is especially true when expectations of a variable are used as part of a model in which the actual value of that variable is determined.

These last two arguments can be illustrated by the liquidity trap version of Keynes's IS–LM model in which expectations of the rate of interest help to determine the actual value of the rate of interest. The Keynesian IS–LM model can, of course, be viewed as a theory of the process by which the rate of interest is determined. And if that model or theory is being put forward as the correct one, it is at the same time being identified as the true process determining the rate of interest. In which case rational people should forecast the rate of interest in line with that process. Yet in the standard textbook version of Keynes's model the expected rate of interest is not the same as the rate of interest that the model predicts. Rather the normal or expected rate of interest is arbitrarily assumed to be a constant which is slightly above the actual rate of interest. Thus expectations are not being formed in accordance with the process identified by Keynes as determining the rate of interest. To have within the same model one process determining the expectation of a variable and quite another determining its actual value is highly unsatisfactory. At the very least it suggests that the process identified as determining the actual variable is unstable; it will change as people change their ideas until the process determining expectations and the process determining the actual variable become one and the same.

A final justification of the assumption that the process determining a variable is known is the empirical one mentioned above. The ultimate test of the assumption is the accuracy of the predictions to which it leads. If it leads to predictions which are consistently inaccurate it should be discarded; if it does not then it can be usefully retained.

Of course even if the process determining a variable is not known there is no obvious reason why this should lead to forecasting errors which do not have a mean of zero and which exhibit some discernible pattern. Thus there are still reasons for believing that typical forecasts will exhibit two of the key features of rational forecasts: an average error of zero and no pattern to the errors. For if they do not it implies that forecasters are not fully exploiting the costless information provided by their own errors.

(c) The limits to the applicability of rational expectations

As we have emphasized the rational expectations hypothesis is seen as applying to variables which are determined by recurring processes which are stochastic. The characteristic features of the errors of rational forecasters were derived above from an analysis of just such a process. But in many instances in economics the variable about which expectations are being formed may not be of this type.

A recent example is provided by the early years of the Thatcher Government in the UK. This government was committed to 'tight' monetary and fiscal policy. Yet many people doubted that government's ability to maintain such policies for very long and there was much speculation about whether, indeed when, Mrs Thatcher herself or a replacement would abandon them. And there were good reasons for believing that such a 'U-turn' was not far away. A significant number of Conservative MPs and even Cabinet Ministers were known to be unsympathetic to the policies being pursued; unemployment was rising at what was for the post Second World War period a spectacularly high rate; and the government was performing badly in by-elections. After the Falklands crisis of course speculation about a 'U-turn' largely vanished. But before then it would have been perfectly reasonable for an intelligent observer to expect higher monetary growth in the future than actually occurred. And, moreover, it would have been perfectly reasonable to go on expecting it even though it kept not occurring. So over the period until the Falklands crisis a perfectly rational person might have persistently overestimated future monetary growth because he attached a non-zero probability to a 'U-turn'. His expectational error over this period at least would not have averaged zero.

A much earlier example is provided in the following quotation.

> One incidental by-product of our analysis is to illustrate a limitation of much recent work on rational expectations. One way that concept has been made operational is by regarding rationality of expectations as requiring that on the average expectations are correct and hence by testing rationality of expectations by direct or indirect comparisons of expectations with the subsequent values of the variables about which expectations were formed. But consider the period from 1880 to 1896. It was surely not irrational according to a commonsense interpretation of that term for participants in the financial markets to fear that growing political support for free silver would lead the United States to depart from the gold standard and to experience subsequent inflation. Indeed, the longer the deflation proceeded, the more pressure built up for free silver, and the higher

an intelligent observer might well have set his personal probability of inflation within, say, three years.

As it happened, the departure from gold was avoided. That does not prove that the persons who bet the other way were wrong – any more than losing a two to one wager that a fair coin will turn up heads proves that it was wrong to take the short end of the wager. Given a sufficiently long sequence of observations, of course, it could be maintained that all such events will ultimately average out, that in the century of experience our data cover, for example, there are enough independent episodes so that it is appropriate to test rationality of expectations by their average accuracy. But that is cold comfort, since few studies cover so long a period, and our aim is surely to derive propositions that can be applied to shorter periods . . . (Friedman and Schwartz, 1982, pp. 556–7)

The general point which these two specific examples illustrate is that many events about which expectations have to be formed cannot easily be seen as the result of a recurring process which it is possible to discern and exploit. On the contrary many important economic events can genuinely be seen as unique, or at least exceptional or unusual. In what sense can the rational expectations hypothesis be said to apply to these exceptional cases?

The first point to make here is that it is perfectly true that the rational expectations hypothesis can best be applied to variables or events which can be seen as part of a recurring process. However, this class of events may be a larger one than is commonly thought. For example, in the last 30 years in the UK government policy has tended to oscillate between tight and loose fiscal and monetary policy. At the beginning of each expansionary phase the switch of policy has often been presented as unique, as a new and bold experiment, a 'dash for growth'. And, of course, it is always possible to analyse it in terms of the personalities of the politicians involved in its design, the particular political circumstances of the day and so on. Such analysis would emphasize its unique or exceptional nature. But at a deeper level such switches of policy could be seen as part of a fairly regular and reasonably predictable process, one element in which is the desire by governments to have a high level of economic activity at the time of a general election. So an event which could be portrayed as unique may well from another viewpoint be part of an underlying recurring process.

Even where events cannot be seen in this way there is no obvious reason for abandoning the assumption that all the relevant, available information will be used in forming expectations. The belief, mentioned above, that the Thatcher Government was likely to perform a 'U-turn' was presumably prompted by an examination of the political circumstances of the day plus some 'feel' for the likely force they would exert and the resistance they would meet. This 'feel' was almost certainly partly determined by previous experience of the same sort of circumstances, in the case of the Thatcher Government the experience of the previous Conservative administration which *had* performed a 'U-turn' in its economic policy. Even in these cases then expectations are likely to be formed from an intelligent appraisal of circumstances (after all no-one was seriously predicting a drastic *tightening* of the policies being pursued by the Thatcher Government), though the process behind such circumstances may be a lot harder to discern.

(d) The testability of the rational expectations hypothesis

Some have criticized the rational expectations hypothesis on the grounds that it is not testable. There are a number of layers to this criticism. First, if the rational expectations hypothesis is taken rather loosely to imply that people make the best of their available information then it may always be possible to define the available information so that the hypothesis becomes immune from falsification. This criticism would be perfectly valid if tests of the rational expectations hypothesis tended to employ the loose form of the hypothesis. But they do not. On the contrary they tend to employ very strong versions of the hypothesis in which people's knowledge of the process determining a variable is assumed to be the same as the best estimate that can be made of that process by standard econometric techniques. A theme of this book is that this frequently made assumption leads to predictions which are both clear and different from the predictions derived from other theories about expectations. To put that another way, the imposition in a wide variety of contexts of the strong version of rational expectations leads to significant restrictions on what we should and should not observe. One can therefore test the rational expectations hypothesis in a wide variety of contexts by seeing whether we do observe what the rational expectations hypothesis predicts we should not, and whether we do not observe what the rational expectations hypothesis predicts we should. This first criticism of the testability of the rational expectations hypothesis is hardly a strong one.

A more subtle criticism is that expectations about a variable are almost always only *part* of a model. Tests of models which incorporate the rational expectations hypothesis are therefore always *joint* tests of the rational expectations hypothesis itself *and* the rest of the model. If the model fails the tests to which it is subjected one can always 'rescue' the rational expectations hypothesis by arguing that it is the rest of the model which is wrong. For example, as we shall see in a later chapter, when combined with the assumption that consumption expenditure is a constant proportion of permanent or expected income the rational expectations hypothesis produces some quite distinctive predictions. If the data find these predictions are very wrong then it would always be possible to argue that the form of the relationship between consumption and permanent income was misspecified and that it was this misspecification rather than the assumption of rational expectations which was causing the model to be rejected.

This criticism has some force, though of course it applies equally to other theories about how expectations are formed. However, it is at times possible, as we shall see later in the book, to distinguish between the restrictions imposed on the data by the rational expectations hypothesis itself and the restrictions imposed by the rest of the model. It is then possible to go some way towards testing the rational expectations hypothesis itself. However, this may not always be possible and the usefulness of the rational expectations hypothesis can then only be tested informally and less satisfactorily. For example, as we have said, the rational expectations hypothesis can be applied in a wide variety of contexts; if, time after time, the models incorporating rational expectations were rejected then this would almost certainly force a rejection of the rational expectations hypothesis.

A related, and even more subtle, criticism of the testability of rational expectations models is what is known as 'observational equivalence'. We shall discuss this more fully in later chapters, but it is worth giving a brief description of it here. In fact it is a general problem, not only in economics but in other subjects too, but it has been much discussed in the context of rational expectations where it takes the following form. For any rational expectations model which 'fits the data' there will always be a non-rational expectations model which fits the data equally well. For it is always possible to devise a non-rational expectations model which has exactly the same implications for any given set of data as the rational expectations model. The data themselves cannot discriminate between the two theories which are said therefore to be observationally equivalent. The obvious implication of this is that even if a rational expectations model 'passes' conventional empirical tests that does not necessarily imply that one should accept the hypothesis. Whether you do or do not depends not so much on the test but on whether you find it more 'plausible' on some other unspecified grounds than the non-rational expectations model.

SUMMARY

At the end of this chapter it is worth summarizing its main themes since their development or application in different contexts constitutes the rest of the book. Many economic variables can be thought of as being determined by processes. A rational expectation of a variable is one which is formed in accordance with the process determining that variable and which uses all the available information relating to that process. It is more natural to think of such expectations being formed about variables which are determined by recurring processes rather than variables which are unique or 'unusual' events since the recurrent nature of the process is what allows it to be discerned. Rational expectations are in this sense an equilibrium concept in that they are best seen as applying to processes which have recurred sufficiently often to have been discerned. Rationality of expectations thus helps to define full equilibrium.

The characteristic features of the errors of rational forecasts are that their mean is zero, that they exhibit no pattern and that their variance is at least as low as the variance of errors produced by any other method of expectations formation. Because of the pervasive role of expectations in macroeconomics it is possible to apply the theory of rational expectations in a wide variety of macroeconomic contexts. Such application reveals that the theory of rational expectations has some very strong implications for the general characteristics of macroeconomic models, for the individual components of those models and for government economic policy. And because of its strong and distinctive predictions it is possible to test it and thereby come to some conclusions about its usefulness. In the next three chapters we apply the rational expectations hypothesis in a number of macroeconomic contexts to illustrate the implications of rational expectations mentioned above. After that we consider methods of testing the rational expectations hypothesis and some of the results of so doing.

SUGGESTIONS FOR FURTHER READING

Shiller (1978), Fellner (1980) and Friedman (1979) contain various criticisms of the rational expectations hypothesis. The Friedman reference is particularly relevant to the first two chapters of this book in that it suggests that under certain assumptions about the sensible use of available information rational expectations and adaptive expectations become very similar. Lucas (1977) presents a very simple application of the idea of rational expectations to the problem of the business cycle.

3

Rational Expectations and a Flexible Price Macroeconomic Model

Some of the most controversial implications of the rational expectations hypothesis occur when it is combined with a flexible price version of the standard aggregate demand/aggregate supply macroeconomic model incorporating the natural-rate hypothesis, for the result is a model which suggests that the post-war emphasis on the manipulation of fiscal and monetary policy to stabilize real output and employment has been misplaced and that a different approach to macroeconomic policy will produce results which will be at least as good and probably better. In this chapter we shall explain this major result in detail, maintaining throughout the assumption that prices move freely to equate supply and demand. In the next chapter we shall examine the attacks on this major result and on the model on which it is based. We begin the present chapter with a brief revision of the aggregate demand curve.

3.1 THE AGGREGATE DEMAND CURVE

In Figure 3.1 we have drawn a conventional IS–LM diagram. The IS curve shows combinations of the level of real income and the level of the nominal interest rate (i) for which it is true that the aggregate demand for output equals the actual quantity of output. It is drawn for given levels of certain key variables such as the level of real government expenditure, tax rates and the level of autonomous expenditure. The LM curve shows combinations of the level of real income and the level of the nominal interest rate for which it is true that the quantity of money demanded equals the quantity of money supplied. It too is drawn on the assumption that the values of certain key variables are given, in this case the quantity of money and, importantly, the general level of prices.

Let the relevant IS curve be the one labelled IS_0, and the relevant LM curve be initially the one drawn for the general level of prices (P_0) and

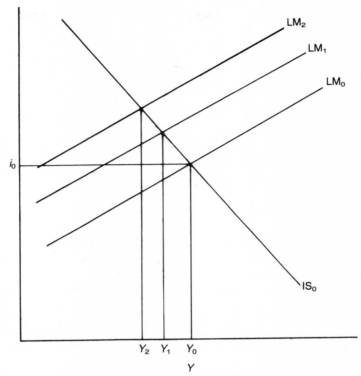

FIGURE 3.1   Equilibrium output at different prices.

labelled LM_0. The point at which these two curves intersect gives the equilibrium interest rate and the equilibrium level of aggregate demand, i_0 and Y_0 respectively. This level of aggregate demand, Y_0 is the equilibrium level in the sense that if that level of output, Y_0, is actually produced each period then all that output and no more will be willingly demanded each period. Clearly the equilibrium level of aggregate demand is dependent on the positions of the IS and LM curves. In particular if the general level of prices is higher at, say, P_1 the LM curve will be to the left of LM_0 at, say, LM_1 and the equilibrium level of aggregate demand will be lower at Y_1. And if the general level of prices is higher still at, say, P_2 the LM curve would be even further to the left at, say, LM_2 giving an even lower equilibrium level of aggregate demand, Y_2.

In Figure 3.2 we draw the line which plots the different values of P, the general level of prices, against the equilibrium levels of aggregate demand which they generate, given the values of all the other variables which determine the positions of the IS and LM curves, such as the level of real

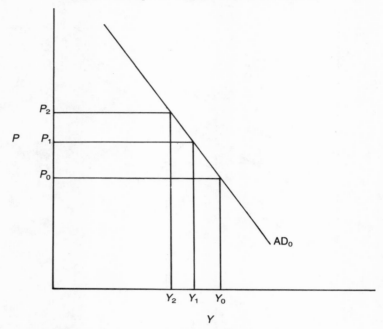

FIGURE 3.2   Aggregate demand curve.

government expenditure and the nominal quantity of money. We label this line AD_0 and shall refer to it as the Aggregate Demand curve. It shows for any general level of prices what the equilibrium level of aggregate demand is, *ceteris paribus*. Clearly, (P_0, Y_0), (P_1, Y_1), and (P_2, Y_2) are combinations of P and Y lying on this line.

The intuitive explanation for the negative slope of the Aggregate Demand curve is that a higher price level implies, *ceteris paribus*, a lower real quantity of money in the economy since the real quantity of money is defined to be the nominal quantity of money, M, divided by the general level of prices, P, that is M/P. One way in which people may respond to finding themselves with less real money than they had before is by selling off holdings of bonds to rebuild their holdings of money. But this can only work at the individual level, it cannot work for the economy as a whole since the quantity of nominal money is fixed and so one person obtains more money by selling bonds only with the result that someone else – the person who buys the bonds – finds himself with less. The general attempt to sell bonds will tend to drive down the price of bonds and raise their rate of interest and this will help eliminate the excess demand for money since the higher the rate of interest the lower the demand for money. But the rise in the rate of interest will do something else too: it will depress investment expenditure and thereby cause a fall in aggregate demand. As a consequence the equilibrium level of aggregate demand will fall. Thus a rise in the price level leads to a fall in the equilibrium level of aggregate demand.

The position of the Aggregate Demand curve is determined by the values of all the variables other than the general level of prices which determine the positions of the IS and LM curves, such as real government expenditure and the nominal quantity of money in the economy. A rise in either government expenditure or the quantity of money will shift the Aggregate Demand curve to the right, the exact sizes of the effects depending upon the slopes of the IS and LM curves. The effects on the Aggregate Demand curve of a change in real government expenditure or the quantity of money can be derived diagrammatically by shifting the IS or LM curves whichever is appropriate, or intuitively along the following lines. A rise in government expenditure adds directly to aggregate spending and hence will tend to increase the equilibrium level of aggregate demand. Of course the financing of such an increase in government spending by the sale of an equivalent quantity of government bonds will tend to raise interest rates and thus choke off some private expenditure but unless the interest elasticity of private expenditure is very high, or the interest elasticity of the demand for money very low the net effect of an increase in government spending will be significantly to raise the equilibrium level of aggregate demand for any price level. Thus a rise in real government expenditure shifts the Aggregate Demand curve to the right.

A rise in the nominal quantity of money will have the same effect, though the route here is a little different. The rise in the quantity of money leads, *ceteris paribus*, to a rise in the real quantity of money. One way people might respond to finding themselves with more real money than they want would be to use their excess holdings of money to buy bonds. The general attempt to do this will drive the interest rate on bonds down and thereby stimulate investment expenditure and hence aggregate demand. Provided investment expenditure is significantly influenced by changes in the rate of interest, the rise in the quantity of money will significantly shift the Aggregate Demand curve to the right.

There are many differences of opinion amongst economists about the relative power of fiscal and monetary policy to influence the position of the Aggregate Demand curve, but these debates are of no great concern to the question we are dealing with here. What is more important for our purposes is the way in which the Aggregate Demand curve interacts with the Aggregate Supply curve to determine the equilibrium general level of prices and the equilibrium level of output; we are especially interested in the nature of that interaction when expectations are rational. To understand that interaction we must first analyse the flexible price, natural rate version of the Aggregate Supply curve.

3.2 THE FLEXIBLE PRICE – NATURAL RATE AGGREGATE SUPPLY CURVE

Imagine the economy as consisting of a large number of geographically separate markets. It may help to think of each of these markets as being located on its own island. On every island, i.e. in every market, the same type of good is bought and sold each period. It is a one-good economy, but the good is traded in many separate markets. Furthermore on each island the price of the good adjusts each period to equate the supply of the good *on that island* and the demand for the good *on that island*. In each period on each island a large number of suppliers and demanders are located. They trade with each other and then next period may find themselves on different islands and the whole process is repeated. Prices throughout this economy are thus fully flexible and competitively determined, that is they move to equate supply and demand, and no individual exerts any significant influence on price. In the previous section we analysed the factors determining aggregate demand in this economy, i.e. the Aggregate Demand Curve. To derive an Aggregate Supply curve we shall assume that suppliers are primarily influenced by the relative price of the good on their island. If the price of the good on their island is, for whatever reason, known to be higher than the average price of it on all other islands they will take advantage of this high relative price and supply a higher quantity of the good than they otherwise would. The total level of output supplied when the relative price of the good on all islands is correctly perceived we shall call the normal or natural level of aggregate output.

But why should the price of the good established on one island ever be any different from the price of the good established on any other island – after all it is the same type of good which is being traded on each island? Because of the *relative demand* shifts between islands which we shall assume are a significant feature of the economy. One way of conceiving of this is that in any period there are in some islands a greater than average number of demanders, and in others a smaller number than average. This produces in some islands higher than average demand and in others lower than average demand. Of course over the whole economy these relative demand changes sum to zero and aggregate or average demand is given by the Aggregate Demand curve derived in section 3.1. But any individual market or island may experience somewhat higher or lower demand than average, those with lower than average demand cancelling out those with higher than average demand. (If these perturbations around the average do not cancel each other out, they cannot be reflecting purely relative demand changes because there would be some net *aggregate* effect.)

In those islands where demand is relatively high the equilibrium price of the good will be relatively high and in those islands where demand is relatively low the price of the good will be relatively low. So, given the set-up of the model, in particular given that in any period people can only buy or sell in the island on which they are located, different equilibrium prices can be established for the *same* good. What would be the relationship between the general level of prices, or the average price of the good in this economy and the total or aggregate quantity of output supplied? The answer to this question depends upon the amount of information people have about what is happening in the economy. If suppliers know not only the current equilibrium price in their own market but also the current equilibrium price in all other markets the aggregate level of output will be *independent* of the average level of prices, for if their own equilibrium price rises by 10 per cent and the average of all other prices rises by 10 per cent too then they will not increase output because they know that there has been no increase in the relative price of the good on their island.

If their own price rises by 10 per cent and they know that on average other prices have risen by 5 per cent then they will increase their output. But in the nature of averages the price on some other island(s) must have risen by less than 5 per cent. For simplicity imagine that on one island the price of the good has not risen at all. On this latter island output will be lower than normal because of the known fall in the relative price of the good on that island. Given symmetric behaviour aggregate output in this case too will remain at its normal level: the increase in output in one market cancelling out the fall in output on the other. So in both cases *aggregate* output is likely to remain at its normal level in the face of a change in the general level of prices.

On the other hand if we assume that there is imperfect information in the sense that suppliers and demanders know the current equilibrium price for the good in *their* island but only get to know the equilibrium price in *other* markets with a one-period time lag the relationship between aggregate supply and the general level of prices becomes much more subtle. For now if you, as a supplier, observe a rise in the price of the good in your island of 10 per cent you cannot be certain whether all other markets on average are experiencing the same rise. If they are you would not want to raise output above normal because there has been no rise in your relative price. But if they are experiencing on average a *smaller* rise, you would want to raise output *above* normal, taking advantage of the high relative price on your island, and if they are experiencing a *larger* rise you would want to *reduce* supply below normal. So in order to decide what quantity to supply you would have to form an *expectation* of the average, economy-wide price of the good. You would then compare this with the actual price on your island and depending upon whether your actual price is higher, lower or the same as your expectation of the average price you would supply a quantity of output which is higher, lower or the same as your normal or natural level. And what is true for you would be true for every other supplier: they too will supply more than normal if the price on their island is above what they expected the average price to be, and less if it is below. So the aggregate level of output will be above its natural or normal level if the average price level is above the economy-wide expectation of it, below it if the average price level is below the economy-wide expectation of it, and equal to its natural level if the average level of prices equals the economy-wide expectation of it.

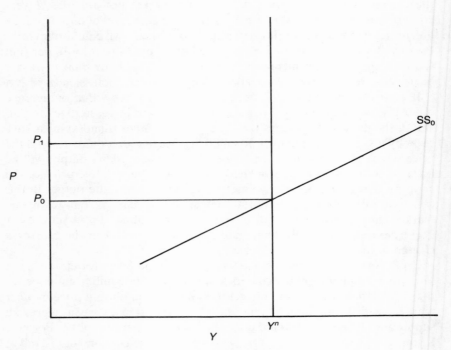

FIGURE 3.3   The long- and short-run aggregate supply curves.

For an economy like the one we have imagined in which there is impefect information in the sense we have described, the relationship between aggregate supply and the general level of prices can be depicted as it is in Figure 3.3. The aggregate normal or natural level of output is labelled Y^n. The vertical line from Y^n shows the relationship between output and the price level when the actual price level is correctly forecast. As we have shown this implies that aggregate output will equal its normal level. (This is quite consistent with some suppliers who face relatively low level of demand producing below normal whilst those who face a relatively high level of demand producing above normal, the two groups offsetting each other.)

The line labelled SS_0 is drawn on the assumption that the general expectation of the average level of prices is P_0. If this expectation is correct and the average price level is P_0 then of course the aggregate level of output will equal its normal or natural level, that is why this line cuts the vertical line from Y^n at P_0. But if the average level of prices is above the level generally expected, P_0, then as we have shown the quantity of output will be above its normal or natural level, whereas if the general level of prices is below the level expected then aggregate output will be below its normal level. Thus the relationship between the general level of prices and aggregate output when the expected price level is held constant at P_0 can be depicted as an upward-sloping line which cuts the vertical line from Y^n at price level P_0. If we had assumed that the expected level of prices was P_1 and drawn the relationship between the general level of prices and aggregate output on that assumption we would have drawn an upward-sloping line which cuts the vertical line from Y^n at P_1.

This aggregate supply curve is of fundamental importance to the macroeconomic policy conclusions often drawn from the rational expectations hypothesis. The crucially important aspect of it is that changes in the level of prices which are foreseen or are expected have no effect on the level of real output. Only unforeseen or unexpected price changes will cause output to deviate from its natural or normal level. To understand this result we have to combine the Aggregate Demand curve derived in section 3.1 with our Aggregate Supply curve and consider how the equilibrium level of prices and the equilibrium level of real output are determined.

3.3 AGGREGATE DEMAND AND EQUILIBRIUM OUTPUT

Imagine that an economy's Aggregate Demand curve is AD_0 in Figure 3.4 and that its normal or natural level of output is Y^n. If the expectation of the general level of prices in this economy is P_0 the relationship between the actual level of prices and the aggregate quantity of output supplied is given by the line labelled SS_0. It is clear from the diagram that if the price level is P_0, the economy is in full equilibrium in the sense that the expected price level is equal to the actual price level and the level of output is therefore equal to its normal or natural level. From this initial position of full equilibrium consider what happens if there is a shift in the Aggregate Demand curve from AD_0 to AD_1. If expectations of the price level remain at P_0 then the economy will move up the line SS_0. Output will rise to Y_1 and prices will rise to P_1. It is this rise in the average level of prices above the level people are in general expecting, P_0, which stimulates the rise in output: on the typical island suppliers are tending to find a price higher than they guess the average price level to be and are responding by

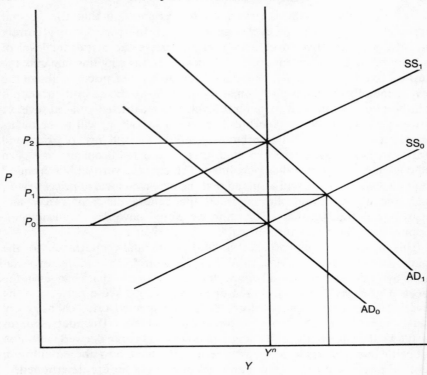

FIGURE 3.4   The interaction of aggregate supply and demand.

increasing their output and since this is happening typically and not merely on one island *aggregate* output is stimulated.

But this is not the only possible way in which the economy might respond to the upward shift of the Aggregate Demand curve. Another possibility is that as the Aggregate Demand curve rises from AD_0 to AD_1 the expected level of prices rises to P_2, and the relationship between the actual level of prices and aggregate output is shown by the line labelled SS_1. In this case there is no increase in output. Output remains at its normal or natural level, whilst prices rise from P_0 to P_2. The reason why there is no increase in output is that the typical supplier has correctly realized that the price on his island is rising at the same rate as the average level of prices and there has therefore been no relative change in his price and so no incentive to raise output above its normal level.

Whilst these two possibilities are interesting special cases they by no means exhaust the ways in which the economy *could* respond to the shift in the Aggregate Demand curve we have assumed. If expectations of the general level of prices rose to some level between P_0 and P_2 then there would be some stimulus to output and some rise in prices. If expectations of the general level of prices rose above P_2 then there would be a fall in output and a rise in prices above P_2. And if expectations of the general level of prices actually fell below P_0 there could be a fall in prices and a rise in output. All these cases can be simply illustrated using the apparatus depicted in Figure 3.4; we leave it to the reader to do so.

The important point for our purposes is that until *some* assumption is made about the generally expected price level we cannot rule out *any* response of the economy to the upward shift in the Aggregate Demand curve. By imposing the assumption that expectations of the general price level are rationally formed we severely restrict the possible ways in which the economy can respond to the assumed change in aggregate demand. We thus turn a model which is untestable, since no conceivable data could prove it wrong, into a testable one.

To see what these restrictions are we must first recall the emphasis placed in chapter 2 on variables being determined by *processes*. The variable we are interested in here is the variable which has caused the shift in the Aggregate Demand curve. It may be a change in government expenditure, it may be a change in the quantity of money, or it may be a change in some other variable. It does not really matter for our purposes what the variable is. What does matter is that the variable can be seen as being determined by a process as can all the other variables which determine the position of the Aggregate Demand curve. Therefore the Aggregate Demand curve itself can be seen as the result of a continuing process and shifts in the Aggregate Demand curve occur in line with this process. Of course they may be due to the stochastic component of that process and therefore be unpredictable, or they may be due to the systematic or predictable component. But any shift in the Aggregate Demand curve should not be treated as a unique event which can be separated from the process determining the position of the Aggregate Demand curve – rather it should be seen as part of a stable but stochastic process. From this point of view the relevant question to ask about the shift of the Aggregate Demand curve in Figure 3.4 from AD_0 to AD_1 is, was it predictable on the basis of the available information relating to the process determining aggregate demand? To put that another way, would a person who was using all the available information concerning the process determining aggregate demand have predicted that the position of the Aggregate Demand curve was going to be AD_1?

If the answer to that question is yes, then the rational expectations hypothesis implies that the generally expected position of the Aggregate Demand curve will be AD_1. In which case the rational expectation of the average price level must be P_2. For if the generally expected price level is

P_2 the relevant Aggregate Supply curve will be the one labelled SS_1 which cuts the expected Aggregate Demand curve AD_1 to give a price level equal to the one that is expected, P_2. So if the rational person thinks that the Aggregate Demand curve will be at AD_1 he must also expect a price level of P_2. If he expected any other price level he would not be acting rationally since he would not be forming his expectation of the price level in line with the process determining it, that is the aggregate demand and supply process depicted in Figure 3.4. For example, if despite expecting the Aggregate Demand curve to be at AD_1 people in general expected a price level of P_0 they would be acting irrationally since the process determining the price level clearly shows that if the Aggregate Demand curve is AD_1 and the expected price level is P_0, the actual price level will not be P_0. The only price level which it is rational to expect if the position of the Aggregate Demand curve is expected to be AD_1 is P_2, since only this expectation will generate an actual price level equal to it.

So if the shift in the Aggregate Demand curve from AD_0 to AD_1 is predictable on the available information relating to the process determining aggregate demand the expected price level will be P_2, the relevant Aggregate Supply Curve will be the one labelled SS_1 and the upward shift in the Aggregate Demand curve *will have no effect on the aggregate level of output*. This is an extremely important result, both because of its policy implications which we shall consider later in this chapter and because of the scope it offers for testing the rational expectations hypothesis. For it implies that those movements in aggregate demand which are predictable will have no effect on real output and by implication employment or unemployment, but will only affect prices. Rational people will predict them and thereby annul any effect they might have on real variables.

Now consider the results of assuming that the shift in the Aggregate Demand curve from AD_0 to AD_1 was entirely unpredictable, the result, say, of a positive value for the random error term in the process determining aggregate demand. Since the shift in demand was not predictable even rational people would not have expected it and so the typical supplier would be finding the price of the good on her island higher than she was initially expecting the average price to be. This might lead her to change her expectation of the average level of prices, after all, if she is rational, she must know that unpredictable movements in aggregate demand can occur and one symptom of them is that the price on her island is higher than she was expecting the average to be. So the very fact that she observes her price to be higher than the average price level she was expecting may make her adjust upwards her expected average price level. But she also knows that *relative* shifts in demand occur and these too can lead to her price being higher than the average. So it is perfectly reasonable for her to believe that her price is higher than she expected the average to be because of a relative demand shift in her favour which she might just as well take advantage of by supplying more output.

She faces what is known as a *signal extraction* problem. The signal she wishes to extract, or the information she wants is the precise size of the random aggregate influence on her good in that period and the precise size of the random relative demand influence. But the information she actually obtains from observing the price of her good tells her the total effect of these two influences and not their individual effects. Somehow she has to try to extract the information she wants from the information she gets. This is the signal extraction problem. Exactly how a rational person will solve it we shall show later on. For the moment notice that if the *typical* supplier infers that her price is higher than she was initially expecting the average to be solely because of a relative demand shift in her favour then the expected average price level will remain at P_0 and the rise in the Aggregate Demand curve will lead to a rise in output equal to $Y_1 - Y^n$. If, on the other hand, she infers that there has been a random upward shift in the Aggregate Demand curve which by its very nature affects all markets alike she will infer that the average level of prices has risen to P_2. The typical expectation of the average level of prices will rise to P_2 and the shift in aggregate demand will have no effect on real output. If she *partly* infers a higher average price level than she was originally expecting and *partly* infers a relative demand increase then the generally expected price level will be somewhere between P_0 and P_2, and hence there will be some increase in aggregate output above its natural level.

As we have said, later on in the chapter we shall consider what might determine the extent to which the observation that the price in your market is higher than the average you were originally expecting leads you to raise your expectation of what that average is. But for the moment we just emphasize that a random increase (decrease) in aggregate demand is likely to produce a positive (negative) deviation of aggregate output from its natural level. This occurs to the extent that the *typical* supplier confuses the higher price that the increase in aggregate demand implies for the good on her island for a relative demand shift in her favour.

We can now state the central result of applying the rational expectations hypothesis to the Aggregate Demand–Aggregate Supply model we have been using this chapter. *Only random changes in aggregate demand can affect the level of real output; predictable, systematic changes in aggregate demand will affect prices but not output.* In the next section we discuss the policy implications of this key result.

3.4 RANDOM AND SYSTEMATIC AGGREGATE DEMAND POLICY

Imagine a government which follows the typically Keynesian approach to macroeconomic policy of raising its own expenditure whenever the economy moves into a recession and (somewhat less typically) reducing its own expenditure when the economy is booming. The idea behind such an approach to policy is that governments can thus soften economic fluctuations in output and employment and thereby produce a more stable economic environment. Many governments have pursued this general approach to economic policy since the last war and a vast amount of economic research has gone into forecasting recessions and booms so that the government can take the measures necessary to offset them in good time.

The model that we have explained in section 3.3 suggests that this approach to policy, and by implication the economic research undertaken to improve it, is fatally flawed. The essence of the flaw is that as the process by which aggregate demand is determined becomes known and therefore predictable, rational people will predict the changes in aggregate demand that governments engineer. And as we have seen, predicted changes in aggregate demand will have no effect on real output, or real economic activity – they will only affect prices. Thus Keynesian economic policy is either impotent or approaching impotence as the process by which aggregate demand is determined becomes known. This impotence is *inherent* in the Keynesian approach to policy and not merely a feature of a specific version of that aproach. For by its very nature, it makes government aggregate demand policies predictable in that it links government policy changes to the current or past state of the economy. Even if government policy is linked to the *future* state of the economy in the sense that it is influenced by the predictions of some government economic model, these predictions can be *currently* ascertained and used to make government policy predictable. And it is precisely its predictability which renders it impotent.

The only possible way in which a government might try to use aggregate demand policies to influence the level of aggregate output would be to introduce random movements in its policy instruments. These would produce random movements in aggregate demand which, as we have shown in section 3.3, would produce deviations of aggregate output away from its normal level. But to be effective these random changes in government expenditure or the money supply or whatever, would have to be unpredictable and that means unpredictable to the government too, for if the government could predict them so could others. Their effect would be not to stabilize output but to increase the fluctuations of output around its normal level, the precise opposite of what Keynesian policies aim to achieve.

So a key implication of the rational expectations hypothesis when combined with the Aggregate Demand–Aggregate Supply model developed in section 3.3 is that the Keynesian approach to macroeconomic stabilization policy is fatally flawed. Much of the controversy which surrounds the rational expectations hypothesis is because of this implication.

A more positive feature of the hypothesis, again in the context of the Aggregate Demand–Aggregate Supply model derived in section 3.3, is the apparent support for the approach to macroeconomic policy, especially monetary policy, advocated by a number of economists notably Friedman (1959). In sharp contrast to Keynes and his followers these economists have suggested that monetary policy should not be changed in response to any booms or recessions which the economy experiences: it should not be more expansionary in a recession and more restrictive in a boom. Rather, the government should bind itself (or even be constitutionally bound) to expand the quantity of money each period at some specified percentage rate of growth, x per cent. The precise value of x in any year should be announced well in advance, say in a 5-year plan, and should be strictly adhered to. The actual state of the economy should not, barring quite exceptional circumstances, induce the government to depart from its announced strategy, its x per cent rule.

The proponents of this approach to policy claim that it will encourage a more stable background in which the private sector can make its own investment and spending plans with greater certainty about future government policy; that it will prevent abrupt and damaging shifts of policy; and that it will make government manipulation of monetary policy for electoral purposes more difficult. They also believe that government attempts to vary monetary policy in order to stabilize the economy are very likely to destabilize it because the precise timing of the effects of monetary policy are hard to pin down and as a consequence are not well understood. This destabilization would be avoided if monetary policy was conducted in accordance with the x per cent rule described above. For all these reasons some economists have for many years advocated this approach to monetary policy and during the 1970s a number of governments began to pay at least lip service to it by announcing target rates of growth for the money supply over the coming year.

However, within the simple aggregate supply and demand framework we have developed in sections 3.2 and 3.3, it has always been possible to show that if expectations of inflation are not rational then Friedman's x per cent growth rule for the quantity of money is bound to be inferior to some other policy which links monetary growth to the current or past state of the economy. Inferiority here means that Friedman's x per cent growth rule would imply greater fluctuations of real output around its natural level than would a policy of appropriately varying monetary policy as the economy moved into boom or recession.

The intuitive reason for this inferiority is that *irrational* expectations always offer some scope for a government to 'fool' people systematically. We have already seen a number of examples of this. Take the case where the price level expected next period is always equal to last period's actual price level. Then if there is, for whatever reason, a large permanent fall in aggregate demand there will be an immediate fall in prices and drop in output. Expectations of the price level will fall only gradually to their new equilibrium level and whilst they do so output will be below its natural level. If the government is locked into a policy of expanding the money supply at some preannounced rate it cannot do anything about this possibly severe recession. But if it is not bound by such a policy it can induce a large increase in the money supply and prevent the recession or at least bring it to an end quickly. Thus the more flexible monetary policy is superior to the Friedman *x* per cent growth rule.

But if expectations are rational then this superiority disappears, for if the fall in aggregate demand assumed above was predictable, it would have no effect on real output and would not need to be countered by a change of monetary policy. And if it was unpredictable, then whilst it would have an immediate effect on output, this could not be prevented by government policy since the government would not be able to foresee the fall in aggregate demand either. Furthermore the effect on real output would disappear after one period since the fall in aggregate demand would then be known and would be fully taken into account in the setting of prices, giving output equal to its natural rate. So once again no change in monetary policy would be of any advantage.

The result that Friedman's approach to monetary policy is no longer inferior to a more 'flexible' approach once one incorporates rational expectations into the basic aggregate supply and demand model was demonstrated more formally and generally by Sargent and Wallace (1975) and is sometimes known as the Sargent–Wallace proposition.

In fact the rational expectations hypothesis is sometimes seen as providing suport for the 'strong' version of the Friedman approach to monetary policy which argues that the *x* per cent rule should be made constitutionally binding. For from the model derived in section 3.3 it is clear that output will be raised above its normal rate only if people in general are fooled into believing that the average price level is lower than it actually is. If expectations are irrationally, say adaptively, formed then it is always possible to specify a rule for government policy which will consistently fool people. For example if the expected price level always equals last period's actual price level then by linking the change in the money supply to last period's price level it will always be possible to ensure that the actual price level exceeds the expected price level and hence output is kept above its normal level. Such a policy would work even if it was fully announced, provided expectations were formed in the way we have assumed. Thus there is no incentive for the government to cheat on this way of conducting monetary policy, that is to follow a different policy from the one that it has announced; for it can fool people without cheating. Consequently there is little need to prevent cheating by making the government's announced monetary policy constitutionally binding.

But if expectations are rationally formed the government cannot expect a policy of linking the change in the money supply to the previous price level to succeed, for people will not be fooled by it. On the contrary they will change their method of forming expectations in line with the process announced for determining the money supply and hence aggregate demand. This will be true whatever the process determining monetary policy is. Thus the only way in which the government might achieve a higher level of output would be by cheating, or by not following the rule it says it is following. The fact that governments could cheat like this will clearly be known to rational agents and might introduce some uncertainty about government policy. This uncertainty could be partly removed by making government policy constitutionally binding. (But only 'partly' since constitutions can be changed too.)

The possibility of cheating raises an issue referred to as the 'time inconsistency' of policy. Loosely speaking a policy is said to be 'time inconsistent' if there is an incentive to renege or cheat on the part of the policy-maker. For example, the promise of an investment subsidy at some future date may encourage many firms to invest: when the future date arrives, there is nothing to be gained from actually paying the subsidy, but every incentive to cheat. Such a policy is said to be time inconsistent. A policy is time consistent if the incentive to cheat does not arise (as it did not in the case of adaptive expectations).

It may now be clear that under rational expectations, policies will be time inconsistent as the following example illustrates. Imagine that the government has been following a simple (no growth) money supply rule which gives the aggregate demand curve AD_0, so that the economy is at Y^n and P_0 in Figure 3.5 Now suppose that we can define the government's 'indifference' curves for output and the price level by a series of lines, labelled v_0, v_1 and v_2 in the figure. It may help to conceive of these as 'iso-vote' lines, combinations of P and Y along each line producing a given level of government popularity in the opinion polls. They take the shape they do in Figure 3.5 because generally voters prefer higher output and lower overall prices, so v_0 implies fewer votes than v_1.

If expectations were given, the government could select an optimal policy by maximising v along SS_0 (which is constructed on the assumption

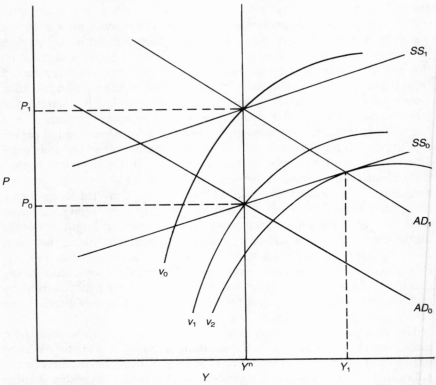

FIGURE 3.5   Aggregate demand policy and government popularity

that expectations of the price level are P_0). To do this, the government would expand aggregate demand to AD_1 (by increasing the stock of money to M_1, for example) and achieve the highest number of votes possible (labelled v_2). If agents are rational, however, and they know both the government's objective (to maximize v) and the positions of the iso-vote lines, they would anticipate the expansion in M and revise their expectations of the price level to P_1, so that output would remain at Y^n. Note this implies a lower level of votes than that enjoyed initially (v_0 compared with v_1). It is clear that an optimal policy under rational expectations would be to make no attempt to expand aggregate demand to AD_1.

However, whilst this may be optimal policy over the long run, there is always a temptation to cheat (i.e. the policy is still time inconsistent). Imagine, for example, that having adopted a policy of $M=M_0$ for some time, the government unexpectedly raised aggregate demand to AD_1, thus achieving – albeit temporarily – a higher level of votes (v_2). This may be considered a 'discretionary policy' in contrast to the 'rule' that set $M=M_0$.

Having observed the government renege, agents will now revise their price expectations to P_1. As there is nothing more to be gained from a high level of M, the government will subsequently reduce M to M_0, the combination of higher price expectations (P_1) and lower money supply restoring the original aggregate demand curve (AD$_0$) will cause the level of votes to fall below v_0. Agents will realize the old money rule is re-established and revise their price expectations downwards to P_0 The benefit of reneging (to the government) is the higher number of votes in the first period; the cost is the even lower number of votes which followed. The incentive to cheat clearly will depend upon the relative costs and benefits of so doing. Some have argued that these incentives may be higher just before elections, when more votes may mean re-election (the so-called 'U-turn' referred to in chapter 2), the loss of popularity once re-elected being a small price to pay. However, repeated instances of such behaviour will eventually be predictable by rational agents so that such short-term gains may not be available to governments.

3.5 THE VARIANCE OF AGGREGATE DEMAND POLICY

One other important result can be derived from the application of the rational expectations hypothesis to the aggregate demand – aggregate supply model of section 3.3. This result has implications for policy and also can be used as a test of the validity of the rational expectations hypothesis. It is a subtle result; we shall first state it and then explain how it is derived. It says that the greater the variance of the random component of the process determining aggregate demand the smaller the effect on real output of any given value for the random component of aggregate demand. Thus in an economy where aggregate demand is highly unpredictable in the sense that random aggregate demand has a high variance, a 5 per cent random increase in aggregate demand will have a much lower effect on real output than the same (5 per cent) random increase in aggregate demand would have in an economy in which aggregate demand is significantly less unpredictable.

To understand how this result is obtained recall from section 3.3 the way in which a random increase in aggregate demand induces an increase in output. It does so by raising demand in the typical market above the level expected, thereby inducing a price in the typical market which is higher than the average price expected by the typical supplier in the market. Since the supplier is rational and knows that a higher than average price can either be due to an unpredictable increase in aggregate demand or to a relative demand shift in favour of his market he will infer from the unexpectedly high price for his good *partly* that there has been a random increase in aggregate demand which of course affects all markets alike, and *partly* that there has been a relative demand shift in his favour. At one limit if he attributes all the unexpectedly high price in his market to a random increase in aggregate demand he will merely change his expectation of the general level of prices in line with the price in his own market and produce no more output than normal. At the other limit if he attributes *all* the unexpectedly high price in his market to a relative demand shift in his favour he will not adjust his expectation of the general level of prices at all and will produce a higher level of output than normal. And in between these limits he will partly raise his expectation of the average level of prices and partly produce more output.

In general the more the unexpectedly high price in his market leads the typical supplier to infer a random aggregate demand increase the less effect there will be on aggregate output. So a random increase in aggregate demand which leads to an unexpectedly high price in the typical market or island will have less effect on aggregate output in economies in which the observation of an unexpectedly high price leads suppliers to infer a random movement in aggregate demand.

But what will determine the extent to which the observation of an unexpectedly high price in one's own market leads to the inference of a random aggregate demand increase rather than a relative demand shift? If expectations are rational the inference should be related to the true process determining the unexpectedly high price, that is the true likelihood of any unexpectedly high price being due to a random aggregate demand increase rather than a favourable relative demand shift. Thus in an economy in which relative demand shifts are typically small and infrequent but random movements in aggregate demand are typically large and occur often it would be rational for you to attribute most of an unexpectedly high price in your market to a random increase in aggregate demand. As a consequence, in this economy any random increase in aggregate demand will be seen for what it is and will have little effect on aggregate output. But in an economy in which random movements in aggregate demand are typically small but relative demand shifts typically large it is rational to attribute most of an unexpectedly high price in your market to a relative demand shift. As a consequence in this economy any random increase in aggregate demand will *not* be seen for what it is; it will be misinterpreted as a favourable relative demand shift and it will induce a large increase in aggregate output.

If we assume for the moment that the variance of relative demand shifts is more or less constant across economies it follows from the analysis above that economies in which the random element in aggregate demand has a high variance, i.e. is highly volatile, will be those economies in which random movements in aggregate demand have little effect on real output.

This is the result we set out to prove.

Apart from the scope that this result offers for testing the rational expectations hypothesis, something we consider in chapter 7, its policy implications are worth considering. It is generally agreed that a policy which produces large fluctuations of output around its natural level is inferior to one that produces small fluctuations. On the basis of the analysis developed in section 3.4 this would seem to suggest that aggregate demand policies should be as predictable as possible, the aim of government should be to reduce the random, unpredictable element in the aggregate demand as far as it can by making its procedures more efficient etc., for it is only this unpredictable element which sets up fluctuations of output around its natural rate.

But the analysis that we have just explained might appear to challenge this intuitively attractive result that policies should be made as predictable as possible, for it suggests that by making aggregate demand as *unpredictable* as possible you would achieve complete stability of aggregate output at its natural rate. As aggregate demand becomes more volatile unexpectedly high prices are increasingly likely to be attributed by rational suppliers to random movements in aggregate demand, and therefore are increasingly less likely to induce changes in real output. Any random movement in aggregate demand would be seen for what it was; it would be perfectly predicted and would therefore have no effect on aggregate output. So why not make aggregate demand completely *volatile*? The answer to this question is that in doing so you would make the economy less efficient. For not only would suppliers correctly interpret random movements in aggregate demand as random movements in aggregate demand and therefore not produce anything different from normal, they would also incorrectly interpret *relative* demand shifts as random shifts in aggregate demand. They would therefore not respond to relative demand shifts by varying output simply because they did not interpret them as relative shifts. It is a sign of an efficient economy that it does respond to relative demand shifts, and so the economy would be inefficient if aggregate demand policy was made extremely volatile.

So the analysis of this section too supports the idea that predictable aggregate demands are better than unpredictable ones. This need for policy to be made as predictable as possible is sometimes seen as being more easily satisfied under a simple Friedman-type rule than under a Keynesian policy linking government policy instruments to the state of the economy. For the Friedman policy is extremely simple to understand, the only unpredictability in it coming from the government's inability, perhaps as a result of technical inefficiencies, to achieve its aims precisely. The same technical inefficiencies will presumably dog a Keynesian policy too but here there might be further problems. For example imagine that the money supply is linked to the level of aggregate income so that when income is low the change in the quantity of money is high. There are a number of ways of measuring aggregate income and they all should in theory give the same answer but occasionally because of accounting errors or deliberate concealment of income they do not, and sometimes they differ by quite large amounts. A rational person who knew that monetary policy was linked to aggregate income might be puzzled if the different measures of income gave different estimates and be uncertain as to which measure policy might be linked to. What is more his uncertainty might be well founded if the government itself was unsure which measure of income to use and made a more or less random choice between the different measures. This increased scope for making rational mistakes implies a higher variance for the errors of rational forecasts, and thereby a higher variance for the fluctuations of real output about its normal level. It seems likely that complex rules are likely to offer more scope for such misunderstandings than simple ones, and are therefore likely to create more unpredictability.

3.6   A FORMAL STATEMENT OF THE RATIONAL EXPECTATIONS MODEL

We end this section with a formal statement of a simplified version of the rational expectations aggregate supply and demand model developed in the previous sections. We use this model primarily to demonstrate rigorously the results we have obtained more intuitively above, but we also use it to illustrate a mathematical technique which is often used in rational expectations models. The mathematics in this section may appear to be a little difficult, though in fact it involves only fairly simple algebra.

As we have explained above we are imagining the economy consists of a large number of geographically separate markets or islands. We shall index these markets or islands by the subscript z, where z can be any number between 1 and the number of islands in the economy, N. We begin the model by writing down the supply of output in the zth market as

$$y^s(z)_t = \beta_0 + \beta_1 [p(z)_t - E_t(z)p_t] \tag{3.1}$$

where $y^s(z)_t$ = the quantity of output supplied in market z in period t
$p(z)_t$ = the price of output in market z in period t
$E_t(z)p_t$ = the expectation formed in market z of the economy-wide average price of output in period t, p_t, using all the information available in the zth market at the beginning of period t
β_0 and β_1 = coefficients; β_1 is positive.

All variables are defined as natural logarithms

This equation is merely a formal statement of the idea that the quantity of output supplied is primarily determined by the local price relative to suppliers' expectations of the economy-wide average price of output. If the local price and the expected price are the same then output will equal its normal or natural level, β_0. Remember that the information available in the zth market at the beginning of period t includes knowledge of all past aggregate and local variables and of $p(z)_t$ but does not include knowledge of any other current price.

The next equation of the model formally states a simple hypothesis about demand in each market.

$$y^d(z)_t = \alpha_0 + m_t - E_t(z)p_t + \varepsilon(z)_t \tag{3.2}$$

where $y^d(z)_t =$ the quantity of output demanded in the zth market

$m_t =$ the economy-wide average quantity of nominal money holdings in period t

$\varepsilon(z)_t =$ a random, serially uncorrelated variable with a mean of zero and constant variance, σ^2_ε

$\alpha_0 =$ a coefficient.

Once again all variables are defined as natural logarithms.

This equation states that there are two major influences on demand in the zth market. The first is common to all markets, it is the average nominal quantity of money in the economy deflated by the expectation held in the particular market of the average price level. This is the term $m_t - E_t(z)p_t$, the expected real value of the money balances held by demanders in the zth market. The second influence, $\varepsilon(z)_t$, is a random variable whose value can be positive or negative in any period but has a mean value of zero. The first of these influences represents the influence of aggregate demand since the key term, m_t, is an economy-wide average; its influence is not specific to one particular market, it affects all markets and hence is not indexed on z. In terms of the Aggregate Demand curve developed in section 3.1 this specification is a simplification: it ignores the influence on aggregate demand of variables other than the quantity of money. The second influence represents relative demand shifts between markets. If $\varepsilon(z)_t$ is positive then the zth market is experiencing a relative demand shift in its favour – demand is higher than average. If $\varepsilon(z)_t$ is negative then the zth market is experiencing an unfavourable relative demand shift – demand is lower than average. Of course if we were to add up the $\varepsilon(z)_t$ term in every market/island in the economy we would get the answer zero – the markets with below average demand cancel out those with above average demand.

The third equation of the model describes the process by which the average quantity of nominal money holdings is determined. To keep things as simple as possible we shall assume that the quantity of money is determined by the government in accordance with the following process

$$m_t = m_{t-1} + g + u_t \tag{3.3}$$

where g is a constant and u_t is a random, serially uncorrelated error with zero mean and constant variance, σ^2_u

This equation states that the average quantity of money in the economy equals its value last period, m_{t-1}, plus a constant, g, plus a random serially uncorrelated error term, u_t. Since the term m_t is a logarithm it follows that $m_t - m_{t-1}$ is a measure of the proportionate rate of growth of the quantity of money. We shall assume that g is known and we shall therefore treat g as the predictable component of monetary growth; u_t on the other hand is not known and is therefore the unpredictable component.

As we explained in section 3.2 the model we are considering assumes that prices on each island/market move each period to equate supply and demand on each island. Thus for each island we can write the following

$$y^s(z)_t = y^d(z)_t \tag{3.4}$$

Combining equations (3.1) to (3.4) and solving for the equilibrium price in the zth market gives

$$p(z)_t = (1/\beta_1) [(\alpha_0 - \beta_0) + m_{t-1} + g + (\beta_1 - 1)E_t(z)p_t + u_t + \varepsilon(z)_t]. \tag{3.5}$$

As we emphasized a key feature of the model is that participants in any market observe the current price in their market but do not observe the current price in any other market. Thus suppliers and demanders in the zth market observe $p(z)_t$ and can use their knowledge of that single current equilibrium price to help form some expectation about the two random influences on their market, u_t and $\varepsilon(z)_t$. Remember that suppliers would like to know whether their price is unusually high because of a positive value for u_t or because of a positive value for $\varepsilon(z)_t$ since they would wish to respond differently in the two cases: they do not want to respond to u_t at all but do want to respond to $\varepsilon(z)_t$. We can now use equation (3.5) to show formally how suppliers will try to extract the information they want from the information provided by their observation of the current price in their market. First rewrite equation (3.5) in the following way

$$p(z)_t - (1/\beta_1)[\alpha_0 - \beta_0 + m_{t-1} + g + (\beta_1 - 1)E_t(z)p_t] = (1/\beta_1)[u_t + \varepsilon(z)_t]. \tag{3.6}$$

Then note that all the variables on the left-hand side of equation (3.6) are known to participants in the zth market. They know the price of the good in their own market, $p(z)_t$; they know the values of the coefficients; they know the values of all past values of m and so they know the value of m_{t-1}; they are assumed to know the value of g ; and of course they know what they are expecting for the average price level. But because equation (3.6) is an equation, knowledge of the value of the left-hand side implies knowledge of the value of the right-hand side, i.e. $(1/\beta_1)[u_t + \varepsilon(z)_t]$. And since participants in the zth market know the value of β_1 it follows that they can deduce from their knowledge of m_{t-1}, g etc., the value of the 'composite' disturbance term $[u_t + \varepsilon(z)_t]$. What they do not know, but would like to find out, are the individual values of u_t and $\varepsilon(z)_t$. This is the signal extraction problem mentioned above.

Given that rational agents know the composite disturbance that is currently affecting their market, $[u_t + \varepsilon(z)_t]$, how might they extract from this an estimate of its individual components? In other words how much of this composite disturbance will they attribute to u_t and how much to $\varepsilon(z)_t$? It turns out that the best they can do is form their expectation of u_t and of $\varepsilon(z)_t$ in accordance with the following formulae

$$E_t(z)u_t = \gamma[u_t + \varepsilon(z)_t] \qquad (3.7)$$

$$E_t(z)\varepsilon(z)_t = (1-\gamma)[u_t + \varepsilon(z)_t] \qquad (3.8)$$

$$\text{where } \gamma = \frac{\sigma_u^2}{\sigma_u^2 + \sigma_\varepsilon^2}.$$

The intuitive explanation for this has already been discussed in section 3.4: the greater the proportion of the variance of the composite disturbance which is due to the variance of u, the more sensible it is to attribute most of any period's composite disturbance to u. The variance of u is σ_u^2, and the variance of the composite disturbance is $\sigma_u^2 + \sigma_\varepsilon^2$ provided we assume that u and ε are uncorrelated. Hence the formulae given above.

More formally, if one were to use all the past values of u and $[u + \varepsilon(z)]$ in a regression of u on $[u + \varepsilon(z)]$ one would by the conventional ordinary least squares formula estimate the coefficient on $[u + \varepsilon(z)]$ to be γ, and one would estimate a constant term of zero. This is the best equation one could use to forecast the current value of u, u_t, given knowledge of the current composite disturbance, $[u_t + \varepsilon(z)_t]$, and is therefore the one which rational agents will use to forecast u_t given their information.

From equation (3.7) we have the expectation of u_t in market z formed on the basis of all the information available to participants in market z. The expectation of u_t formed in any other market/island will be derived in the same way, though of course the actual value of the composite disturbance will differ from market to market because of the different values of ε in each market. The economy wide average expectation of u_t, $E_t u_t$, is the sum of all the individual market expectations divided by the number of markets, that is

$$E_t u_t = \gamma u_t \qquad (3.9)$$

Notice here that the $\varepsilon(z)_t$ terms have dropped out because they sum to zero. Thus the economy wide expectation of u_t is some fraction of the actual value of u_t. We can now use this result to solve the whole model. First write the economy wide average price from equation (3.5) as

$$p_t = (1/\beta_1)[(\alpha_0 - \beta_0) + m_{t-1} + g + (\beta_1 - 1)E_t p_t + u_t] \tag{3.10}$$

where $E_t p_t$ is the economy wide expectation of p_t.

Once again the economy wide average of, in this case, p_t is found by summing equation (3.5) over all markets and dividing by the number of markets and hence the relative demand terms – the $\varepsilon(z)$'s – will cancel out. Equation (3.10) is not yet a solution for p_t since it includes on the right-hand side the expectation $E_t p_t$ which is a variable whose value is yet to be determined. To obtain a solution we shall employ one method which is often used to solve (usually more complex) rational expectations models – this is known as the method of undetermined coefficients. The first step in this technique is to write a general solution for p_t, that is to express p_t as a function of all the predetermined and exogenous variables. Since all the equations of the model are linear in logs (i.e. there are no squared terms etc.) then it seems reasonable to conjecture that the solution will also be linear. Thus we write

$$p_t = \pi_0 + \pi_1 m_{t-1} + \pi_2 g + \pi_3 u_t \tag{3.11}$$

where the π_i's are coefficients whose values are as yet unknown.

If equation (3.11) is the solution for p_t then the rational expectation of p_t should be formed in accordance with it. Thus from rational expectations we can write

$$E_t p_t = \pi_0 + \pi_1 E_t m_{t-1} + \pi_2 E_t g + \pi_3 E_t u_t. \tag{3.12}$$

But m_{t-1} and g are both known when the expectation is being formed and we have just derived what $E_t u_t$ will be, so we can write equation (3.12) as

$$E_t p_t = \pi_0 + \pi_1 m_{t-1} + \pi_2 g + \pi_3 \gamma u_t. \tag{3.13}$$

We now have two equations which both describe the process determining p_t, equation (3.11), and equation (3.10) with equation (3.13) substituted in for $E_t p_t$. Since they both describe the process of the same variable they must give the same answer as each other for p_t whatever the values of m_{t-1}, g, and u_t. Thus for all possible values of these three variables the following must be true.

$$\pi_0 + \pi_1 m_{t-1} + \pi_2 g + \pi_3 u_t = \frac{a_0 - \beta_0}{\beta_1} + \frac{m_{t-1}}{\beta_1} + \frac{g}{\beta_1}$$

$$+ \left(\frac{\beta_1 - 1}{\beta_1} \right) (\pi_0 + \pi_1 m_{t-1} + \pi_2 g + \pi_3 \gamma u_t) + \frac{u_t}{\beta_1}. \qquad (3.14)$$

This equality will always hold whatever the values of m_{t-1}, g, etc., if the constant terms on both sides of the equality are identically equal, and if the coefficients attached to each variable are identically equal. These conditions hold where the following are true:

$$(1) \quad \pi_0 = \frac{a_0 - \beta_0}{\beta_1} + \left(\frac{\beta_1 - 1}{\beta_1} \pi_0 \right)$$

$$(2) \quad \pi_1 = \frac{1}{\beta_1} + \left(\frac{\beta_1 - 1}{\beta_1} \pi_1 \right)$$

$$(3) \quad \pi_2 = \frac{1}{\beta_1} + \left(\frac{\beta_1 - 1}{\beta_1} \pi_2 \right)$$

$$(4) \quad \pi_3 = \frac{1}{\beta_1} + \left(\frac{\beta_1 - 1}{\beta_1} \pi_3 \gamma \right)$$

These four conditions can be solved for the four π_i's giving,

$$\pi_0 = a_0 - \beta_0; \qquad \pi_1 = 1; \qquad \pi_2 = 1; \qquad \pi_3 = 1/[\gamma(1 - \beta_1) + \beta_1].$$

(The reader is advised to check this result before proceeding.)

Substituting these values for the π_i's in equations (3.11) and (3.13) and using the economy-wide version of equation (3.1), we can derive the solution for aggregate or economy-wide output as

$$y_t = \beta_0 + \frac{\beta_1 (1 - \gamma) u_t}{[\gamma(1 - \beta_1) + \beta_1]} \qquad (3.15)$$

where y_t is aggregate output. This expression can be written in more convenient form as

$$y_t = \beta_0 + \frac{\beta_1 \sigma_\varepsilon^2}{\beta_1 \sigma_\varepsilon^2 + \sigma_u^2} u_t \qquad (3.16)$$

The two major results we derived more intuitively in the earlier sections of this chapter are apparent from equation (3.16). First, only the unpredictable component of monetary growth u_t affects real output. The predictable component, g, does not appear in equation (3.16), i.e. it does not influence real output. And secondly the greater the variance of u i.e. the greater the unpredictability of monetary growth, the less the influence of any given value of u on real output. This result is apparent from the presence of the term σ_u^2 in the denominator of the second term in equation (3.16).

SUMMARY

In the next chapter we shall examine some of the criticisms of the model we have developed in this chapter and of the major results we have derived from that model. It is worthwhile restating what those major results are.

Shifts in aggregate demand will only affect real output if they are random and therefore unpredictable. Furthermore such shifts will have less effect on output the more unpredictable aggregate demand is. Attempts to stabilize an economy's real output by systematic manipulation of aggregate demand will fail since by making aggregate demand predictable they also render it ineffective. Governments should aim to make their policy instruments as predictable as possible so as to minimize confusion and hence undesirable fluctuations in output. This all provides some support for an approach to policy quite different from that associated with Keynes which has dominated policy makers over the last 30 years. This new approach to policy emphasises the need for governments to operate macroeconomic policy in accordance with simple and predetermined rules which on the whole do not link policy to the current or past state of the economy.

SUGGESTIONS FOR FURTHER READING

Friedman (1968) and Phelps (1967) (see also Phelps, (1970)) are the seminal statements of the natural rate hypothesis. Barro (1976), Lucas (1972, 1975) are equally influential, formal statements of the rational expectations hypothesis within a natural rate framework. Kydland and Prescott (1977) analyse in some detail the problem of the time inconsistency of policy. A useful introduction to the more technical aspects of the application of rational expectations can be found in Minford and Peel (1983).

4

Criticisms of the Flexible-Price Rational Expectations Model

It is hardly surprising that the attack on conventional macroeconomic policy outlined in the previous chapter has itself provoked a number of counter-attacks. We shall consider these counter-attacks under two broad headings: those which maintain the assumption of price flexibility; and those which do not.

4.1 CRITICISMS WHICH MAINTAIN PRICE FLEXIBILITY

In this first category we consider three main criticisms: (a) that the model developed in chapter 3 cannot account for a major feature of all economies, (b) that the model relies for all its results on very simple specifications of the aggregate supply and demand curves, and (c) that even if one accepts the model as it stands governments might effectively stabilize the economy if they possess better information about the economy than the private sector, or if some parts of the private sector possess better information than others.

(a) Serial Correlation in Aggregate Real Variables

The model developed so far suggests that only random movements in aggregate demand will cause real aggregate output to deviate from its natural or normal level. These random movements in aggregate demand are of course unpredictable and exhibit no clear pattern. The model therefore implies that the deviations of output from its natural rate should also be unpredictable and exhibit no pattern. But it is a common and easily observed fact that measures of aggregate output in any economy tend to be positively *serially correlated*, that is a higher than average value for aggregate output in any period is more often than not followed by a higher than average value next period and similarly a low value in any period is more likely to be followed by another low one than by a high one. To put it in common parlance, all economies experience booms and slumps many of which are quite drawn out or persistent. This persistence has been seen by many as an obvious contradiction of the prediction that deviations of output from its natural level should be random and hence a clear refutation of the rational expectations version of the aggregate supply and demand model developed above.

However, it is in fact easy to modify the model we have developed and thereby make it immune from this criticism whilst ensuring that all the important features of it are retained. Such modification involves specifying some form of *propagation mechanism* which converts serially *uncorrelated* shifts in aggregate demand into serially *correlated* movements in aggregate output. One obvious propagation mechanism is provided by stocks of finished goods. Firms might hold such stocks so that when faced with an unexpectedly high level of demand they can meet it without recourse to a sharp and possibly very costly increase in production. So if an unexpected rise in demand occurs they meet it partly by producing more and partly out of their stocks of goods. But such a response implies that next period their stocks of goods will be lower than they feel is optimal and they will therefore want to build them up again by producing more next period than they otherwise would. If they do this slowly then production will be higher than normal for a number of periods until stocks of goods are back at their optimal level. But this implies that a single random increase in aggregate demand in the current period can set up a serially correlated movement or boom in real output over a number of subsequent periods. Similarly, a single random decrease in aggregate demand could set up a multiperiod recession. (See Blinder and Fischer (1981)).

All the results derived from the simpler model explained in the previous chapter (see pp. 39–52) could also be derived from one which allows stocks of finished goods to play this role. It will still be the case that only random aggregate demand will affect real output and the more unpredictable aggregate demand is the less effect it has on output. The policy conclusions drawn from the simpler model will also still follow. Other propagation mechanisms could be introduced with much the same result. For example if it is costly for firms to hire more labour or adjust their capital stock it will be optimal for them to spread out over time their response to any relative price signals they receive. So in these cases too a random increase in aggregate demand will typically produce a 'strung out' response in aggregate output. None of the major implications derived from the simple model would be affected by the introduction of these mechanisms.

This criticism of the model is thus more a criticism of the form in which it is put than of its substance; the form can be changed to take account of the criticism without changing any matter of substance.

(b) The Simplicity of the Model

A more telling set of criticisms of the results we have derived from the rational expectations Aggregate Demand–Supply model concerns their reliance on extremely simple specifications for the Aggregate Supply and Demand curves. Minor, but realistic changes in specification alter the implications of the model significantly. For example, imagine a rise in income tax which is fully announced and anticipated. Standard economic theory suggests that this is likely to have an effect on the willingness of the population to work. The exact size or direction of the effect does not matter, what does is that there is a possibility of *some* effect. Thus a fully anticipated change in fiscal policy is quite likely to have some effect on real output in that it affects the willingness of the population to work to produce output.

Another and more important possible change of specification concerns the relative price term which determines what each supplier will supply. Up to now we have defined this relative price term as the current price in the local market relative to the expected *current* average price across all markets. In fact it is theoretically more likely that suppliers will respond to their local price relative to their expectation of *next period's* average price. If this (expected) relative price is high then it will pay suppliers to produce and sell more this period and hold the proceeds in monetary form in anticipation that their real value will increase as the average price level falls next period. If the (expected) relative price is low then it will pay suppliers not to supply as much because they will be anticipating a drop in the real value of the proceeds. This specification of the supply function emphasizes the 'intertemporal substitution' aspect of supply in that suppliers consider current and future time periods when deciding what quantities of output to supply. One implication of it is that a permanent rise in the rate of growth of aggregate demand and hence in the rate of inflation may permanently reduce the quantity of output supplied since it permanently reduces the real rate of return on holding the proceeds from sales in the form of money. Thus fully anticipated changes in the rate of growth of aggregate demand may affect the level of real output.

This point can be made formally by a simple modification to the model developed in the previous chapter. Rewrite the supply function – equation (3.1) in chapter 3 – as equation (4.1),

$$y^s(z)_t = \beta_0 + \beta_1[p(z)_t - E_t(z)p_{t+1}] \tag{4.1}$$

The only difference between this specification of the supply function and that in chapter 3 is that the expected current average price, $E_t(z)p_t$, has been replaced by the average price expected to prevail next period,

$E_t(z)p_{t+1}$. If we retain the rest of the model as outlined in chapter 3 and repeated for convenience here,

$$y^d(z)_t = \alpha_1 + m_t - E_t(z)p_t + \varepsilon(z)_t \qquad (4.2)$$

$$y^s(z)_t = y^d(z)_t \qquad (4.3)$$

$$m_t = m_{t-1} + g + u_t \qquad (4.4)$$

then the expected value of the random aggregate demand shock, u_t, will be the same as before, i.e.

$$E_t u_t = \gamma u_t \qquad (4.5)$$

where $\gamma = \sigma_u^2/[\sigma_u^2 + \sigma_\varepsilon^2]$ Using the same method described in chapter 3 we conjecture the solution for the aggregate price level to be as before,

$$p_t = \pi_0 + \pi_1 m_{t-1} + \pi_2 g + \pi_3 u_t. \qquad (4.6)$$

Given the rationality of expectations we can write the economy-wide or average expectation of p_t to be,

$$E_t p_t = \pi_0 + \pi_1 m_{t-1} + \pi_2 g + \pi_3 \gamma u_t. \qquad (4.7)$$

But now, because of the presence of $E_t p_{t+1}$ in the supply function, we have also to derive the economy wide rational expectation of p_{t+1} formed on the basis of the information available at the beginning of period t. Since it is a rational expectation it will be formed in accordance with the process determining p_{t+1}. From equation (4.6) we can deduce that p_{t+1} will be determined as follows,

$$p_{t+1} = \pi_0 + \pi_1 m_t + \pi_2 g + \pi_3 u_{t+1}. \qquad (4.8)$$

All that we have done here is lead equation (4.6) by one period, so m_{t-1} becomes m_t and so on. If this is the process determining p_{t+1} the rational expectation of p_{t+1} formed on the information available at the beginning of period t will be,

$$E_t p_{t+1} = \pi_0 + \pi_1 E_t m_t + \pi_2 E_t g + \pi_3 E_t u_{t+1}. \qquad (4.9)$$

Since the value of g is known it follows that $E_t g$ equals g; and since at time period t there is no information relating to the value of the random aggregate demand shock next period, u_{t+1}, the best guess that can be made at the beginning of period t about u_{t+1} is that it will equal zero, so

$E_t u_{t+1}$ equals zero. That leaves only $E_t m_t$; but since the process determining m_t is given in equation (4.4), the rational expectation of m_t will be formed in accordance with that process as

$$E_t m_t = E_t m_{t-1} + E_t g + E_t u_t \tag{4.10}$$

which equals

$$E_t m_t = m_{t-1} + g + \gamma u_t. \tag{4.11}$$

It follows that we can write $E_t p_{t+1}$ as

$$E_t p_{t+1} = \pi_0 + \pi_1 m_{t-1} + \pi_1 g + \pi_1 \gamma u_t + \pi_2 g. \tag{4.12}$$

To deduce the values of the 'π' coefficients we proceed as explained in chapter 3. First use the economy wide equivalents of equations (4.1) to (4.4) to obtain the following expression for the economy wide price level p_t,

$$p_t = (1/\beta_1)(\alpha_0 - \beta_0 + m_{t-1} + g + u_t - E_t p_t + \beta_1 E_t p_{t+1}). \tag{4.13}$$

Then substitute for $E_t p_t$ and $E_t p_{t+1}$ from equations (4.7) and (4.12) respectively to obtain,

$$p_t = (1/\beta_1)(\alpha_0 - \beta_0 + m_{t-1} + g + u_t - \pi_0 - \pi_1 m_{t-1} \\ - \pi_2 g - \pi_3 \gamma u_t) + \pi_0 + \pi_1 m_{t-1} + \pi_1 g + \pi_1 \gamma u_t + \pi_2 g. \tag{4.14}$$

Now set equation (4.14) equal to the solution for p_t given by equation (4.6) and obtain expressions for the π's in the way explained in chapter 3. The resulting values for the π's are as follows:

(1) $\quad \pi_0 = \alpha_0 - \beta_o$

(2) $\quad \pi_1 = 1$

(3) $\quad \pi_2 = 1 + \beta_1$

(4) $\quad \pi_3 = \dfrac{1 + \beta_1 \gamma}{1 + \beta_1}.$

(Again the student may wish to check this result before proceeding.) Using these values for the π's we can deduce from equations (4.6) and (4.12) the following

$$p_t - E_t p_{t+1} = -g + \left(\frac{1-\gamma}{1+\beta_1}\right) u_t. \tag{4.15}$$

Using this expression in the economy-wide equivalent of equation (4.1) gives the expression for aggregate output as

$$y_t = \beta_0 + \beta_1 \left(\frac{1-\gamma}{1+\beta_1} \right) u_t - \beta_1 g \qquad (4.16)$$

The important difference between this expression for aggregate output and the equivalent expression derived in chapter 3 is that in equation (4.16) the predictable component of money growth, *g*, *does* now appear. Thus if the supply function is specified by equation (4.1) one of the major results derived in chapter 3 is contradicted: predictable money growth, or more generally predictable movements in aggregate demand *will* have an effect on aggregate real output.

However, the method by which a change in predictable monetary growth leads to a change in aggregate real output is not the familiar one – a higher rate of monetary growth does not fool people into supplying more output. Indeed it does not lead to a rise in output at all but a fall. Variations in predictable monetary growth cause changes in aggregate real output because they cause changes in the normal or natural level of output and not deviations of output around its natural level. An increase in the anticipated growth of the money supply will raise the anticipated inflation rate, and this will lower normal output as is clear from equation (4.1). Thus the result derived in chapter 3 – that predictable changes in aggregate demand do not lead to deviations in real output around its natural level – can also be derived from a model which has the supply function as specified in equation (4.1).

There are other ways in which predictable changes in the rate of growth of aggregate demand might affect the aggregate level of output by affecting the natural level of output. For example, if a high rate of change of aggregate demand stimulates a high rate of inflation it may encourage people to hold less money and more physical assets. The accumulation of such assets, some of which could be new machinery and plant, may raise the natural level of output. Such effects, which operate through the rate of inflation and the resulting change in the rate of return from holding money are sometimes referred to as 'Tobin effects' after the article by Tobin (1961) who analysed some of them.

(c) Asymmetric Information

One assumption that we implicitly made when we derived the standard results of the rational expectations Aggregate Demand–Aggregate Supply model was that the private sector and the government sector have the same information. If they do not, in particular if the government sector has significantly better information it may be able to exploit that advantage in order to stabilize real output.

The point can be made quite simply. Imagine a random decrease in aggregate demand which for the private sector is unpredictable. In the absence of any change in government policy this unpredictable downward shift in the Aggregate Demand curve would induce a fall in real output. If the aggregate demand shift was also unpredictable to the government, then clearly the government could not take any measures to offset it. But if it had better information about what was likely to happen in the economy than the private sector, the government could take such measures. In the case we are considering this would involve some increase in government spending or some increase in the quantity of money or some combination of both. The result would be, provided the government acted efficiently, that the Aggregate Demand curve would not shift down: the tendency for it to do so being offset by government action. Hence there would be no fall in real output, the government would have stabilized it.

There is no doubt that where the government has such an advantage it can exploit it to stabilize output, though in the context of a rational expectations model it could achieve the same result by releasing the information to the private sector. The question is how important are such differences or asymmetries in information likely to be? On the whole it is difficult to believe that they are very important. Most macroeconomic data are published fairly quickly and any delay is usually due more to the time it takes to collect them than a strict publication lag. Government models of the economy have their counterpart in private sector models of the economy which although not exactly the same nevertheless exhibit much the same features. Besides it is standard practice for the government model to be known to those outside government. Furthermore of course if the government did possess an important information advantage there would be a strong incentive for the private sector to obtain the same information, so one might expect the advantage to be eroded.

The same objections might also be applied to the assumption that some groups in the private sector have better information than others. However, some interesting results have emerged from models which incorporate that assumption: in particular, within such models government stabilization can be effective. To illustrate this result we shall look at one version of such a model. (The analysis is somewhat mathematical, but we attempt a more intuitive explanation after explaining the mathematics of the model.)

In chapter 3 all economic agents were assumed to have information about *aggregate* or economy-wide variables dated $t-1$ and before but not to have information about any *current aggregate* variable. (The only current variable they observe is their own local price.) In the model described below we shall assume that *some* agents – consumers – have information about all the relevant current aggregate variables whereas other agents – suppliers – do not.

The economy is seen as having an aggregate supply curve similar to the one explained in chapter 3: deviations of aggregate supply from its natural rate are explained by the departure of the price level from the level suppliers expect it to be. Suppliers are assumed to form their expectations on the basis of aggregate information dated $t-1$ and before. To distinguish them from consumers who have more up-to-date information we shall write their expectation of p_t as $E_{t-1} p_t$. Assuming for convenience the natural level of output to be zero we write the aggregate supply function as

$$y_t^s = \beta(p_t - E_{t-1}p_t) \tag{4.17}$$

where
$\quad y_t^s$ = real aggregate supply
$\quad p_t$ = the general level of prices
$\quad E_{t-1}p_t$ = the general level of prices expected by suppliers
$\quad \beta$ = a positive constant
All variables are in logarithms.

Imagine that the major determinants of real aggregate demand are the real quantity of money in the economy and the expected rate of inflation. The reasons for the former variable influencing aggregate demand should be well known, the reason for the influence of the latter variable may be less so. Its influence can be explained in the following way: a high rate of expected inflation raises the cost or lowers the return of holding money and therefore makes the acquisition of goods more attractive. So the higher the expected rate of inflation the greater will aggregate demand be. We shall assume that unlike suppliers consumers do possess information about current aggregate variables. As a result they do not have to form an expectation about any current variables, they know their values. Furthermore when the forming expectations in period t about variables in periods after period t consumers will use all the information they possess at period t. Since the latter includes in their case current values of variables in period t their expectations will be written as E_t rather than E_{t-1}. So we write the aggregate demand function as:

$$y_t^d = m_t - p_t + \delta(E_t p_{t+1} - p_t) + \eta_t \tag{4.18}$$

where m is the nominal quantity of money and δ is a positive constant. All variables again are in natural logarithms.

In equation (4.18), η_t is a random error with mean zero. It can be thought of as representing random unpredictable movements in aggregate demand. $E_t p_{t+1} - p_t$ is the expected rate of inflation. Notice that the expectation on p_{t+1} is dated at t, and that there is no expectation term on the current price level. Both these results arise from the assumption that consumers have contemporaneous aggregate information.

Of course the absence of any relative demand terms in equation (4.18) is because it refers to an aggregate rather than to any individual market. Combining equations (4.17) and (4.18) we obtain the 'solution' for the price equation as

$$p_t = \left(\frac{1}{1+\beta+\delta}\right) m_t + \left(\frac{\beta}{1+\beta+\delta}\right) E_{t-1}p_t + \left(\frac{\delta}{1+\beta+\delta}\right) E_t p_{t+1}$$

$$+ \left(\frac{1}{1+\beta+\delta}\right) \eta_t \qquad (4.19)$$

Suppliers' expectations of p_t will be the rational expectation of equation (4.19) using all the information available at the end of period $t-1$, $E_{t-1}p_t$. This will be as follows:

$$E_{t-1}p_t = \left(\frac{1}{1+\beta+\delta}\right) E_{t-1}m_t + \left(\frac{\beta}{1+\beta+\delta}\right) E_{t-1}p_t$$

$$+ \left(\frac{\delta}{1+\beta+\delta}\right) E_{t-1}p_{t+1}. \qquad (4.20)$$

Notice that in forming this expression we have assumed that the suppliers' expectation of their own expectations of p_t equals their expectation of p_t, i.e. $E_{t-1} E_{t-1} p_t = E_{t-1}p_t$. And similarly that their expectation of the consumers' expectation of prices next period is equal to their own expectation of prices next period, i.e. $E_{t-1} E_t p_{t+1} = E_{t-1}p_{t+1}$. Both these assumptions are implied by rationality. In the first case because suppliers know their own expectation; and in the second because they do not have the information consumers have, and therefore the best guess that they can make is that consumers will make the same forecast as they do: any other guess would carry with it the implication that they themselves were wrong or consumers irrational.

Taking equation (4.20) from (4.19) yields:

$$p_t - E_{t-1}p_t = \left(\frac{1}{1+\beta+\delta}\right) (m_t - E_{t-1}m_t)$$

$$+ \left(\frac{\delta}{1+\beta+\delta}\right) (E_t p_{t+1} - E_{t-1}p_{t+1}) + \left(\frac{1}{1+\beta+\delta}\right) \eta_t \qquad (4.21)$$

It is clear from this equation that the price 'surprise' term, $p_t - E_{t-1}p_t$ depends upon the revision of future price expectations as more information becomes available between periods $t-1$ and t. This revision term is $(E_t p_{t+1} - E_{t-1}p_{t+1})$. The reason for its presence is that if, between period

$t-1$ and t, some new piece of information becomes available which leads consumers to change their expectation of price next period this will imply a change in aggregate demand in period t and hence a change in prices in period t. But since suppliers are assumed not to have that information when forming their expectations it follows that their expectations will not be changed by it. Therefore such information will alter the gap between actual prices and the prices suppliers are expecting.

The interesting feature about models which allow such revisions to be important is that monetary policy can have stabilizing effects. To show this we shall assume that the government devises a 'rule' by which it proposes to set the quantity of money in the economy. Imagine that it chooses to link the quantity of money to last period's aggregate demand shock, i.e.

$$m_t = \mu \eta_{t-1} \tag{4.22}$$

where μ is a policy parameter whose value can be chosen by the government in such a way as to minimize fluctuations of output around its natural rate. If equation (4.22) defines the money supply rule and agents are aware of it, then, under rational expectations, $E_{t-1}m_t = m_t$ because η_{t-1} is known to agents at the end of $t-1$. This allows us to re-write equation (4.21) as:

$$p_t - E_{t-1}p_t = \left(\frac{\delta}{1+\beta+\delta}\right)(E_t p_{t+1} - E_{t-1}p_{t+1}) + \left(\frac{1}{1+\beta+\delta}\right)\eta_t. \tag{4.23}$$

From the aggregate demand function (4.18) we can write

$$p_t = \left(\frac{1}{1+\delta}\right)(m_t - y_t + \delta E_t p_{t+1} + \eta_t) \tag{4.24}$$

and from this and the assumption of rationality we derive the following expectations

$$E_t p_{t+1} = \left(\frac{1}{1+\delta}\right)E_t m_{t+1} - \left(\frac{1}{1+\delta}\right)E_t y_{t+1} + \left(\frac{\delta}{1+\delta}\right)E_t p_{t+2} \tag{4.25}$$

$$E_{t-1}p_{t+1} = \left(\frac{1}{1+\delta}\right)E_{t-1}m_{t+1} - \left(\frac{1}{1+\delta}\right)E_{t-1}y_{t+1} + \left(\frac{\delta}{1+\delta}\right)E_{t-1}p_{t+2} \tag{4.26}$$

Since the natural level of output is assumed to be zero, the expected value for output in period $t+1$ is also zero whether expectations are dated at t or $t-1$, for neither consumers nor suppliers have any reason to think in period t that η_{t+1} will be other than its mean value of zero. Since the money supply is assumed to depend on only the lagged demand shock, it follows that no new information will become available to consumers between periods $t-1$ and t that will lead them to change their expectations of p_{t+2}. These two results together imply that the last two terms are the same in both the price expectation equations and so we can derive the following expression for the price expectation revision term:

$$E_t p_{t+1} - E_{t-1} p_{t+1} = \left(\frac{1}{1+\delta}\right)(E_t m_{t+1} - E_{t-1} m_{t+1}) \qquad (4.27)$$

Now $E_{t-1} m_{t+1}=0$ since at period $t-1$ the aggregate demand shock is expected to be zero in period t. However, $E_t m_{t+1}=\mu\eta_t$ since η_t is known when expectations are being formed. Therefore equation (4.27) may be written:

$$E_t p_{t+1} - E_{t-1} p_{t+1} = \left(\frac{1}{1+\delta}\right)\mu\eta_t \qquad (4.28)$$

The price surprise term $p_t - E_{t-1} p_t$ which determines aggregate supply may thus be written as

$$p_t - E_{t-1} p_t = \left(\frac{\delta}{(1+\beta+\delta)(1+\delta)}\right)(\mu\eta_t) + \left(\frac{1}{1+\beta+\delta}\right)\eta_t. \qquad (4.29)$$

It should now be clear that the government could, by the appropriate choice of μ set the right-hand side of (4.29) to zero and thereby remove all output fluctuations. By setting $\mu = -(1+\delta)/\delta$, the reader can verify that the right-hand side of (4.29) becomes zero and the output equation can be written $y_t = 0$ which is the assumed natural rate of output. Thus governments may have a role to play in stabilizing the economy even where expectations are fully rational provided different groups within the private sector have access to different information. The importance of different groups having different information is easily seen by noting that if we had assumed that everyone had information dated at period $t-1$ equation (4.27) would be zero and there would be no terms involving μ in equation (4.29). In other words the choice the monetary authorities made about μ would be of no importance in determining the degree to which aggregate output fluctuates around its natural level: government policy would be irrelevant.

The mathematics of this result is complicated and it is therefore worthwhile attempting an intuitive explanation of it, though not surprisingly, since the mathematics is complicated, so too is the intuitive explanation. Imagine that for whatever reason the aggregate demand shock, η_t, is positive. Suppliers do not observe this shock and are therefore fooled by it into supplying a higher level of output than they would have done if they had forecast the rise in demand. Consumers on the other hand do observe the current value of η_t. Being rational, they will realize that suppliers will not have anticipated it and will therefore be selling their output in period t at a lower price than they would have done if they had anticipated it. This implies that the rise in prices between period t and period $t+1$ will tend, *ceteris paribus*, to be higher than it otherwise would be as suppliers become aware in period $t+1$ of the mistake they made in period t and raise their prices accordingly. The threat that prices in period $t+1$ will be sharply higher provides another reason for consumers to buy now, in period t, rather than in period $t+1$.

So there will be two distinct effects increasing aggregate output. One is the initial shock to aggregate demand which suppliers do not predict and which opens up a gap between actual prices and those expected by suppliers. The other is the recognition by consumers that suppliers have not anticipated what has happened and that this implies a higher rate of inflation between periods t and $t+1$: this effect will further widen the gap between actual prices and those expected by suppliers and therefore further raise aggregate output.

But if the monetary authorities are known to be following a rule of decreasing the quantity of money in period $t+1$ if there is a positive value for η in period t, rational consumers will infer from their knowledge that η_t is positive that the government will reduce the quantity of money in period $t+1$. This in turn implies some reduction in the tendency described in the previous paragraph for prices to rise at a fast rate between period t and $t+1$. Provided the authorities select appropriately the amount by which they promise to decrease the quantity of money in response to a positive value for η_t they can even make consumers realize that a positive demand shock in period t implies a fall in prices between periods t and $t+1$ because of the policy response it will evoke in period $t+1$. But if consumers expect a fall in price between periods t and $t+1$ this will lower their aggregate demand in period t. The authorities can thus drive down aggregate demand in period t to the point where it is just sufficient to ensure an actual level of prices equal to the one suppliers are expecting. This, of course, means that aggregate output is stabilized at its natural level. Thus differential information between groups within the private sector can restore the effectiveness of government policy in stabilizing the economy's output. The analysis above is based partly on Turnovsky (1980) and Weiss (1980).

4.2 THE IMPLICATIONS OF ASSUMING PRICE STICKINESS

In the previous chapter the theory of rational expectations was combined with a macroeconomic model which assumed full price flexibility: on each island, each period the price of the good moved to equate supply and demand. A major result was that *systematic* aggregate demand policies would be ineffective in stabilizing real output, employment and other real variables. It is commonly agreed that whilst in some markets prices move in the way this model assumes – very quickly to equate changes in supply and demand, in other markets they do not. For example, in the foreign exchange market or the stock markets the prices of currencies or stocks and shares change by the hour to equate supply and demand. The prices of certain goods like vegetables also seem to respond very promptly to changes in supply and demand. Even in certain labour markets, for example casual day labour, the price of labour can move apparently very freely. But there are other markets in which prices appear to move sluggishly and to be, at least in the short run, unresponsive to changes in supply and demand. Many labour markets appear to fall into this category with wage rates being determined through complex institutional arrangements and bargaining processes which seem to imply that they will be less than fully flexible. The prices of certain goods too – notably manufactured goods – appear to be 'administered' or set for some time so that they do not respond immediately to changes in supply and demand.

Of course prices may appear to be more sticky than they in fact are, for there are many ways of changing the 'price' of a good without changing the amount of £s printed on the good's label. For example, a firm could offer better after-sales service for the microcomputer, a longer guarantee for the television; it could waive delivery charges for the new table, or throw in a set of free wine glasses with the petrol. All such measures can be seen as changing the terms on which a good is bought, a broad interpretation of its price, without necessarily changing the quoted price of the good. Thus the fact that quoted prices appear inflexible may not necessarily imply that prices broadly interpreted are.

Furthermore pointing to inflexibility in some prices does not by itself show that the assumption of general price flexibility is unreasonable. It may be that the cited deviations from price flexibility are empirically unimportant, that is they do not significantly affect the 'average' behaviour of prices.

However, most economists would agree that there is at the very least prima-facie evidence that a significant number of prices are not fully flexible and that one ought therefore to consider the implications of sticky prices in macroeconomic models. In the rest of this chapter we shall drop the assumption that prices are fully flexible and examine the implications of assuming that they are either fixed or at least move only slowly to their 'equilibrium' values. We shall maintain the assumption that expectations are rational and show that it is not this assumption *per se* which guarantees the ineffectiveness of systematic stabilization policy but its combination with (inter alia) the assumption of price flexibility. Thus even if expectations are fully rational there may be a role for systematic stabilization policy provided prices are sufficiently inflexible.

(a) The McCallum Model

We begin the analysis of sticky prices by recalling the policy implications of the flexible price model developed in the previous chapter. In figure 4.1 AD_0 represents the level of aggregate demand (rationally) expected to prevail at time t. The typical expectation of the general price level is therefore P_0. If the actual level of aggregate demand is greater than that expected (say AD_1 in figure 4.1) the actual level of prices will move above P_0 to equate supply and demand and output will rise above Y^n. The reason

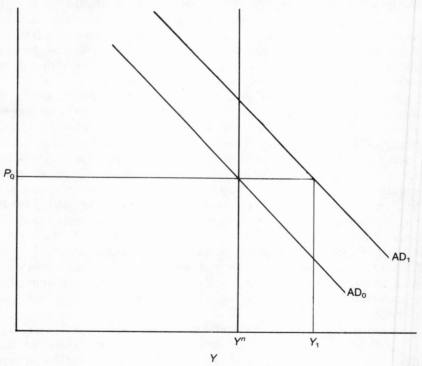

FIGURE 4.1   Sticky prices and excess demand.

for the rise in output is that the unexpectedly high level of aggregate demand has led to the typical supplier observing an unexpectedly high price. Partly misinterpreting this as due to a favourable relative demand shift the typical supplier increases output to take advantage of what (wrongly) appears to be a high relative price. Any rise in aggregate demand which was rationally anticipated would have had no such effect – it would merely have led to a rise in prices. Systematic changes in the instruments of monetary and fiscal policy would produce only predictable changes in aggregate demand and therefore cannot be used to stabilize real output – policy is ineffective.

How would the implications of this model be changed if prices were temporarily fixed or 'sticky'? The answer depends upon the precise nature of price rigidity. The definition of price stickiness which we shall employ in this section does not in fact alter very much the policy implications of the model developed in the previous chapter though it does have implications for tests of that model. This definition was suggested by McCallum (1977, 1978). In his model firms set prices at the end of period $t-1$ to cover period t. Once set, prices cannot be changed within period t. At the end of period t prices are then set for period $t+1$, and so on. In this sense prices in period t are sticky: they are set one period in advance and are then unresponsive to the level of demand which actually occurs in period t. McCallum assumes that firms set their prices for period t in the following way. Given all the information available to them at the end of period $t-1$ firms expect that the position of the Aggregate Demand curve in period t will be AD_0 in figure 4.1. Firms aim to set prices so that their expected level of production is in each period (in total) Y^n. Given that the typical firm expects the Aggregate Demand curve to be AD_0 it follows that the general level of prices set at period $t-1$ for period t will be P_0.

If the actual Aggregate Demand curve is AD_0 the general level of prices will be P_0 and the level of output will be Y^n, but what happens if the Aggregate Demand curve is higher than expected, say at AD_1? Of course such a shift in the Aggregate Demand curve can only occur, given rational expectations, if it is the result of a random, unpredictable movement in, for example, monetary and fiscal policy, It cannot occur through any systematic movement or it would have been predicted. But if such a random movement occurs how will firms react to it? In particular, given that prices have already been set and cannot be changed what will happen to real output? The answer requires some specification of a 'quantity rule' – i.e. a description of agents' behaviour when, because of price stickiness, disequilibrium prevails.

To understand the need for some quantity rule consider figure 4.1 again. It is clear from that figure that at the price level P_0 the level of actual aggregate demand is Y_1 whereas firms initially wanted to produce Y^n, in other words there is excess demand. Output could be as high as Y_1 if firms adopt the rule of producing whatever is demanded, or as low as Y^n if firms decide to produce only what they planned initially. The quantity rule determines where between these two extremes the level of actual output will be.

A frequently invoked quantity rule is that if there is disequilibrium, that is a difference between the quantity demanded and the quantity supplied, the actual quantity traded will equal the minimum of demand or supply. So if there is excess supply the quantity actually traded will be the quantity demanded, and if there is excess demand the quantity actually traded will be the quantity supplied. The rationale for this quantity rule is that it implies that no agents are forced to buy or sell quantities in excess of their wishes, so the rule preserves the principle of voluntary exchange. In the present context this rule would imply that output will equal Y^n in figure 4.1 with the gap $Y_1 - Y^n$ being unsatisfied excess demand. So the result of the unanticipated movement in aggregate demand is merely to create excess demand: prices are already fixed at P_0, and the quantity rule implies that output remains at Y^n.

An alternative quantity rule sets output equal to the level of demand. The rationale here is that firms may wish to preserve customer goodwill by preventing shortages. They may therefore agree to sell at price level P_0 whatever is demanded. In figure 4.1 this implies that output would rise to Y_1 if aggregate demand unexpectedly rose to AD_1.

Clearly then different quantity rules imply different solutions for output. With the 'minimum' quantity rule, unexpectedly high levels of aggregate demand do not raise output above Y^n but unexpectedly low levels of aggregate demand will depress output below Y^n (the reader may wish to verify this by imagining an actual Aggregate Demand curve to the left of AD_0.) Setting output equal to aggregate demand means that output will exceed Y^n when aggregate demand is unexpectedly high and output will fall below Y^n when aggregate demand is unexpectedly low. Whatever the rule the mechanism by which random movements in aggregate demand lead to fluctuations in output is not the same as the one explained in chapter 3. There the random movement in aggregate demand leads to an unexpectedly high price and it is this which induces a rise in output. But here such a change in price cannot occur since prices are fixed at the end of period $t-1$ and their values are therefore known. Thus in McCallum's model unexpected fluctuations in aggregate demand can cause changes in real output even though they do not cause unexpected movements in prices.

What happens to the 'policy ineffectiveness proposition' in this model? McCallum assumes that the government decides its monetary and fiscal policies for period t at the end of period $t-1$, and cannot or does not change them in period t. In this sense he assumes that government policy is subject to the same degree of stickiness as prices. Since aggregate demand policies are decided on the basis of the information available at the end of period $t-1$ it follows that the systematic component of aggregate demand will as before have no effect on real output. For by definition the systematic element in aggregate demand can be predicted at the end of period $t-1$ and will be reflected purely in the prices firms set at the end of that period for next period. The stickiness in prices assumed in the model is not sufficiently severe to change the key result of chapter 3: only the random component of aggregate demand can affect real output. Thus the policy ineffectiveness proposition can survive in a model where prices exhibit some degree of stickiness provided the policy instruments exhibit the same degree of stickiness.

More generally prices could be sticky and yet the major implications of the flexible price model developed in chapter 3 could still be true. The shorter the period over which *prices* are sticky in relation to the period over which *government policy instruments* are sticky the more likely it is that the policy implications of chapter 3 will remain true.

(b) The Fischer–Phelps–Taylor Model

As we have just seen the policy ineffectiveness proposition derived from a flexible price model can also occur in a sticky price model provided that the period over which firms, or more generally the private sector, agree to fix prices is no longer than the period over which the authorities cannot or will not change their policy instruments. In a contrasting approach, a number of writers have introduced the possibility that private agents, e.g. firms or workers, may bind themselves to fix prices over periods long enough to permit within-period reaction by the policy-makers. In such models the policy ineffectiveness proposition no longer results, even though expectations are assumed to be rational. The original application of rational expectations to this type of sticky price model was by Fischer (1977), Phelps and Taylor (1977) and later by Taylor (1979). The models developed in these articles are fairly technical in nature but their important features and policy implications can easily be illustrated with the Aggregate Demand–Aggregate Supply model of chapter 3.

Imagine an economy where firms, for whatever reason, agree to fix prices at the end of period t to cover periods $t+1$ and $t+2$, and not to alter these prices in either period $t+1$ or $t+2$ if cicumstances differ from those expected at the close of period t. Similarly at the end of period $t+2$ firms set prices to cover periods $t+3$ and $t+4$, and these prices may not be altered in periods $t+3$ and $t+4$. In other words prices are set at the end of every even period (0, 2, 4, etc.) to cover the next two periods. In deciding what prices to set firms form an expectation (which of course we shall assume is rational) of what the price level is likely to be in the next two periods.

Using figure 4.1 again we might imagine firms at the end of period 0 expect that the position of the Aggregate Demand curve will be AD_0 in period 1. For simplicity we shall also assume that firms expect the position of the Aggregate Demand curve in period 2 will also be AD_0. Given their (rational) expectations firms agree to set prices at P_0 in periods 1 and 2, and therefore expect to produce a level of output in both periods equal to Y^n. If the position of the Aggregate Demand curve in periods 1 and 2 turns out to be as expected then obviously in both periods the general level of prices will be P_0 and the aggregate level of output will be Y^n. But imagine that the aggregate demand curve is at AD_0 in period 1 but shifts out to AD_1 in period 2, what will happen then? The answer of course depends upon the quantity rule firms employ, in particular how they react to a higher level of demand than they were expecting. If firms are anxious to maintain customer goodwill and therefore agree to produce whatever is demanded at the set price then the effective supply curve for periods 1 and 2 is the horizontal line from P_0. Thus in period 2 if the Aggregate Demand curve is in fact AD_1 output will rise to Y_1, price remaining at P_0. Of course if aggregate demand fell below the level indicated by AD_0 then the level of output would fall below Y^n.

It is now straightforward to show how government policies, even anticipated ones, can stabilize real output in this model of 'sticky' prices. Imagine that firms have set their prices at the end of period 0 to give a price level of P_0 in periods 1 and 2. They have done this because they rationally expect the Aggregate Demand curve to be AD_0 in periods 1 and 2. Imagine that private sector investment, a component of aggregate demand, turns out to be unexpectedly high in period 2, so that in period 2 the Aggregate Demand curve is in fact AD_1. In the absence of any change in government policy, and if firms are following the quantity rule of setting output equal to demand, output will rise to Y_1 in period 2. It is important to realize that firms may have enough information at the end of period 1 to predict the rise in aggregate demand in period 2 so that the rise in aggregate demand from period 1 to period 2 is anticipated at the end of period 1. But the rise in aggregate demand was not anticipated at the end of period 0.

But despite their ability to predict the coming rise in aggregate demand firms are obliged to keep prices at P_0 and to produce Y_1. Thus in this model even anticipated movements in aggregate demand may affect the level of output. Whether they do or not depends upon their timing. If they can be anticipated at the end of one of the even periods they will have no effect on real output: prices will merely adjust to keep output at its natural rate Y^n. But if they can only be anticipated at the end of one of the odd periods they will have an effect on real output because prices are fixed.

Furthermore, government policy can now be used to stabilize real output. For if at the end of period 1 a rise in aggregate demand is predictable the government could reduce its own spending and thereby maintain the position of the aggregate demand curve at AD_0, and hence maintain aggregate real output at Y^n. Such a policy would work even if, at the end of period 1, it was perfectly predictable. It does not rely for its efficacy on the government having access to better information, for as we have said firms may well be able to anticipate the rise in aggregate demand between periods 1 and 2. What it does rely on is the government's ability to change its policy instruments more quickly than firms can change prices.

To summarize the argument so far: if price stickiness is of the 'McCallum type' so that firms' price-setting and authorities' policy-setting are defined over the same period (one period) the major implications of applying rational expectations to the flexible price model developed in chapter 3 still apply. Anticipated shifts in aggregate demand will have no real output effects and therefore systematic monetary and fiscal policy cannot be used to stabilize real output. By contrast if prices are rigid over periods longer than the planning period of policy-makers, anticipated policies can have real effects and therefore can be used by the government to iron-out perturbations caused by fluctuations in the other determinants of aggregate demand. The effectiveness of policy in this case arises because the private sector limits its own behaviour by binding itself to set prices for a certain number of periods ahead, whereas the government is assumed to be free to act to remove the disequilibrium to which price stickiness can lead.

(c)   'Partly Flexible' Prices

The sticky price models explained above assumed that prices are set at fixed levels for a given period of time; whatever the realized level of aggregate demand, nothing can be done to change the price level in either model. In the two-period 'contract' model firms set prices at the end of period 0 to cover periods 1 and 2, and can only adjust them again at the end of period 2 to cover periods 3 and 4. This assumption may seem unduly restrictive. One can imagine, for example, an expansion (or contraction) in aggregate demand sufficiently severe for firms to have an incentive to abrogate their agreement or contract to keep prices at the level decided two periods ago. Or one might imagine the contract formally or informally recognizing that in certain circumstances prices will be changed within periods. One way of incorporating this idea is to assume that prices are 'partly flexible'. Suppose, for example, that prices adjust part way to their equilibrium levels, but are not free to adjust fully each period. We can represent the adjustment of prices in the following equation:

$$P_t - P_{t-1} = \beta(P^* - P_{t-1}) \tag{4.30}$$

where β = a positive fraction
     P^* = the equilibrium price level.

One justification for this equation is that all firms adjust their prices slowly (possibly in order to maintain goodwill with their customers, or because there are other costs to price adjustment). Another is that whilst some prices adjust fully each period others are fixed for different lengths of time and equation (4.30) represents the resulting movement in average prices.

Consider the implications of adding equation (4.30) to our aggregate supply and demand model. Let the initial state of the economy be the equilibrium given in Figure 4.2 with the price level P_0 and the level of output Y^n. Now let this equilibrium be disturbed by an anticipated rise in government expenditure which shifts the aggregate demand curve to AD_1.

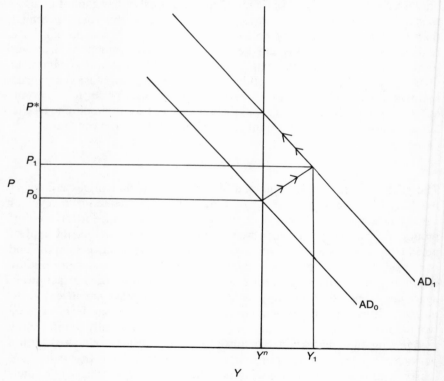

FIGURE 4.2   The response of output to a rise in aggregate demand when prices are partly flexible.

Since this shift is assumed to be rationally anticipated the expected price level would rise to P^* if prices were believed to be fully flexible. But from equation (4.30) prices are not fully flexible; in fact equation (4.30) indicates that in period 1, the period in which the shift in aggregate demand occurs, the price level adjusts to P_1, that is $P_1 - P_0 = \beta(P^* - P_0)$.

Rational forecasters will know that prices are sticky in this way and with their knowledge of the aggregate demand shift etc. they will expect the price level to be P_1. And since P_1 is both the actual and the expected price level firms will wish to produce in aggregate Y^n. However, the level of aggregate demand at P_1 is Y_1. As with the other sticky price models disequilibrium prevails and the solution for output requires a quantity rule. If output were determined by the minimum of supply and demand, the level of output in this case would be Y^n. Alternatively, firms may wish to minimize customer inconvenience by agreeing to supply whatever is demanded at each price, in which case output would rise to Y_1. If this second quantity rule applies the timepath for prices and output would be given by the arrows in Figure 4.2. Notice that in this model output again deviates from its natural level Y^n in periods of high aggregate demand because of the inflexibility of prices even though price expectations are rationally formed and the changes in aggregate demand are fully anticipated. And it is straightforward to show that in this model too anticipated monetary and fiscal policies can stabilize output. With each anticipated increase (decrease) in aggregate demand, the authorities simply adjust their own policy instruments to maintain the original Aggregate Demand curve and thereby achieve real output (and also price) stability.

(d) Sticky Prices and General Equilibrium

The sticky price models we have so far considered tend merely to 'tack on' the assumption of sticky prices to the sort of model developed in chapter 3. In recent years a number of economists have developed models which make price stickiness and the ensuing failure of markets to clear central to their analysis. In these models much attention has focused on the *interaction* between markets which fail to clear and the mechanisms by which agents' actions are co-ordinated when prices are sticky. Early macroeconomic models with quantity rationing were developed by Solow and Stiglitz (1968), Barro and Grossman (1971) and Malinvaud (1977). In what follows the main ideas of these models are discussed in general terms and the implications of allowing expectations to be rational within them are very briefly mentioned. We cannot in this book discuss the models in any depth: the interested reader is referred to Muellbauer and Portes (1978).

The central contribution of these models has been to focus on the 'spill-over' effects that result from the failure of markets to clear. If one market fails to clear, this will have repercussions in other markets and these in turn may further affect the disequilibrium in the initial market. These 'spill-over' effects require a 'general equilibrium' analysis – that is one in which the interaction between all markets is considered.

As an illustration of such 'spill-over' effects, imagine an economy with only two markets – a labour market and a goods market. Households supply labour and demand goods; firms supply goods and demand labour. Because wages and prices are rigid both markets fail to clear. Initially we assume that there is excess supply in both markets. Once again we note that the failure of each market to clear requires a quantity rule for each. We shall assume that output is determined by the minimum of supply and demand so that with excess supply in both markets, the quantities traded in each will be determined by *demand*. In the labour market employment is determined by the demand for labour by firms; in the goods market actual output is determined by the demand for goods by households.

Excess supply of labour means that households are *rationed* in the labour market: they cannot sell the quantity of labour services they wish to at current wages and prices. This may mean that some workers are unemployed or that all workers are underemployed or a combination of both. Because households do not realize their desired labour supply, they will not be able to achieve their desired demand for goods. This arises from the fact that unemployment or underemployment will reduce the household's income and *constrain* the demand for goods. The *effective* demand for goods (to use a familiar Keynesian term) is below what households would optimally choose *given current wages and prices*. The rationing of the household in the labour market spills over into the goods market by constraining the household's demand for goods.

Similarly, consider the effects of rationing in the goods market. Here excess supply of goods means that output is determined by demand and firms cannot sell the desired volume of output. Firms are *rationed* in the goods market. Because of this (and assuming for simplicity that firms do not carry inventories) they will demand only enough labour to produce the output they *can* sell, for any additional inputs of labour will either be idle or else will produce output which will remain unsold. It is therefore only profitable for the firm to demand just enough labour to meet the demand for output. The demand for labour is therefore *constrained* by the fact that the firm is rationed in the goods market. In this way a ration in the goods market spills over into the labour market by constraining the demand for labour.

Since the constrained demand for goods (by households rationed in the labour market) will exacerbate the ration of firms in the goods market, and since the constrained demand for labour will further ration the household in the labour market, it is natural to ask whether the behaviour of both sets of agents can be mutually consistent. To be mutually consistent the constrained demand for goods must ration firms in a manner that constrains their demand for labour to give rise to the initial constrained demand for goods. The nature of such a 'quantity constrained equilibrium' is discussed in the references cited above. The coexistence of excess supplies of labour and goods is referred to as a 'Keynesian' quantity constrained equilibrium. Depending on the precise values assumed for the (fixed) levels of wages and prices, other non-market clearing regimes are:

(1) Classical: Excess supply of labour; excess demand for goods.
(2) Repressed inflation: excess demand for goods and labour.
(3) Underconsumption: Excess demand for labour; excess supply of goods.

The significance of these regimes for economic policy has been explored in a number of papers, especially in Muellbauer and Portes (1978) and Malinvaud (1977). In these and other models, households save for future consumption (by accumulating money balances) and firms can accumulate inventories for future sales. Because of this, expectations of the future have important effects on the present. For example if the household expects to be rationed in the goods market in the future, there is less reason to save out of current income and consequently current demand for goods will rise. If a firm expects to be rationed in the future in the goods market, it is more likely to increase its current sales rather than produce for inventories. There is of course no reason why expectations of future rations should not be rational (i.e. based on current information including the economic model of how these rations arise). Indeed Neary and Stiglitz (1983) have introduced the idea of 'rational constraint expectations' into a model characterized by rationing and constrained equilibrium.

The analysis of such models under rational expectations is too compli-cated to discuss in detail here, but the main implications of the Neary and Stiglitz model are worth sketching. When Keynesian quantity constrained equilibrium exists in the current period (i.e. excess supply of both labour and goods) the multiplier effect of government spending (whether that spending is anticipated or otherwise) is greater under rational expectations than under 'static' (non-rational) expectations. Similarly an increase in the supply of money will have real output effects whether it is anticipated or otherwise. The allowance for spill-over effects between markets does not alter the policy implications discussed in simpler models earlier in this chapter, *viz.* that anticipated policies (both monetary and fiscal) can be used to 'stabilize' output. Moreover, the increase in the expenditure multiplier led Neary and Stiglitz to argue that the introduction of rational expectations into 'quantity constrained' models 'actually enhances the effectiveness of government policy' (p. 224).

4.3   MICRO-FOUNDATIONS FOR STICKY PRICES

The previous section has shown that the precise nature of price stickiness is of major importance to the results usually derived from rational expectations macroeconomic models. For if prices are rigid in the McCallum sense the main results of flexible price models carry through, in particular systematic attempts to stabilize real output, employment and other real variables will fail. Whereas if prices are sticky over periods long enough to permit policy adjustments by the government the case for the type of stabilization policy advocated by Keynesian economists is restored even if expectations are rational.

Proponents of the view that Keynesian stabilization policies are futile have been quick to point out the key role that wage and price rigidity play in justifying such policies and the need for supporters of such policies to provide some theory of why prices should be rigid in the way they claim they are. Imposing exogenously a particular form of price rigidity which happens to produce the result that Keynesian stabilization policies can work is hardly enough by itself to justify such policies. After all it seems likely that the form of wage and price rigidity in an economy will reflect the economic environment, one component of which is likely to be the behaviour of aggregate demand. For example, in the two-period model described in section 4.2(b) above it would seem likely that if aggregate demand became more volatile firms would become much more reluctant to agree to set prices two periods in advance and so perhaps they would set prices only one period in advance: the nature of price rigidity would change in response to a change in the economic environment.

It is for this reason that Keynesian stabilization policies have been criticized for relying on the 'unexplained postulate' of wage rigidity, and for assuming that the form of wage and price rigidity, the form of wage and price contracts, is exogenously given rather than determined by, amongst other things, the type of monetary and fiscal policies being carried out.

This point has been forcefully expressed by two of the leading proponents of rational expectations, Lucas and Sargent:

> So the issue here is really the fundamental one involved in the dispute between Keynes and the classical economists: is it adequate to regard certain superficial characteristics of existing wage contracts as given when analysing the consequences of alternative monetary and fiscal regimes? Classical economic theory denies that those characteristics can be taken as given. To understand the implications of long term contracts for monetary policy, one needs a model of the way those contracts are likely to respond to alternative monetary policy

regimes. An extension of existing equilibrium models in this direction might well lead to interesting variations, but it seems to us unlikely that major modifications of the implications of these models for monetary and fiscal policy will follow from this.

(Lucas and Sargent, 1978 p. 65)

The need to find a sound theoretical basis for wage and price stickiness has inspired a large and growing literature on what has become known as contract theory. Some of the early contributions (for example by Azariadis (1975); Baily, (1974); Gordon, (1974)) emphasized that in their very nature employers are likely to be more willing to undertake risk than are workers. If firms offered to remove or take on themselves some of the risk which otherwise workers would have to undertake they would be able to obtain workers for somewhat lower average wages. One way in which firms could do this would be to guarantee workers a fixed wage over some specified period on the understanding that if conditions deteriorated there would be layoffs but no reduction in the wage paid to those not laid off, and if conditions improved workers would be rehired at the same wage rate. Such a contract might appeal to workers in that it makes their earnings a little more certain and hence their employment conditions less risky, and might also appeal to firms because it allows them to hire workers for average wages which are lower than they otherwise would be because of the lower risk associated with the form of contract assumed. There have been many extensions and other ideas in the literature on contract theory which it is beyond the scope of this book to review. One problem for most of the theories is that they usually explain why real wages might be fixed over some period and do not explain why nominal wages might be similarly fixed. Another problem, particularly important in the context we are considering, has been raised by Barro (1977b). His argument centered on long-term contracts in the labour market but its force can be appreciated by examination of fixed-price contracts as illustrated in Figure 4.1.

Suppose that a contract to sell at a given price for a specified period is, for whatever reason, advantageous to both buyers and sellers. A contract is therefore concluded to sell at a price P_0 for a set period (the exact length of this period is of no immediate concern). If unpredictable changes in aggregate demand occur, disequilibrium results: for example an unexpectedly high level of aggregate demand would cause excess demand to arise. In such a circumstance a quantity rule has to be adopted in order to determine what actual output will be, and one which we adopted was that actual output would equal the level of demand, thus obliging firms to produce and sell more than they initially considered optimal at the price set. If they are rational, firms will realize that such disturbances can occur even though they cannot forecast their precise timing. Furthermore they will know that such disturbances will force them to produce a level of output which is not the optimal one in the sense that it is not what they would in advance choose to produce at a price P_0. Barro's question is why should firms agree to a course of action which they know in certain circumstances will force them to do something which in advance or *ex ante* appears suboptimal? To put this a slightly different way: a contract which fixes price but specifies that output will equal whatever demand turns out to be must *ex ante* be suboptimal for firms.

A similar question can be asked about consumers when the quantity rule is that output equals the minimum of demand and supply. For this implies that if there is an unexpected rise in demand in period t consumers will not be able to buy the quantity of the good they at time period $t-1$, or *ex ante*, considered optimal at the set price. Knowing that such disturbances can occur why should consumers agree to a form of contract which, in such circumstances, forces them to acquire a quantity of goods at the agreed price which they consider suboptimal? Such a contract must *ex ante* be suboptimal.

As Barro points out the only quantity rule which does not carry with it the implication that at times buyers or sellers will, *at the price set*, trade a quantity of the good they consider *in advance* to be suboptimal is a rule which sets output equal to the value it would take in the absence of any unanticipated disturbances, i.e. Y^n. For then if the price is set at P_0 the quantity traded will equal the quantity that buyers at the end of period $t-1$ thought optimal at that price, and also the quantity which firms at the end of period $t-1$ thought optimal to produce at that price. Of course if disturbances occur to aggregate demand buyers or sellers who have agreed on a price of P_0 and a quantity to be traded of Y^n will find themselves buying more or less than they now think is optimal, but that is not the point. At the time they agreed the contract, period $t-1$, it appeared optimal to trade the quantity Y^n if the price level was P_0. And since that is what the contract binds both sides to do it is at period $t-1$ an optimal contract.

The force of Barro's point should now be clear: in order to explain quantity movements when prices are sticky Keynesian economists must provide some theoretical justification for the quantity rule they use. A quantity rule which fixes price but not output appears to be suboptimal. If economic agents are assumed to be rational optimizers when forming expectations why should they not also be rational optimizers when drawing up contracts? And if they are, why should they draw up contracts which fix prices but not output? But if they fix output how do quantity movements occur? As we have said these questions are the subject of a large amount of current research which it is beyond the scope of this book to consider.

SUMMARY

In this chapter we have dealt with the major criticisms of the model developed in chapter 3, in particular we have shown the implications of applying rational expectations to a variety of sticky price macroeconomic models. What emerges is that some of the key conclusions of the model developed in chapter 3 survive the assumption of sticky prices only if the period over which prices are sticky is relatively short. In particular the implication derived in chapter 3 that systematic manipulation of monetary and fiscal policy must fail to stabilize real output is rejected if prices are sticky over periods within which government can alter fiscal and monetary policy. However, we have also shown that the theoretical basis for sticky prices is rather poorly developed, and that on these grounds advocates of rational expectations have criticized the ability of sticky price models to explain output fluctuations in a way which is consistent with rational behaviour. None the less the presence of sticky prices and asymmetric information led one notable advocate of rational expectations to write 'the potential usefulness of activist policy rules in dampening fluctuations . . . may survive the rational expectations revolution' (McCallum, 1980 p. 738).

SUGGESTIONS FOR FURTHER READING

Buiter (1980) summarizes and develops a number of criticisms of the rational expectations equilibrium macroeconomic model. Marini (1985) demonstrates that stabilization through monetary policy is possible in Barro's (1976) model. Gray (1976) analyses certain conditions under which 'sticky' wages might be optimal.

5

Rational Expectations and the Open Economy

In the previous two chapters we applied rational expectations to a closed-economy macroeconomic model, i.e. to a model of the economy which ignores any trade in goods or financial assets which takes place between different countries. In this chapter we shall consider the implications that rational expectations may have for open-economy macroeconomic models.

There are two main reasons for considering open-economy models. The first is a practical one: most countries are very open to influences from the rest of the world either because a large proportion of their output is sold to other countries, or because the demand by foreigners for domestic financial assets affects the domestic interest rate. So open-economy models are likely to be of practical importance and therefore worth analysing. Secondly, the very fact of foreign trade implies the existence of a world-wide foreign exchange market – a market in which one country's currency can be bought for another's; and, of course, the existence of a market implies the existence of a price, the price of one currency in terms of another, or the foreign exchange rate. Typically the current value of this price is well publicized which suggests that it will be part of the information which agents use to form expectations. And so within an open-economy model we can illustrate the general implications of assuming that all agents, when forming expectations, not only have information on their own current local price as in chapter 3, but also on one current economy-wide price – in this case the foreign exchange rate.

5.1 THE AGGREGATE DEMAND CURVE IN THE OPEN ECONOMY

The introduction of trade in goods and financial assets with the rest of the world necessitates important modifications to the Aggregate Demand Curve derived in chapter 3. The trade in goods suggests that the demand for domestic output will come partly from the home country and partly from abroad. The demand from the home country for domestic output will equal total domestic demand for all goods less imports since the latter represents domestic demand for foreign output. The demand from abroad for domestic output will equal exports since this is the quantity of domestic goods brought by foreigners. Thus the demand for *domestic* output will be total domestic demand plus exports and minus imports. What determines 'net' trade' (i.e. exports minus imports)? We shall assume that the demand for imports depends on domestic national income (Y) and on the price of foreign goods *relative* to the price of domestically produced goods. Because imported goods are priced in foreign currencies their prices must be adjusted by the exchange rate for comparison with domestic prices. The price of foreign goods relative to domestic goods (both expressed in units of the *domestic* currency) is given by the expression:

$$R = \frac{P^f S}{P} \tag{5.1}$$

where P^f is the price of foreign goods denominated in units of the foreign currency, e.g. \$s; S the price of one unit of foreign exchange, e.g. one \$, in units of the domestic currency, e.g. £s; and P is the domestic price level. $P^f S$ is therefore the price of imports in units of the domestic currency. We shall refer to R as the 'terms of trade' between the domestic economy and the rest of the world. The higher is R, the lower, *ceteris paribus*, will be the demand for imports since domestic consumers will switch from higher-priced imports to domestically produced goods.

Similarly we shall assume that the level of exports depends upon two factors: first exports will be higher the greater is world income (Y^f); secondly exports will be greater the lower are domestic prices relative to those in the rest of the world (i.e. exports will depend positively on R). 'Net trade' with the rest of the world (i.e. the volume of exports minus the volume of imports), will thus depend negatively on domestic income, positively on foreign income and positively on the relative price of foreign and domestic goods as expressed in the term R. It follows that the position of an economy's *IS* curve – which plots combinations of output and the interest rate at which output and the demand for domestic output are equal – will depend upon the level of world income (Y^f) and the relative price term, R. An increase in world income or an increase in R will shift the *IS* curve to the right since both imply an increase in the demand for domestic output. (Students unfamiliar with the derivation of the *IS* curve in the open-economy case should refer to standard texts; e.g. Parkin and Bade (1982) gives a full treatment of the open economy and develops the simple analytical framework used in this chapter.)

In the open economy an additional equilibrium condition is required – that of balance-of-payments equilibrium. For our purposes it is convenient to follow the conventional practice of dividing the balance of payments into the balance on current account and the balance on capital account. The balance-of-payments surplus on current account is the value of exports minus the value of imports. Our discussion above suggests that three variables are likely to be major influences on the current-account surplus. The first is world income: the higher this is, the greater the demand for exports and so the greater the current-account surplus. The second is domestic income: the higher this is, the greater the demand for imports and hence the lower the current-account surplus. And the third is the terms of trade, R: the higher this is, the greater the current-account surplus is likely to be.

The capital-account surplus is the difference between the value of purchases of domestic financial assets by foreigners and the value of purchases of foreign financial assets by domestic residents. In general, one would expect that for any given level for interest rates in the rest of the world (i^f), higher domestic interest rates (i) would attract funds from overseas, thereby increasing the capital-account surplus. To simplify matters in this chapter, and because it seems a fairly close approximation to reality, we shall assume that such 'capital flows' between countries are perfectly mobile. This means that if the expected return on holding a domestic interest-bearing asset is greater than that on a foreign one, foreign demand for domestic financial assets will be so great that the expected return on domestic financial assets will be driven down until it equals the expected return on foreign financial assets. Perceived from abroad, the return to holding a domestic asset is the rate of interest on that asset minus the expected depreciation of the domestic currency. Perfect capital mobility implies that the domestic rate of interest must therefore equal the world rate plus any expected depreciation of the currency. We write this as:

$$i_t = i_t^f + E_t x_{t+1} \tag{5.2}$$

where $E_t x_{t+1}$ is the expected depreciation rate of the domestic currency between period t and $t+1$.

Now that we have specified the characteristics of the current and capital accounts individually we can analyse the overall balance of payments. With a given level of world income and a given level of the terms of trade (R), the higher the level of domestic output the greater will be the balance of payments deficit on current account. But if the expected depreciation of the domestic currency is zero, capital is perfectly mobile and the world interest rate is i^f, a domestic interest rate of $i=i^f$ will attract sufficient funds into the country to ensure that the surplus on the capital account is just enough to offset any deficit on the current account, i.e. to ensure overall equilibrium in the balance of payments whatever the value of domestic

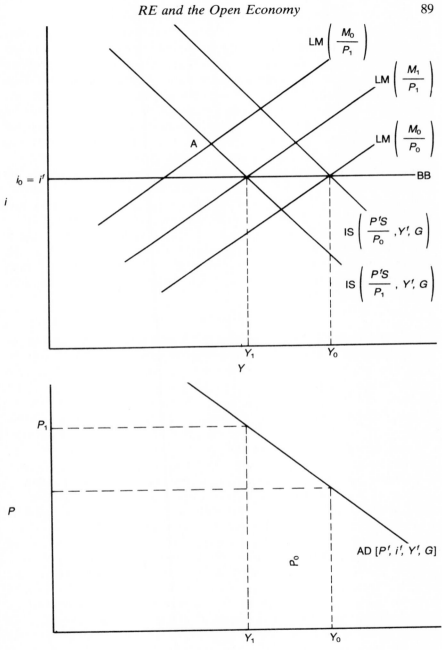

FIGURE 5.1   Aggregate demand under fixed exchange rates

output, Y. The combinations of i and Y that describe balance-of-payments equilibrium are therefore given by a horizontal line labelled BB in figure 5.1. Notice that this locus indicates that for an overall balance of payments of zero the domestic interest rate cannot depart from the world rate. This result is due to the assumption of perfect capital mobility and our assumption that the expected depreciation of the domestic currency is zero. We shall maintain both these assumptions in the interests of simplicity; effectively the latter assumption means we shall be considering 'equilibrium' states only, i.e. states where the exchange rate is at rest.

We are now in a position to derive the Aggregate Demand curve for the open economy. But before we can do this we have to state explicitly whether the exchange rate is fixed at a given value or whether it is allowed to fluctuate. In this chapter we shall examine the open economy under two extreme 'exchange-rate regimes': in the first the exchange rate is completely free to fluctuate; in the second it is completely fixed by the government. In practice exchange rates may be flexible within certain limits (so-called 'managed floats'). Again the polar cases are dealt with here to simplify the analysis.

(a) The Fixed Exchange Rate Case

If the exchange rate is fixed, the term $P^f S$ is fixed exogenously; its value is not determined by our model. For any given value for $P^f S$, the terms of trade (R) will fall when P (the domestic price level) rises. As we have explained such a fall in R will imply a fall in the volume of exports and a rise in the volume of imports, and hence a shift of the country's IS curve to the left. The assumed rise in the domestic price level will also, for the reasons given in chapter 3, shift the LM curve to the left in the usual way.

These two effects are shown in figure 5.1. Initially the domestic price level is P_0 and the relevant IS and LM curves are IS $(P^f S/P_0, Y^f, G)$ and LM (M_0/P_0), intersecting at i_0, Y_0 (G is the level of government spending in real terms). A rise in the domestic price level from P_0 to P_1 will shift the IS and LM curves to IS $(P^f S/P_1, Y^f, G)$ and LM (M_0/P_1) so that they intersect at A. The domestic interest rate will thereby be raised and this will attract foreign funds into the country. (Of course if the relative shifts in the IS and LM curves were different, they could intersect at a lower interest rate, inducing a balance of payments deficit.) Foreigners wishing to buy domestic securities will need units of the domestic currency to do so. The fixity of exchange rates implies that the government is prepared to supply whatever quantity of domestic currency is demanded by foreigners (in exchange of course for foreign currency). As foreigners obtain this domestic currency and use it to purchase domestic financial assets from domestic residents it will lead to an increase in the holdings by domestic residents of units of the domestic country's currency, in other words it will produce a rise in the domestic country's money supply, and produce a shift to the right of the *LM* curve. Such a tendency will persist until the *IS* and *LM* curves intersect once again on the *BB* curve, that is until the *LM* curve is $LM(M_1/P_1)$.

Once we take account of the international repercussions of a rise in the domestic price level, it is clear that the equilibrium level of aggregate demand will fall from Y_0 to Y_1 if the price level rises from P_0 to P_1. This is shown in the lower half of figure 5.1. More generally, in the case where the exchange rate is fixed the level of aggregate demand at each domestic price level is given by the intersection of the *IS* curve and the *BB* curve. Internationally induced changes in the domestic money supply will ensure that the *LM* curve moves to cut the *IS* and *BB* curves where they intersect. The position of the Aggregate Demand curve depends upon the variables that determine the positions of the *IS* and *BB* curves, i.e. the exchange rate (S), foreign price level (P^f), the foreign rate of interest (i^f), foreign income (Y^f), together with the other domestic influences on the *IS* curve (like government expenditure, G).

(b) Flexible Exchange Rate Case

If the exchange rate is flexible it moves freely to ensure an overall balance-of-payments equilibrium. The derivation of the Aggregate Demand curve in this case is set out in figure 5.2. The initial *IS* and *LM* curves are labelled by the initial values assumed for the exchange rate, S_0, and the domestic price level, P_0. A rise in the domestic price level to P_1 will shift the *LM* curve to the left and with an unchanged exchange rate a rise in P will also shift the *IS* curve to the left as imports become more attractive. However, the resulting intersection of the *IS* and *LM* curves (at A) implies a balance-of-payments deficit. Foreigners are demanding less domestic currency with which to purchase domestic goods and financial assets than domestic residents are willing to supply in exchange for foreign currency. This excess supply of the domestic currency will lead to a depreciation of the domestic currency. That is S, the price of one unit of foreign exchange in terms of the domestic currency, will rise.

This rise in S or depreciation of the domestic currency will make imports less attractive and thereby shift the *IS* curve to the right. Such a tendency for the *IS* curve to shift to the right will persist so long as there is an implied deficit on the balance of payments. It will be eliminated when the *IS* curve has shifted far enough to the right to intersect the *LM* curve where the *LM* and *BB* curves intersect. (If the rise in the domestic price level had led to a balance-of-payments surplus, which it would do if the *LM* curve shifted by a large amount to the left relative to the leftward shift of the *IS* curve, the exchange rates (S) would of course fall to give an overall equilibrium in the

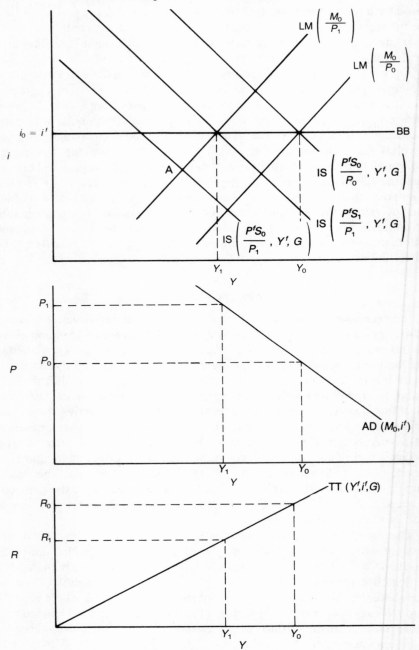

FIGURE 5.2   Aggregate demand under flexible exchange rates

balance of payments. The *IS* curve would thereby be shifted to the left until it intersected the *LM* curve where the *LM* and *BB* curves intersect.)

So once we take account of the international repercussions of a rise in the domestic price level, it is clear that as the price level rises from P_0 to P_1 aggregate demand will fall from Y_0 in figure 5.2 to Y_1. More generally, in the flexible exchange rate case the Aggregate Demand curve is given from the intersection of the *LM* and *BB* curves at the different levels of domestic prices. Movements of the exchange rate ensure that the *IS* curve will intersect the *LM* curve where the *LM* curve intersects the *BB* curve. It follows that if exchange rates are flexible the position of the Aggregate Demand curve is dependent upon all the factors which influence the position of the *LM* and *BB* curves, but not on the factors which only influence the position of the *IS* curve. Thus only a change in the domestic money supply or a change in i^f shift the Aggregate Demand curve.

At the foot of figure 5.2 the relationship between the terms of trade, R, and the level of output is traced (labelled $TT(Y^f, i^f, G)$ in the figure). We shall be using this relationship later on. Its derivation can be explained as follows. At price level P_0 aggregate demand is Y_0, and so the *IS* curve is the one labelled *IS* $(P^f S_0 / P_0, Y^f, G)$. The terms of trade at price level P_0 must, given everything else, be $P^f S_0 / P_0$, that is R_0. At a higher price level P_1 aggregate demand is Y_1 and the *IS* curve which cuts the *LM* curve at this level of output is to the left of the initial one. By implication then there must have been a fall in R, the terms of trade, for only a fall would produce the rise in imports or fall in exports implied by the shift to the left of the *IS* curve. So the lower the level of aggregate demand, *ceteris paribus*, the lower the equilibrium terms of trade. Note also that changes in foreign income (Y^f), the foreign interest rate (i^f) and government expenditure (G) now influence the terms of trade. An increase in G, for example, will shift the *IS* curve to the right. This creates a balance of payments surplus and the resulting revaluation of the currency (fall in S) will cause R to decrease and will return the *IS* curve to its original intersection with the *LM* curve. R will be correspondingly lower at each output level.

5.2 OUTPUT AND THE PRICE LEVEL: FIXED EXCHANGE RATES

Armed with an extended analysis of aggregate demand in the open economy, we are now in a position to analyse the determination of domestic output and the price level. In the first case, we shall assume that the economy is under a fixed exchange rate regime; the analysis is set out in figure 5.3. With fixed exchange rates, the Aggregate Demand curve is influenced by the foreign price level (P^f), the world interest rate (i^f), world income (Y^f) and domestic fiscal policy (say government expenditure, G).

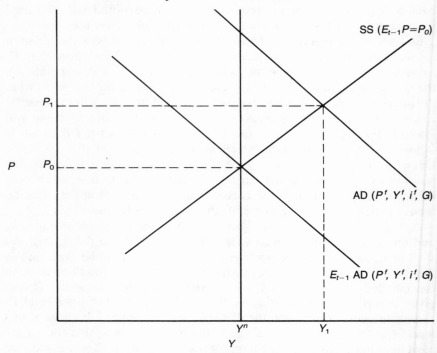

FIGURE 5.3   Output and the price level: fixed exchange rates.

The actual domestic price level is determined by the intersection of aggregate demand and aggregate supply. The short-run supply curve, as in chapter 3, is constructed on the assumption of a given level of price expectations. A higher, unexpected price will cause an increase in output as agents confuse aggregate and relative price signals. Clearly rational agents will derive their expectations of the price level from their information about the position of the Aggregate Demand curve. Imagine that, given their information, agents expect the levels of foreign prices, foreign income, the foreign interest rate and government expenditure to be $E_{t-1}P^f$, $E_{t-1}Y^f$, $E_{t-1}i^f$ and $E_{t-1}G$ respectively. The expected Aggregate Demand curve is labelled $E_{t-1} AD(P^f, Y^f, i^f, G)$. Rational agents will therefore expect a price level of P_0, and they will supply output along $SS(E_{t-1}P=P_0)$.

The extension to the open-economy model has complicated the forma-tion of expectations in that expectations must now be formed about the main world variables such as income and interest rates, but the framework developed in chapter 3 remains relevant. In particular systematic and, therefore, predictable changes in domestic or world influences on aggre-gate demand will, under rational expectations, not affect real output, only random, unpredictable movements in these variables will have real effects. If the realized values of the determinants of aggregate demand listed above correspond to their expected values, the price level would be P_0 and output would be at Y^n. A random increase in world income which shifted the Aggregate Demand curve to the right would raise output to, say Y_1 as shown. Similarly a random increase in government expenditure would have real output effects. A similar but predictable change in Y^f or G would cause agents to revise their price expectations and no deviation in output from its natural level would occur.

Two implications can be drawn from the open-economy model under fixed exchange rates and rational expectations. First the informational requirements for rational forecasts of aggregate demand are more demanding. Agents will require knowledge of developments in the 'rest of the world'. Consequently they may make more mistakes and the disturbances in the level of output about its natural level may be more pronounced even when domestic prices are assumed perfectly flexible. Secondly attempts by the government to stabilize the economy through, say, adjustments in government expenditure, must, as before, take into account the fact that systematic changes will be anticipated and will, therefore, have no output effects. Since only unpredictable, and therefore random changes, in policy will have output effects, the policy implication of rational expectations in this case are the same as before: governments should minimize the unpredictability of their behaviour. However, it may be argued that asymmetric information is more likely to occur in the open-economy case; if the government had privileged access to information concerning foreign developments, the use of government spending to stabilize output might then prove effective.

5.3   OUTPUT AND THE PRICE LEVEL: FLEXIBLE EXCHANGE RATES

Flexibility in the exchange rate will complicate our model in two respects. First, we now require a solution for the exchange rate – its value is not exogenously fixed by the government. Secondly, since the exchange rate is a well-publicized, economy-wide price its current value will form part of the information set used by economic agents when forming their expectations. In other words the value of the current exchange rate will convey certain information to economic agents which they would not otherwise have and which they can use to make better forecasts of, for example, the current price level. Because of this, in the flexible exchange rate open-economy case a distinction will have to be made between expectations before trading begins (i.e. before agents have observed the exchange rate) and expectations following observation of the exchange rate.

For this reason two expectations operators will have to be used. The first, E_{t-1}, is already familiar: it defines the rational expectation given lagged aggregate information. In this section E_{t-1} will be used for expectations formed before trading takes place, i.e. before agents know the current exchange rate (S). Once agents know the current value of the exchange

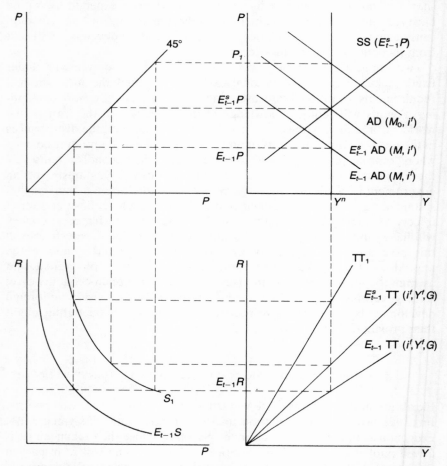

FIGURE 5.4 Output and the price level: flexible exchange rates.

rate, the extra information may cause them to revise their expectations, so the operator E_{t-1}^s will be used to denote a rational expectation conditional on lagged aggregate information *and* knowledge of the current exchange rate. The basic model outlined in this section is developed in Parkin and Bade (1982); as we shall be using it to explain further features of open economies with flexible exchange rates we shall only outline the model here and refer students unfamiliar with the territory to its development in Parkin and Bade.

The situation immediately before trading commences is described in figure 5.4. The two right-hand diagrams are simply those given in figure 5.2, but the position of the expected AD curve is determined by expectations of agents before they observe the exchange rate. This is labelled $E_{t-1}AD(M, i^f)$. Note that the position of this Aggregate Demand curve depends only upon expectations of the money supply and the foreign interest rate. Likewise the expected position of TT will depend upon expectations of the foreign interest rate $(E_{t-1}i^f)$, foreign income $(E_{t-1}Y^f)$ and domestic government expenditure $(E_{t-1}G)$. Again note that these expectations are formed before knowledge of the exchange rate is obtained. The initially expected TT line is $E_{t-1}TT(i^f, Y^f, G)$. Given these expectations before trading commences in foreign exchange, rational agents will expect a domestic price level of $E_{t-1}P$ and terms of trade $E_{t-1}R$. From the definition of R given above, the values of $E_{t-1}P$ and $E_{t-1}R$ imply a unique expectation of the exchange rate, $E_{t-1}S$. This is shown by the two left-hand diagrams in figure 5.4.

The upper diagram is merely a 45° line with the domestic price level on both axes. It enables us to convert a variable from the vertical to the horizontal axis, and requires no further explanation. The lower of these diagrams is more complex. From the definition of R given above, it follows that $R \cdot P = S \cdot P^f$. Thus if P^f is given, the product of R and P will be constant for a given rate of exchange, S. Rationality implies that this equality will hold *as an approximation* if every term in it is interpreted as an expected term, that is

$$E_{t-1}R \cdot E_{t-1}P = E_{t-1}S \cdot E_{t-1}P^f$$

Thus if $E_{t-1}P^f$ is given, the line labelled $E_{t-1}S$ is a rectangular hyperbola, the area bound by the curve being $E_{t-1}S \cdot E_{t-1}P^f$. Figure 5.4 should therefore be interpreted in the following way: given their expectations of the determinants of AD and TT, agents will expect output to be Y^n and the terms of trade to be $E_{t-1}R$ – the upper and lower right-hand side diagrams of figure 5.4 show this. And given the domestic price level that agents rationally expect from their expectations about the position of the Aggregate Demand curve, and given their expectations about foreign prices and the value of R, they will expect to find an exchange of $E_{t-1}S$ when they enter the market for foreign exchange. We now proceed to analyse what happens when trading occurs and the exchange rate is actually observed.

We begin by assuming that the determinants of the position of TT, i^f, Y^f and G, are known with certainty. The only uncertain variable is the quantity of money. Our reason for making this assumption will shortly become apparent. Its immediate implication is that the actual TT curve will coincide with the expected one shown in figure 5.4 and labelled $E_{t-1}TT(i^f, Y^f, G)$. Now imagine that agents enter into foreign exchange transactions and observe that the actual exchange rate is greater than expected (i.e. the domestic currency has devalued relative to expectations). Imagine that the actual exchange rate is S_1. Since TT cannot have changed, rational agents will now infer that their initial conjecture about the money supply ($E_{t-1}M$) was incorrect. For if it were correct the Aggregate Demand curve would be, as initially expected, at $E_{t-1}AD(M, i^f)$, the level of output would be Y^n, the price level, $E_{t-1}P$, and the terms of trade would equal their expected value, $E_{t-1}R$. But such a combination of values is not consistent with an observed exchange rate of S_1. Thus the Aggregate Demand curve cannot be at the position it was initially expected to be.

In the simplified model we are examining the only influence on the Aggregate Demand curve which agents might incorrectly forecast is the quantity of money. The rational agent can therefore infer from observing the exchange rate that her initial forecast of the quantity of money was wrong. What is more there is only one price level consistent with the observed exchange rate and correct expectations, that is P_1. For this price level to occur, the Aggregate Demand curve must be the one labelled $AD(M_0, i^f)$. Therefore rational agents can infer from observing the current exchange rate that the actual position of the Aggregate Demand curve is $AD(M_0, i^f)$, and hence can form an accurate expectation of the price level. This will be so, at least in the simple model we are dealing with, even if the Aggregate Demand curve moves randomly. For although the position of the Aggregate Demand curve in period t cannot be accurately predicted from information available at the end of period $t-1$, knowledge of the current value of an economy-wide price, the exchange rate, enables the rational agent to work out what any random shift in aggregate demand has been.

The importance of this result in the simple example presented should now be apparent. In the closed-economy model, or even in the fixed exchange rate open-economy model, a random movement in aggregate demand would cause output and the price level to rise. But a flexible exchange rate conveys information to rational agents about aggregate demand disturbances, and in the simple example we have been using, the exchange rate conveys sufficient information to enable rational agents to become aware of current random aggregate demand shifts. Since the random movements in aggregate demand thereby become anticipated they have no effect on real output.

In the example we have just explained, knowledge of one economy-wide price conveys sufficient information to rational agents to convert an uncertain world into a certain one. This extreme result occurs because we have assumed that there is only one source of aggregate uncertainty – random movements in the money supply. The one piece of current aggregate information is sufficient to eradicate this uncertainty altogether. If we allow for the possibility of more than one source of uncertainty then knowledge of the current exchange rate would still lead to better forecasts but might not eradicate uncertainty altogether: the one piece of information is not then sufficient to allow rational agents to disentangle more than one random disturbance.

An obvious way to illustrate this point is to drop the assumption in the example above – that the TT relationship is known with certainty – and replace it with the assumption that agents' expectations of i^f, Y^f and G are subject to error. This error will of course be random provided expectations are rational. If this assumption is incorporated in the above example then the observed exchange rate S_1 may be due to a range of possible positions of AD and TT. For example, a rational agent who, as before, was initially expecting an exchange rate of $E_{t-1}S$ may, on observing the exchange rate to be S_1, conjecture that the TT curve is in fact exactly where it was expected to be and the exchange rate is higher because the Aggregate Demand curve is higher. Alternatively the agent may assume that her initial conjectures about the money supply and the foreign rate of interest were correct so that the AD curve is where it was expected to be. In this case a higher than expected exchange rate would be explained by an unanticipated change in TT. In this case, price level expectations would remain at $E_{t-1}P$ even after the exchange rate is observed. An unexpected rise in TT to TT_1 in figure 5.4 would equally well 'explain' why the exchange rate S_1 is observed. And of course the unexpected value of the exchange rate could be due to some combination of both shifts in TT and AD.

Of all the possible combinations which explain the unexpected value for the exchange rate which will the rational agent select? The guiding principle determining the choice is in fact the same principle which we introduced in chapter 3 when the rational supplier had to decide whether an unexpectedly high price reflected an aggregate demand shock or a relative demand shock. From knowledge of the past behaviour of S, AD and TT a rational agent will know that on some occasions unexpected 'changes in AD were responsible for 'unexpected' movements in the exchange rate; on other occasions unexpected changes in TT were responsible. At yet other times changes in both were responsible.

Suppose the rational agent knew that on average 50 per cent of past unexpected changes in S could be attributable to unexpected changes in

AD and 50 per cent to unexpected movements in *TT*. Since the agent only observes a higher than expected *S*, he will conjecture that unanticipated changes in *AD* and *TT* were equally responsible. He may not be correct in this conjecture, but he is rational. Given the information available, the conjecture is the agent's 'best guess'. The observation of S_1 thus causes agents to infer an *AD* curve of $E^s_{t-1}AD(M, i^f)$, the expectation of *AD* conditional on the knowledge of S_1 and a *TT* curve of $E^s_{t-1}TT(Y^f, i^f, G)$. The expected price level is therefore $E^s_{t-1}P$ and agents will supply goods in accordance with the short-run supply curve labelled $SS(E^s_{t-1}P)$. The inference on the position of *AD* and *TT*, conditional on the knowledge of

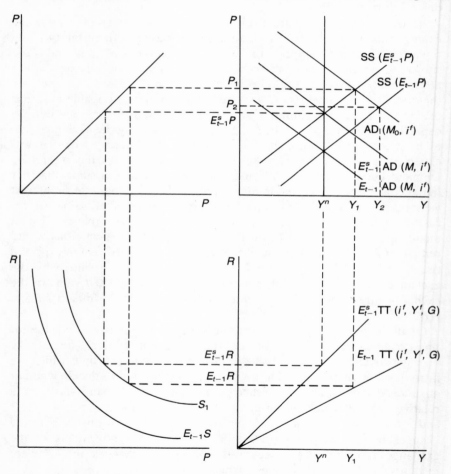

FIGURE 5.5   An increase in money supply with flexible exchange rates.

S_1 is, as we have already mentioned, another example of 'signal extraction'. The agent seeks to extract a 'signal' (i.e. changes in the AD and TT curves) from information on the value of the exchange rate.

This analysis may now be used to explain the effects on output and the price level of an unexpected increase in the money supply if the economy is open and the exchange rate flexible. The effects are explained in figure 5.5. Agents expected M to be $E_{t-1}M$ before observation of the exchange rate. We shall assume that M in fact rises to M_0 and all other variables in fact assume their expected values. This means that the exchange rate is higher entirely because of a higher than expected rise in the money supply. Note that the unexpected nature of the rise in the money supply means that the domestic interest rate will still equal the world rate (i.e. there was no expectation of any change in the exchange rate – see equation (5.2)). Although we know that S is at S_1 only through a higher M, the rational agent will not. His conjecture is that both TT and AD have moved to $E_{t-1}^s TT(Y^f, \; i^f, \; G)$ and $E_{t-1}^s AD(M, \; i^f)$. The expected price level is therefore $E_{t-1}^s P$. The agent is able to anticipate the rise in AD partially, but not fully. The unexpected (even after S_1 is observed) increase in M causes output to rise to Y_1 and the price level to rise to P_1. But note that the output effects of an increase in M are lower and the price effects are higher than they would have been had agents not observed S_1. For in that case output would have been Y_2 and the price level P_2.

So this example illustrates that knowledge of a current economy-wide price will improve rational forecasts but fail to render them perfect so long as there are a number of sources of uncertainty. It also suggests that the real output effects of unanticipated monetary growth, or more generally unanticipated movements in aggregate demand, will be different under different exchange-rate regimes because a flexible exchange rate provides information that a fixed exchange rate does not. A more formal explanation of this feature of the open-economy model has been developed by Duck (1984).

5.4 STICKY PRICES, FLEXIBLE EXCHANGE RATES AND OVERSHOOTING

In the analysis of open economies under flexible exchange rates, we have reintroduced the assumption of flexible prices. We now relax this assumption to illustrate a phenomenon known as exchange rate 'overshooting'. It is well known that exchange rates vary considerably from day to day and month to month. The very flexibility in exchange rates – compared with the relative stickiness of other prices – may cause them to fluctuate beyond their long-run equilibrium solutions, i.e. to 'overshoot'.

A good example of overshooting was given in 1976 by Dornbusch, whose model exploited the fact that exchange rates are likely to be more flexible than other prices in the economy. What follows is a simplified version of the Dornbusch model.

In figure 5.6 the economy is depicted as being in equilibrium at P_0, Y^n. The initial exchange rate is S_0. The equilibrium is disturbed by an unanticipated rise in the money supply – all other variables (like P^f etc.) remaining unchanged. Thus the AD curve shifts to that labelled $AD(M_1, i^f)$. We assume that prices are sticky in the sense that initially they remain at P_0 and only after some time move to their new long-run equilibrium level

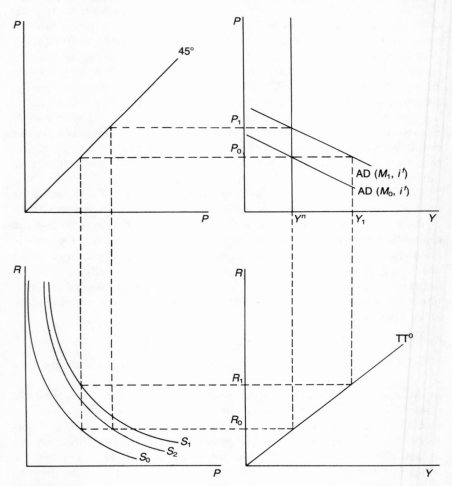

FIGURE 5.6   Price stickiness and exchange rate overshooting.

(P_1). Note that the unexpected nature of the money supply increase means that the change in the exchange rate was also unexpected, so the equality of domestic and foreign interest rates still holds. With prices fixed, disequilibrium results and we again require a quantity rule. Suppose output is always equal to the quantity demanded (see chapter 4): in this case output will rise to Y_1 and the terms of trade must rise to R_1 in order to maintain balance-of-payments equilibrium. Since the price levels at home and abroad are constant, R can only rise if there is an increase in S (i.e. a devaluation). This is shown in the bottom left-hand corner of figure 5.6 where the value of S required for consistency with the foreign and domestic price level and the terms of trade is S_1. An expansion in the money supply thus causes output to rise and the domestic currency to be devalued.

In the long run, however, the price level is free to adjust; prices must rise to P_1 and output will return to Y^n. With output at Y^n the terms of trade return to their original level (R_0). Since both S and P are free to adjust in the long run, the short-run pressure on S to ensure balance-of-payments equilibrium is removed and S falls back to S_2 in long-run equilibrium. An expansion of the money supply has therefore caused S initially to overshoot its long-run value: the domestic currency depreciates more in the short run than in the longer run.

Had the initial increase in the money supply been anticipated, the analysis would still have involved changes in real output in the short run (due to the assumption of sticky prices). But the analysis would be further complicated by the fact that agents would anticipate future devaluations in the currency and the domestic interest would then depart from the world rate. This would cause both the AD and TT curves to shift temporarily, returning to $AD(M_1, i^J)$ and TT_0 in the long run when the exchange rate had attained its long-run equilibrium. It may be clear that the assumption of price stickiness will restore the potential for stabilization policy. An anticipated change in other determinants of aggregate demand (like i^f) will have (undesirable) effects on output. The government can offset such changes with a suitably designed monetary policy.

SUMMARY

In this chapter the application of rational expectations has been extended to incorporate open economies. This not only complicates the model by adding more variables and requiring more solutions but may also affect the information available to rational agents. In particular, the existence of an economy-wide foreign exchange market in an economy with flexible exchange rates provides agents with information they would not otherwise possess. We showed how this information influenced the effects of unanticipated changes in aggregate demand on real output and the price level. The effect on output of an unanticipated increase in the money supply, for example, can be expected to differ in periods when the exchange rate is fixed (when it cannot convey information) and when it is flexible (when it can).

It has not been possible to do justice to the variety of applications of rational expectations in open-economy macroeconomics in a chapter of this size. In chapter 9 we review some of the theory and evidence relating to the direct application of rational expectations to the foreign exchange market itself.

Now that we have introduced and used the idea of rational expectations within some different macroeconomic models we shall turn to examine the evidence on the usefulness of the rational expectations hypothesis within macroeconomics. Before we do so, however, it is first necessary to consider some of the econometric issues which arise when we attempt to test theories which involve rational expectations.

SUGGESTIONS FOR FURTHER READING

The literature on open-economy macroeconomics and rational expectations is both voluminous and wide ranging. In chapter 9 we examine the application of rational expectations to the foreign exchange market and that chapter contains a number of references to tests of the relevance of rational expectations in explaining exchange-rate behaviour. Useful surveys of exchange-rate determination can be found in Dornbusch (1980b) and Krueger (1983). A comprehensive introduction to open-economy macroeconomics is provided by Dornbusch (1980a) and an introduction to the application of rational expectations is given in Parkin and Bade (1982). The role of expectations in a 'sticky price' open-economy model was investigated in an important paper by Dornbusch (1976) and the application of rational expectations to this framework is a feature of Driskill (1981) and Buiter and Miller (1981b). For a discussion of stabilization policy in an open economy with wage indexing, see Weber (1981). Early open-economy models with flexible prices were developed by Barro (1978b) and Cox (1980). A formal extension of Barro's (1976) closed-economy model to the open economy can be found in Duck (1984). 'Overshooting' of the exchange rate without sticky prices is a feature of a model developed by Calvo and Rodriguez (1977).

6

Rational Expectations in Macroeconomics: Some Econometric Issues

We now begin to turn our attention to the empirical issues raised by the rational expectations hypothesis. Wherever expectations play key roles in economic theory – and there is hardly an area where they do not – the introduction of rational expectations must have far-reaching consequences for the design of appropriate empirical tests of the theory. Before we turn to a detailed treatment of some of these tests, it is first necessary to consider some of the more general econometric issues.

This chapter focuses on two of the key econometric issues raised by the rational expectations hypothesis. The first is the question of how to test for the validity of the rational expectations hypothesis within macroeconomics. The central idea introduced is that of *restrictions*: when combined with an economic theory in which expectations are important the rational expectations hypothesis generally implies precise restrictions on what we should observe in the real world, and so its validity can be tested by testing for the validity of these restrictions. Tests of such restrictions are therefore a common feature of tests of the rational expectations hypothesis in a variety of contexts.

The second major issue concerns the practice followed by many economists of estimating macroeconomic models of the economy and then using such models to evaluate different possible macroeconomic policies. Implicit in this practice is the assumption that the estimated model will remain unchanged in the face of different policies and can therefore be used to evaluate different policies. The rational expectations hypothesis suggests that this assumption may not be valid: the coefficients estimated by such models are unlikely to remain unchanged under different policy regimes, and as a consequence the economic policy evaluation based on such models is likely to be misleading.

6.1 DIRECT TESTS OF RATIONALITY

We begin the chapter by considering how, in general, one might test the rational expectations hypothesis. Our starting point is the tests which use direct observations from sample surveys of individuals' expectations.

Imagine that we could *directly* observe a particular person's or group's expectation formed last period of the current period's value of an economic variable. We might think of this variable as the retail price index and label its current value P_t, but it could be any economic variable. Possession of such direct observations on expectations would allow us to test the validity of the rational expectations hypothesis in two ways. The first, and weaker test, would exploit one of the central predictions of the rational expectations hypothesis which we explained in chapter 2: that forecast errors arise from the inherent unpredictability or stochastic nature of the variable and should exhibit no pattern, i.e. they should not be predictable on the basis of any information available at the time the forecast is made; and they should on average be zero. For the variable we are considering, this prediction implies that the difference between the current value of the retail price index, and the expectation of that index formed last period will be a serially uncorrelated random variable with mean zero, that is

$$P_t - E_{t-1}P_t = u_t \tag{6.1}$$

where P_t is the actual value of the current retail price index, $E_{t-1}P_t$ is the expectation of P_t formed in period $t-1$ and u_t is the random forecast error which is uncorrelated with any information available in period $t-1$ or earlier.

If, as we are assuming, we could directly observe $E_{t-1}P_t$ then we could use the data on $E_{t-1}P_t$ and P_t to carry out the following regression

$$P_t = \alpha_0 + \alpha_1 E_{t-1}P_t + v_t \tag{6.2}$$

where α_0 and α_1 are the coefficients to be estimated by this regression and v_t is an error with zero mean.

If the prediction of the rational expectations hypothesis embodied in equation (6.1) is correct then this regression should estimate α_0 to be not significantly different from zero, and α_1 to be not significantly different from one. More formally the regression should yield results such that the joint null hypothesis H_0: $\alpha_0 = 0$, $\alpha_1 = 1$ cannot be rejected. Furthermore the error term in the regression, v_t, should be a serially uncorrelated random error, that is it should exhibit no pattern since on H_0 it is the forecasting error. The test of the null hypothesis, H_0, is called a test of the 'unbiasedness property' of rational expectations. It is also referred to as a 'weak test'.

Direct observations on what people are expecting allow a second and stronger test of the rational expectations hypothesis. This test is based on the following implications of the hypothesis: if expectations of a variable are rational, they are formed in accordance with the process determining that variable and therefore they will depend upon any set of past variables in exactly the same way as the variable itself depends upon that same set of past variables. This property of rational expectations is known as the efficiency property. As an illustration take the link between P_t and its own past values. Imagine that we regress the actual price index on its own past values as shown in equation (6.3)

$$P_t = \beta_1 P_{t-1} + \beta_2 P_{t-2} + \ldots + \beta_k P_{t-k} + u_{1t} \tag{6.3}$$

where the β_i's are the coefficients to be estimated on each variable, and u_{1t} is a random error.

Since we are assumed to have a direct observation on $E_{t-1}P_t$, we can carry out a regression of $E_{t-1}P_t$ on exactly the same variables as those on the right-hand side of equation (6.3). That is, we can carry out the following regression.

$$E_{t-1}P_t = \gamma_1 P_{t-1} + \gamma_2 P_{t-2} + \ldots + \gamma_k P_{t-k} + u_{2t} \tag{6.4}$$

where the γ_i's are the coefficients to be estimated on each variable and u_{2t} is a random error.

If the rational expectations hypothesis is correct we should find in large samples that the coefficient estimated on each variable in equation (6.3) is approximately the same as the coefficient estimated on the same variable in equation (6.4); that is, β_1 should equal γ_1, β_2 should equal γ_2, etc. More formally we can test the rational expectations hypothesis by testing the joint null hypothesis, $H_0: \beta_i = \gamma_i$ for $i = 1, \ldots k$. Rejection of this null hypothesis would imply a rejection of the rational expectations hypothesis. The reason that the two sets of coefficients in equations (6.3) and (6.4) should be the same under rational expectations can be seen clearly if we subtract equation (6.4) from equation (6.3) to obtain

$$P_t - E_{t-1}P_t = (\beta_1 - \gamma_1)P_{t-1} + (\beta_2 - \gamma_2)P_{t-2} + \ldots$$
$$+ (\beta_k - \gamma_k)P_{t-k} + u_{1t} - u_{2t} \tag{6.5}$$

The left-hand side of equation (6.5) must equal a random variable, as shown in equation (6.1), which it will if $\beta_i = \gamma_i$ for all i. Another way of putting this is that under rational expectations the forecast error $P_t - E_{t-1}P_t$ is independent of all lagged information, in this case lagged prices.

Both of the tests we have examined require direct observations of the expected variable. As we explained in chapter 1, for most variables we do not have such direct observations and cannot therefore carry out the tests.

But for some variables we do, and some economists have used the available data to carry out these tests of the rational expectations hypothesis

One of the first studies to test the unbiasedness property was by Turnovsky (1970). He used data from a survey which had asked informed business economists their predictions for 6 and 12 months ahead for a number of economic series which included the consumers price index for the period 1954 to 1969 in the United States. He found that the only period to be consistent with rational expectations was from 1962 to 1969. That is, for the period 1954 to 1964, using the 6-month-ahead predictions, in the regression shown above in equation (6.2) he obtained an estimate of α_0 of 1.137 with estimated standard error of 0.306 and an estimate of α_1 of 0.184 with estimated standard error of 0.17. Therefore α_0 is significantly different from zero and α_1 is significantly less than one which refutes the hypothesis that these expectations were rationally formed. For the period 1962 to 1969, however, he obtained an estimate of α_0 not significantly different from zero and an estimate of α_1 of 1.039 with estimated standard error 0.083 which implies that α_1 is not significantly different from one and so the expectations did satisfy the unbiasedness property of rational expectations for this period. The 12-month-ahead forecasts gave similar results. A number of other researchers have investigated this same data set, e.g. Pesando (1975), Carlson (1977), Pearce (1979), Figlewski and Wachtel (1981) but their conclusions are mixed and no clear case for or against rational expectations emerges.

Another data set consisting of interest rate expectations of a panel of money-market professionals has been extensively analysed by Benjamin Friedman (1980). He found that survey respondents did not make unbiased predictions and that they did not efficiently exploit the information contained in past interest-rate movements and concludes that his results are 'mixed to unfavourable' to the hypothesis that expectations are rational. On the face of it then the direct evidence from sample surveys of businessmen's expectations seems to provide very little, if any, support for the rational expectations hypothesis.

There are, however, a number of reasons why we should be cautious about interpreting the results of tests which use this type of data. First, when the questions asked in the surveys are qualitative in nature (e.g. Do you expect the inflation rate to rise, fall or stay the same?), the quantitative expectation constructed on the basis of the answers is likely to be measured with error. This means, as we show in the next section, that the estimator of, for example, α_1 in equation (6.2) may be biased downwards from its true value of one. Secondly, even if the questions posed in the surveys are quantitative in nature (e.g. What do you expect the inflation rate to be in the next year?) and the average expectations elicited from the surveys in a particular market appear biased and inefficient it could be that only a few 'sophisticated' individuals operating in that market could make the market function *as if* rational expectations were operating even though many individuals in the market are not rational. When attempting to explain *market* behaviour, the rational expectations hypothesis will be valid in such cases.

An alternative method of testing the validity of the rational expectations hypothesis is to incorporate it into an economic model and see if the predictions of the model are consistent with the facts. This approach is made all the more necessary by the lack of direct observations on expectations for most variables, and all the more attractive by the possibility of incorporating the rational expectations hypothesis within an economic model and testing *separately* the rationality of expectations and the structure of the rest of the model.

6.2 MEASURING A RATIONAL EXPECTATION OF A VARIABLE BY ITS ACTUAL VALUE

In this section we shall begin considering how one might estimate a macroeconomic model of the economy which incorporates rational expectations. We shall show first that what might appear to be an obvious way to proceed is not in fact likely to be valid and that a more subtle procedure is required. In the next section we shall show that this more subtle procedure is a valid way of estimating a macroeconomic model which incorporates rational expectations. We also show that this method allows us to test rational expectations *conditional* on the economic model with which it is combined. In the following chapter, we shall consider a special case in which we can test *separately* rational expectations and the structure of the rest of the model.

Suppose the macroeconomic model we are estimating states that consumption expenditure in period t depends upon what people in period $t-1$ expect their income will be in period t, that is

$$C_t = \alpha_0 + \alpha_1 E_{t-1} Y_t + v_t \tag{6.6}$$

where C_t = desired consumption expenditure
$E_{t-1} Y_t$ = expected income
v_t = a random error with mean zero
α_0 = a constant
α_1 = the marginal propensity to consume out of expected income.

And suppose that we wish to estimate the value of α_1 the marginal propensity to consume out of expected income. If we believe that expectations about Y_t are rationally formed then we must also believe that the actual value of Y_t diverges from the value people expect, $E_{t-1}Y_t$, by a random error, which we label u_t. Thus the rationality of expectations implies equation (6.7).

$$Y_t = E_{t-1}Y_t + u_t \tag{6.7}$$

Since the actual value of income diverges from the expected value only by a random error it is tempting to replace the expected income term in equation (6.6) with actual income and rewrite equation (6.6) as

$$C_t = \alpha_0 + \alpha_1 Y_t + v_t - \alpha_1 u_t \tag{6.8}$$

To estimate the marginal propensity to consume, α_1, it might be thought that one could carry out the following regression,

$$C_t = \alpha_0^* + \alpha_1^* Y_t + u_t^* \tag{6.9}$$

where u_t^* is an error term, and treat the value obtained for α_1^* as an estimate of the marginal propensity to consume, α_1. It might appear to be an attractive feature of the rational expectations hypothesis that it suggests such a simple method of incorporating expectations into macroeonomic models, i.e. use the actual value of a variable to measure the expectation of it. Unfortunately this method is not valid, for if expectations are rational then equation (6.7) implies that Y_t is (positively) correlated with u_t. Furthermore, if equation (6.8) is true then u_t^* in equation (6.9) must in fact equal $v_t - \alpha_1 u_t$. Therefore in equation (6.9) Y_t and u_t^* must be correlated since they both depend upon u_t. The consequence of this is that the estimator of α_1^* will be biased away from 'α_1' and towards zero.

The intuitive reason for this is as follows. High (or low) values for u_t imply through equation (6.7) high (or low) values for actual income, but no change in expected income and therefore (from equation (6.6)) no change in consumption expenditure. But we are using actual income to measure expected income, and so a positive value for u_t will suggest that there has been a rise in expected income with no accompanying rise in consumption expenditure.

Similarly a negative value for u_t will suggest a fall in expected income but no accompanying fall in consumption expenditure. So to the extent that changes in Y_t are due to such changes in u_t rather than in $E_{t-1}Y_t$, C_t will appear to be unaffected by expected income as we measure it, and therefore we shall obtain an estimate of α_1 which will tend to be less than the true value of α_1. This downward bias will be more severe the more that changes in actual income are due to changes in u_t rather than changes in expected income; in other words the more inaccurate our measure of expected income is the greater the severity of the bias.

More formally, if equations (6.6) to (6.8) are 'the truth' and we carry out an ordinary least squares (OLS) regression of C_t on Y_t as shown in equation (6.9) then, assuming we have a very large sample, our estimate of α_1^* will be obtained from the conventional formula as

$$\alpha_1^* = \frac{\text{covar}(C, Y)}{\text{var}(Y)} \tag{6.10}$$

where covar (C, Y) is the covariance between C and Y, var(Y) is the variance of Y.

We can derive the term covar (C, Y) as the covariance between Y and the terms on the right-hand side of equation (6.8) since these terms in sum equal C. Thus assuming that Y_t and v_t are uncorrelated we can derive

$$\text{covar}(C, Y) = \alpha_1 \text{var}(Y) - \alpha_1 \text{covar}(Y, u). \tag{6.11}$$

And similarly we can derive from equation (6.7) an expression for covar (Y, u) as the covariance between u and the terms on the right-hand side of that equation. Assuming u_t and $E_{t-1}Y_t$ are uncorrelated we can derive the covariance between Y and u as

$$\text{covar}(Y, u) = \text{var}(u) \tag{6.12}$$

Thus our estimator of α_1^* is

$$\alpha_1^* = \frac{\alpha_1 \text{var}(Y) - \alpha_1 \text{var}(u)}{\text{var}(Y)}$$

$$= \alpha_1 - \frac{\alpha_1 \text{var}(u)}{\text{var}(Y)} \tag{6.13}$$

So our estimator, α_1^*, will equal α_1 only if the variance of u is zero. This will be the case if u_t is always zero and hence from equation (6.7) our measure of expected income is perfectly accurate. If our measure of expected income is perfectly inaccurate in the sense that all changes in Y_t reflect variations in u_t, not $E_{t-1}Y_t$, then our estimate of α_1^* will tend to zero because var(u)/var(Y) will tend to one. The problem essentially is that instead of estimating the true marginal propensity to consume, α_1, in equation (6.6) we are in fact estimating the composite function in equation (6.13). To be able to obtain a separate estimate of α_1 we need more information. One source of information could be knowledge of the variance of u, var(u), for we could obtain the variance of Y, var(Y), from our sample and hence an estimate of α_1 from equation (6.13).

An alternative procedure is to find 'instrumental variables' for Y (which are uncorrelated with u^*) and obtain an instrumental variable estimate of α_1. (For a discussion of instrumental variable estimation see Johnston (1972) and for its application in rational expectations models see Wickens (1982).)

A more important and fruitful method of incorporating rational expectations into a macroeconomic model makes use of the central idea of rational expectations that variables are determined by processes. Suppose that the process determining Y_t in the example above is

$$Y_t = \theta_0 + \theta_1 Y_{t-1} + \theta_2 X_{t-1} + \theta_3 Z_{t-1} + u_t \tag{6.14}$$

where X and Z are whatever variables determine Y and the θ_i's are coefficients.

It follows that if expectations are rational we can write

$$E_{t-1} Y_t = \theta_0 + \theta_1 Y_{t-1} + \theta_2 X_{t-1} + \theta_3 Z_{t-1}. \tag{6.15}$$

Substituting this expression for $E_{t-1}Y_t$ into the consumption expenditure equation (6.6) we obtain

$$C_t = \alpha_0 + \alpha_1 \theta_0 + \alpha_1 \theta_1 Y_{t-1} + \alpha_1 \theta_2 X_{t-1} + \alpha_1 \theta_3 Z_{t-1} + v_t. \tag{6.16}$$

It is clear from equations (6.14) and (6.16) that we could employ a two-stage procedure to obtain estimators of α_0, α_1 and the θ_i's which are 'consistent' in the formal statistical sense that as we use more and more observations we would expect the means of our estimators of α_0, α_1 etc. to tend towards their true values. The first stage of this procedure is to regress Y_t on the set of variables Y_{t-1}, X_{t-1} and Z_{t-1} as in equation in (6.14) and thereby secure estimates of the θ_i's. These estimates of the θ_i's can then be used to measure $E_{t-1}Y_t$, for in accordance with equation (6.15) we could construct the following estimate of $E_{t-1}Y_t$,

$$\hat{E}_{t-1}Y_t = \hat{\theta}_0 + \hat{\theta}_1 Y_{t-1} + \hat{\theta}_2 X_{t-1} + \hat{\theta}_3 Z_{t-1} \tag{6.17}$$

where a ' $\hat{}$ ' over a variable or coefficient denotes our estimate of that variable or coefficient.

The second stage of the procedure would then be to regress C_t on a constant and our estimate of $E_{t-1}Y_t$ given in (6.17). Notice that only one variable, $\hat{E}_{t-1}Y_t$ is being used in this regression. The four elements which together add up to $\hat{E}_{t-1}Y_t$ have been combined to form the single variable $\hat{E}_{t-1}Y_t$, and C_t is regressed on this single variable. The resulting estimates of the constant and the marginal propensity to consume out of expected income would be consistent estimators of α_0 and α_1 respectively. The problem experienced when using actual income to measure expected income would disappear under this two-stage procedure since the source of the problem was the correlation between u_t and the measure used for

$E_{t-1}Y_t$. As equation (6.17) indicates our measure of expected income is no longer correlated with the error term u_t – it does not appear in that equation – and hence the problem no longer occurs.

So the rational expectations hypothesis suggests a valid method of incorporating additional information when estimating macroeconomic models which contain expectation terms. The key element in it is that the process determining the variable about which expectations are being formed has to be estimated alongside the rest of the model. A further and very important advantage of this method is that it suggests a way of testing the validity of the rational expectations hypothesis itself. To see this consider again the consumption expenditure model we have been discussing. If we measure expected income in accordance with our estimate of the process determining income, that is by equation (6.17); and if consumption expenditure is determined in accordance with equation (6.6) then as we have shown it follows that we can write C_t in accordance with equation (6.18).

$$C_t = \alpha_0 + \alpha_1\hat{\theta}_0 + \alpha_1\hat{\theta}_1Y_{t-1} + \alpha_1\hat{\theta}_2X_{t-1} + \alpha_1\hat{\theta}_3Z_{t-1} + v_t. \qquad (6.18)$$

But this implies that if we regressed C_t on the three variables $\hat{\theta}_1Y_{t-1}$, $\hat{\theta}_2 X_{t-1}$, and $\hat{\theta}_3Z_{t-1}$ entered separately (rather than as a single variable, $E_{t-1}Y_t$), we should observe that the coefficients estimated on these three variables are approximately all the same for they are all estimates of α_1, the marginal propensity to consume out of expected income. Thus the rationality of expectations imposes restrictions on what we should find when we estimate equation (6.18). This is a common feature of the rational expectations hypothesis and it provides an obvious way of testing the hypothesis, for if on estimating equation (6.18) we found 'widely different' coefficients on $\hat{\theta}_1Y_{t-1}$, $\hat{\theta}_2X_{t-1}$ and $\hat{\theta}_3Z_{t-1}$ then it would suggest that either equation (6.6) is untrue or expectations are not formed rationally. So to test the rational expectations hypothesis, on the assumption that the rest of the model (in our example equation (6.6)) is true, one tests the validity of the restrictions imposed by the assumption of rational expectations. To do this of course we have to be more precise about the meaning of the description 'widely different', so in the next section we consider precisely how we can test for the validity of the type of restriction that rational expectations imposes.

6.3 TESTING THE RESTRICTIONS IMPLIED BY RATIONAL EXPECTATIONS

The precise statistical formulae for testing the validity of restrictions which we explain in this section may appear complex, but the essential idea behind them is simple. If a restriction is imposed on a model of a particular variable's behaviour, then if that restriction is valid its imposition should not affect the model's success in explaining the variable's behaviour whereas if the restriction is invalid, it should. To make clear how we can formally test for the validity of restrictions we shall consider first of all the following simple linear regression model

$$Y_t = \beta_0 + \beta_1 X_t + \beta_2 Z_t + u_t \tag{6.19}$$

where Y, X and Z are variables β_0, β_1 and β_2 are coefficients, and u is an error term with mean zero.

Suppose we have some *a priori* information suggesting that $\beta_1 = \beta_2$ in equation (6.19). If we had a large enough sample of observations on Y_t, X_t and Z_t we would expect a linear regression of Y_t on X_t and Z_t to yield the result that the estimates of β_1 and β_2 were the same – except for sampling variation – if it is really true that $\beta_1 = \beta_2$. Another way of putting this is that if we impose the restriction that $\beta_1 = \beta_2$ by adding X and Z together to form a single variable, $(X + Z)$, and carry out the regression

$$Y_t = \beta_0 + \beta_1 (X_t + Z_t) + v_t \tag{6.20}$$

if β_1 really is equal to β_2 in the process generating Y_t then the estimates of β_0 and β_1 from equation (6.20), in a large sample, should not differ very much from the estimates from equation (6.19). Furthermore the ability of the regression equation (6.20) to explain the behaviour of Y_t should not be any worse than the ability of equation (6.19) to do the same. If, on the other hand, our hypothesis $\beta_1 = \beta_2$ is false the estimates of β_0 and β_1 from equation (6.20) are likely to be very different from those obtained from equation (6.19), and the ability of equation (6.20) to explain the behaviour of Y is likely to be very much worse than that of equation (6.19).

But what precisely do 'very different' and 'ability to explain behaviour' mean in this context? What precise statistical procedure can be applied to test whether the coefficients and explanatory power of equation (6.19), the unrestricted model, are significantly different from those in equation (6.20), the restricted model? A sensible way to proceed is to compare the estimated sum of squared residuals from equation (6.19), $\Sigma \hat{u}^2$ say, with those estimated from the regression equation (6.20) in which the restrictions have been imposed, $\Sigma \hat{v}^2$, where a '$\hat{}$' over a variable denotes the estimated value of that variable. Intuitively if the hypothesis that $\beta_1 = \beta_2$ is true we would expect $\Sigma \hat{v}^2$ and $\Sigma \hat{u}^2$ to be approximately equal in a large sample since that implies that both models explain the behaviour of Y equally well. And imposing a restriction which is true should not worsen the ability of the right-hand side variables to explain the left-hand side variable, or, alternatively, relaxing the restriction and allowing the estimators of β_1 and β_2 to be different should not lead to a much better fitting equation if β_1 and β_2 are in fact not different.

If it is assumed that u_t and v_t are normally distributed, it can be shown that the ratio $[(n-k)/g][(\Sigma\hat{v}^2 - \Sigma\hat{u}^2)/\Sigma\hat{u}^2$ is distributed as an F-variate with g and $n-k$ degrees of freedom, where g is the number of restrictions – one in our example, i.e. $\beta_1 = \beta_2$; n is the number of observations; and k the number of coefficients in the unrestricted model – three in the example: β_0, β_1, and β_2 (see Maddala, (1977)). Thus to test these restrictions one would estimate equations (6.19) and (6.20) separately and compute the F statistic given above; then compare the result with the critical F value given the appropriate degrees of freedom, and reject the hypothesis that the restrictions are valid if the computed value of the F-statistic is higher than its critical value.

One problem with this particular test of the validity of a set of restrictions is that it can only be applied when those restrictions are linear, that is coefficients are restricted to be linear rather than non-linear functions of each other. Thus if, in our example, the restriction was not that $\beta_1 = \beta_2$ but that $\beta_1 = 1/\beta_2$ the F-test we have given could not be used.

Another test which, like the F test, is based on the sum of squared residuals but which can be used in more general situations is the likelihood ratio test. It can be shown that for large samples the statistic $n(\ln \Sigma\hat{v}^2 - \ln \Sigma\hat{u}^2)$, called the likelihood ratio test statistic, is distributed as a chi-square variate with g degrees of freedom where, once again, g is the number of restrictions on the model, and ln of course stands for the natural logarithm. The intuition behind this result is again that if the restrictions are valid one would expect the sum of squared residuals, and hence their logarithms, to be approximately the same in both the restricted and unrestricted equations. Notice that for small differences $[(\Sigma\hat{v}^2 - \Sigma\hat{u}^2)/\Sigma\hat{u}^2]$ is approximately equal to $\ln \Sigma\hat{v}^2 - \ln \Sigma\hat{u}^2$. With linear restrictions on a single-equation linear model the test using the F distribution is preferable, but in most other cases the likelihood ratio test could be used. The restrictions applied in rational expectations models are often non-linear and are imposed across equations rather than within a single equation. As an example take the consumption function model discussed in section 6.2. There, from the following two equations

$$C_t = \alpha_0 + \alpha_1 E_{t-1} Y_t + v_t \tag{6.6}$$

$$Y_t = \theta_0 + \theta_1 Y_{t-1} + \theta_2 X_{t-1} + \theta_3 Z_{t-1} + u_t \tag{6.14}$$

and the assumption of rationality we derived the following two-equation model:

$$C_t = \alpha_0 + \alpha_1\theta_0 + \alpha_1\theta_1 Y_{t-1} + \alpha_1\theta_2 X_{t-1} + \alpha_1\theta_3 Z_{t-1} + v_t \tag{6.16}$$

$$Y_t = \theta_0 + \theta_1 Y_{t-1} + \theta_2 X_{t-1} + \theta_3 Z_{t-1} + u_t \tag{6.14}$$

As we noted in section 6.2 the coefficients on each variable in the consumption relationship are restricted to equal the coefficients on the same variable in the process determining income multiplied by the marginal propensity to consume, a_1. Because of the non-linearity of the cross equation restrictions we cannot use the F-test in this case but we can use the likelihood ratio. Because the restrictions arise in a two-equation model (rather than the single-equation case considered before), we now require a method of summarizing the variation in both equation errors. We begin by defining the variance-covariance matrix of the equation errors as:

$$E \begin{bmatrix} v_t \\ u_t \end{bmatrix} [v_t, u_t] = \begin{bmatrix} E(v_t^2) & E(v_t u_t) \\ E(u_t v_t) & E(u_t^2) \end{bmatrix} = \begin{bmatrix} \sigma_v^2 & \sigma_{vu} \\ \sigma_{uv} & \sigma_u^2 \end{bmatrix} = \Sigma.$$

Next we define the generalized variance as the determinant of the variance-covariance matrix Σ, which is defined in the two-equation case as

$$\det(\Sigma) = \sigma_v^2 \sigma_u^2 - \sigma_{uv}^2.$$

Now consider the completely unrestricted model

$$C_t = \pi_0 + \pi_1 Y_{t-1} + \pi_2 X_{t-1} + \pi_3 Z_{t-1} + w_{1t}$$

$$Y_t = \pi_4 + \pi_5 Y_{t-1} + \pi_6 X_{t-1} + \pi_7 Z_{t-1} + w_{2t}.$$

(6.21)

We define the variance-covariance matrix of this model's equation errors as

$$E \begin{bmatrix} w_{1t} \\ w_{2t} \end{bmatrix} [w_{1t}, w_{2t}] = \Omega$$

Then the generalized variance of the equation errors for the unrestricted model is given by $\det(\Omega)$. In general it can be shown that for large n the statistic

$$n[\ln \det(\hat{\Sigma}) - \ln \det(\hat{\Omega})]$$

is distributed as a chi-square variate with g degrees of freedom where, once again, g is the number of restrictions in the model. $\hat{\Sigma}$ and $\hat{\Omega}$ are formed from the cross products of the estimated residuals from the relevant equations. The intuition behind this result is much the same as before. If the restrictions are valid we would expect the generalized variance from the restricted and unrestricted models to be approximately the same. The likelihood ratio statistic shown above is a formalization of this. The test can easily be generalized to the case of more than two equations.

The testing of the rational expectations hypothesis in a variety of macroeconomic contexts has often proceeded along the lines suggested above, that is the validity of the restrictions imposed by the rational expectations hypothesis has been tested. A particularly influential series of studies have been carried out by Barro (1977a, 1978a). We shall discuss his empirical results in a later chapter, but here we shall explain the Barro approach and use it first to reinforce the idea that the rational expectations hypothesis imposes testable restrictions, and secondly to illustrate a problem with testing the hypothesis by testing the validity of the restrictions it imposes.

6.4 THE BARRO MODEL

The Barro model is based on the flexible price rational expectations macroeconomic model which we derived in chapter 3. In that model aggregate demand affects real output only if the change in aggregate demand is unexpected. Barro assumes that the quantity of money is the prime determinant of aggregate demand and therefore obtains the result that changes in the quantity of money will affect real output only if they are unexpected. Expected changes in the quantity of money will affect only the level of prices. In a simplified form this first element of Barro's model can be written as

$$Y_t = \alpha W_t + \beta(DM_t - E_{t-1} DM_t) + v_t \tag{6.22}$$

where W_t = a variable or a number of variables which determine the natural level of output

DM_t = the rate of growth of the quantity of money in period t

$E_{t-1} DM_t$ = the expectation of the rate of growth of the quantity of money

α = a coefficient (or vector of coefficients)

β = a positive coefficient

v_t = a random error with mean zero.

Equation (6.22) is merely a formal statement that if monetary growth equals the expectation of it then output will be at its natural level; if monetary growth is greater (less) than expected, real output will be greater (less) than its natural level. Notice that equation (6.22) could be written with expectations formed non-rationally. However, it does assume what is sometimes called 'structural neutrality': that however expectations are formed expected money growth does not affect real output. We mention this here because later on we shall be examining how one might test separately for rational expectations and structural neutrality. In order to derive a rational expectations model incorporating equation (6.22) we must specify a process for monetary growth. Imagine that monetary growth for the economy we are considering is determined by the following process

$$DM_t = \delta_1 X_{t-1} + \delta_2 Z_{t-1} + u_t \tag{6.23}$$

where X and Z = variables whose values in period $t-1$ partly determine monetary growth in period t

u_t = the random, unpredictable component of monetary growth with zero mean

δ_1 and δ_2 = coefficients.

Equation (6.23) is sometimes described as a 'policy regime', that is a rule by which the authorities link a policy instrument, in this case the growth of money, to the behaviour of other variables. In this case these other variables are the lagged values of X and Z which could be, for example, the level of unemployment and the inflation rate, or the balance of payments or the public sector borrowing requirement, or whatever variables the government wishes. The coefficients δ_1 and δ_2 are chosen by the authorities in order, as they see it, to achieve their aims. A change of policy regime can occur either as a result of a change in the values of the coefficients, the δ_i's, or as a change in the choice variables to which the policy instrument is linked. Given the process described by equation (6.23) the rational expectation of DM_t must be

$$E_{t-1}DM_t = \delta_1 X_{t-1} + \delta_2 Z_{t-1} \tag{6.24a}$$

whereas a non-rational expectation would be, for example

$$DM^e_{t-1} = \delta_3 X_{t-1} + \delta_4 Z_{t-1} \tag{6.24b}$$

where δ_3 and δ_4 are any numbers other than δ_1 and δ_2 respectively.

Putting the equations (6.22) and (6.24a) together, i.e. imposing rational expectations, gives the two-equation rational expectations model

$$DM_t = \delta_1 X_{t-1} + \delta_2 Z_{t-1} + u_t$$
$$Y_t = \alpha W_t + \beta u_t + v_t. \tag{6.25}$$

Notice that (6.25) assumes or imposes both structural neutrality (only unexpected monetary growth affects real output) and rational expectations (expected monetary growth equals the predictable component of the process determining monetary growth). The presence in the real output equation of the random component of the money growth equation, u_t, and the absence of any other component of monetary growth in that same equation reflect the imposition of both these assumptions. The restrictions which are imposed on (6.25) by the assumption of rational expectations and which can be used to test for the validity of the rational expectations hypothesis can be most easily seen if we substitute the expression $u_t = DM_t - \delta_1 X_{t-1} - \delta_2 Z_{t-1}$ into the output equation to give an alternative form of the two-equation system

$$DM_t = \delta_1 X_{t-1} + \delta_2 Z_{t-1} + u_t$$
$$Y_t = \alpha W_t + \beta DM_t - \beta\delta_1 X_{t-1} - \beta\delta_2 Z_{t-1} + v_t. \qquad (6.26)$$

In (6.26) there are two restrictions imposed by the assumption of rational expectations: the coefficients on X_{t-1} and Z_{t-1} in the output equation must both be the negative of the product of their respective coefficients in the money growth equation, δ_1 and δ_2, and the coefficient on actual money growth in the output equation, β. Intuitively, if expectations were not rational, but the rest of the model were true, there is no reason why the coefficient on, say, X_{t-1} in the output equation should bear any relationship at all to its coefficient in the money growth equation: the two are quite independent and each can be any number. But if expectations are rational then this independence is lost: expectations must be formed in a way which is restricted to be in accordance with the process which monetary growth actually follows; the coefficient on X_{t-1} in the output equation is therefore restricted by the coefficient on X_{t-1} in the money growth equation. The same argument applies to Z_{t-1}.

We could test for the validity of rational expectations within this macro-model as follows. First compute the likelihood obtained from the system (6.26) in which the coefficients on X_{t-1} and Z_{t-1} in the output equation are forced to be equal to $-\beta\delta_1$ and $-\beta\delta_2$ respectively, that is the rational expectation restrictions are imposed. (The exact method by which this is done need not concern us here. Attfield et al. (1981a, b) outline the procedure and the necessary assumptions.) Next, estimate the non-rational expectations model which combines equation (6.24b) with the non-rational equivalent of equation (6.22) to give:

$$DM_t = \delta_1 X_{t-1} + \delta_2 Z_{t-1} + u_t$$
$$Y_t = \alpha W_t + \beta DM_t - \beta\delta_3 X_{t-1} - \beta\delta_4 Z_{t-1} + v_t. \qquad (6.27)$$

Notice that in this model there are no restrictions on the coefficients estimated on X_{t-1} and Z_{t-1} in the money growth and output equations: the computer can estimate whatever numbers it finds give the best explanation of DM_t and Y_t. The reason for this of course is that by incorporating equation (6.24b) rather than (6.24a) into equation (6.22) we are in effect relaxing the restrictions imposed by the rational expectations hypothesis. The statistical result of this relaxation of restrictions must be to give a model which is more successful, or at least as successful, in explaining the behaviour of DM_t and Y_t. But how much more successful? To find out one would use the likelihoods computed from the two models to construct the likelihood ratio test statistic as described above, and compare it with the chi-square distribution with the appropriate degrees of freedom. Such a comparison would be a test of the rational expectations hypothesis. If the unrestricted model performed significantly better than the restricted model it would imply that the restrictions imposed were invalid. And since these restrictions are due to the assumption of rational expectations, rejection of them implies a rejection of rational expectations, conditional upon the rest of the model being true.

6.5 OBSERVATIONAL EQUIVALENCE

This last sentence hints at a problem with testing the rational expectations hypothesis in the way we have outlined. The problem is a general one but one aspect of it can be illustrated using the Barro model. What if the 'rest of the model' was not as specified in (6.25)? Specifically, what if the normal or natural level of real output depended on the same variables which influence monetary growth? In the simplified version of the Barro model in (6.25) we have excluded as an independent influence on Y_t the variables X_{t-1} and Z_{t-1}. Imagine that in fact these variables influence both money growth and the natural level of output so that the rational expectations system (6.25) becomes:

$$DM_t = \delta_1 X_{t-1} + \delta_2 Z_{t-1} + u_t$$
$$Y_t = \alpha_1 W_t + \alpha_2 X_{t-1} + \alpha_3 Z_{t-1} + \beta u_t + v_t. \tag{6.28}$$

Substituting out for u_t from the money growth equation gives:

$$DM_t = \delta_1 X_{t-1} + \delta_2 Z_{t-1} + u_t$$
$$Y_t = \alpha_1 W_t + (\alpha_2 - \beta\delta_1)X_{t-1} + (\alpha_3 - \beta\delta_2)Z_{t-1} + \beta DM_t + v_t. \tag{6.29}$$

In this model the restrictions which we used to test for rational expectations in (6.25) are no longer binding even though we are still assuming rational expectations: the coefficients on X_{t-1} and Z_{t-1} in the output equation no longer have to equal the negative of the products of their respective coefficients in the money growth equation and the coefficient on DM_t in the output equation. They can equal any number, and the differences between those numbers and $-\beta\delta_1$ or $-\beta\delta_2$ can be attributed to α_2 and α_3 respectively. To put that another way, the model (6.29), which assumes rational expectations, cannot be distinguished from the non-rational expectations model (6.27), because the restrictions which differentiated the rational and non-rational expectations model no longer apply.

Even if we estimated (6.29) and found that the coefficients on X_{t-1} and Z_{t-1} in the output equation did equal the negative products of our estimates of δ_1 and β and, δ_2 and β respectively it would not tell us that expected money growth equalled $\delta_1 X_{t-1} + \delta_2 Z_{t-1}$ as rational expectations predicts. It could still be the case that expected money growth was $\delta_3 X_{t-1}$

+ $\delta_4 Z_{t-1}$, implying non-rational expectations, but α_2 happened to equal $\beta(\delta_3 - \delta_1)$ and α_3 happened to equal $\beta(\delta_4 - \delta_2)$. Of course this may appear to be unlikely but one cannot rule it out unless one knows the values of α_2 and α_3 prior to estimating (6.29). In general one does not have this information and so strictly one cannot test the rational expectations hypothesis in the way we have outlined. Despite having different policy implications the rational expectations model (6.29) and the non-rational expectations model (6.27) are what is called *observationally equivalent*. The data cannot distinguish between them.

The observational equivalence problem in the context of a rational expectations macroeconomic model was first discussed by Sargent (1976a). Barro's method of avoiding the problem is to assume a priori in an equation such as (6.29) that $\alpha_2 = 0$ and $\alpha_3 = 0$, that is he assumes that there are economic variables X_{t-1} and Z_{t-1} which influence monetary growth but which do not have an independent influence on output.

A similar way of overcoming the problem is by using prior knowledge of differing lag lengths of variables in the money and output equations if such information is available. Suppose for example that we have a priori information that two lags of X_t and of Z_t determine monetary growth, but only one lag of these variables plus current and one lag of money growth have an independent influence on output so that the model becomes

$$DM_t = \delta_1 X_{t-1} + \delta_2 Z_{t-1} + \delta_3 X_{t-2} + \delta_4 Z_{t-2} + u_t$$

$$Y_t = \beta_1 u_t + \beta_2 u_{t-1} + \alpha_1 X_{t-1} + \alpha_2 Z_{t-1} + v_t \tag{6.30}$$

Then substituting out u_t and u_{t-1} in the output equation we obtain the model

$$DM_t = \delta_1 X_{t-1} + \delta_2 Z_{t-1} + \delta_3 X_{t-2} + \delta_4 Z_{t-2} + u_t$$

$$\begin{aligned} Y_t = \beta_1 DM_t + \beta_2 DM_{t-1} + (\alpha_1 - \beta_1 \delta_1) X_{t-1} + (\alpha_2 - \beta_1 \delta_2) Z_{t-1} \\ - (\beta_1 \delta_3 + \beta_2 \delta_1) X_{t-2} - (\beta_1 \delta_4 + \beta_2 \delta_2) Z_{t-2} \\ - \beta_2 \delta_3 X_{t-3} - \beta_2 \delta_4 Z_{t-3} + v_t \end{aligned} \tag{6.31}$$

From the first equation in (6.31) we can obtain estimates of $\delta_1, \delta_2, \delta_3$ and δ_4. From the coefficients on DM_t and DM_{t-1} in the output equation we have estimates of β_1 and β_2 Then, from the coefficients on X_{t-1} and Z_{t-1} given β_1, δ_1 and δ_2 we can obtain estimates of α_1 and α_2. The remaining coefficients on $X_{t-2}, Z_{t-2}, X_{t-3}$ and Z_{t-3} contain restrictions which can be tested. In this case then the restrictions on the coefficients in the equations in (6.31) enable the rational expectations model to be distinguished.

A further example of observational equivalence was pointed out by Buiter (1983) who demonstrated that the model of (6.25), that is:

$$DM_t = \delta_1 X_{t-1} + \delta_2 Z_{t-1} + u_t$$
$$Y_t = \alpha W_t + \beta u_t + v_t \tag{6.25}$$

is indistinguishable from a model in which an output shock appears in the money growth equation and there is no money shock in the output equation. He argues that such a model reflects either the behaviour of the authorities through a monetary policy reaction function or the response of the private banking system to changes in the demand for money due to unanticipated changes in income. The essence of his argument can be summarized in the equations

$$DM_t = \gamma_1 X_{t-1} + \gamma_2 Z_{t-1} + \gamma_3 (Y_t - E_{t-1} Y_t) + \varepsilon_{1t} \tag{6.32}$$

$$Y_t = \gamma_4 W_t + \varepsilon_{2t} \tag{6.33}$$

where ε_{1t} and ε_{2t} are contemporaneously and serially uncorrelated random errors. Substituting out the output shock gives

$$DM_t = \gamma_1 X_{t-1} + \gamma_2 Z_{t-1} + \gamma_3 Y_t - \gamma_3 \gamma_4 W_t + \varepsilon_{1t}$$
$$Y_t = \gamma_4 W_t + \varepsilon_{2t} \tag{6.34}$$

It may appear at first sight that the equations in (6.34) place a different set of restrictions on the model than those in (6.25) but this is not the case. If we substitute out the right-hand side endogenous variable, that is Y_t in the money equation in (6.34) we obtain:

$$DM_t = \gamma_1 X_{t-1} + \gamma_2 Z_{t-1} + \gamma_3 \varepsilon_{2t} + \varepsilon_{1t}$$
$$Y_t = \gamma_4 W_t + \varepsilon_{2t} \tag{6.35}$$

Comparison of (6.35) and (6.25) shows that except for the structure of the error terms the models are the same and the likelihood for the model in (6.35) will be idential to the likelihood for the model in (6.25) so we cannot distinguish between them; the models are observationally equivalent.

Buiter goes on to examine models in which current and lagged unanticipated money growth appear in the output equation and where current and lagged unanticipated output appear in the money equation. Although he does suggest certain restrictions which would enable the hypothesis that it is only unanticipated money growth that affects output to be tested, these restrictions depend upon *a priori* knowledge of lag lengths and as such information is not usually available the conclusion from Buiter's work is pessimistic.

The situation, however, is not entirely hopeless since another possible means of overcoming the problem of observational equivalence is provided by breaks or changes in the process determining the variable about which expectations are being formed. To illustrate, consider a change in the process determining monetary growth. What would such a change imply for the rational expectations version of the Barro model (6.29) and its non-rational counterpart (6.27)?

To take a specific example consider what would happen if the value of δ_1 in the money growth equation in (6.27) and (6.29) changed. If expectations were rational the coefficient on X_{t-1} in the output equation should change by a predictable amount since it should equal $(\alpha_2 - \beta\delta_1)$ and hence should change by $-\beta$ times the change in δ_1. But if expectations of monetary growth are formed irrationally then no such change in the coefficient is implied because the process determining a variable does not also determine expectations about that variable. Therefore, if one can identify such changes in policy regime one can test the rational expectations hypothesis since the rational expectations model (6.29) makes a prediction that the non-rational model (6.27) does not. Such changes in 'policy regime' thus offer some scope for testing rational expectations even in the case of models which appear to be observationally equivalent. They do so because changes in policy regime, or more generally changes in the process determining a variable about which expectations are being formed, imply under rational expectations changes in coefficients elsewhere in the model. If changes in policy regime do occur then one can test rational expectations by testing for the occurrence of these changes in other coefficients.

This last point, that changes in policy regimes may themselves lead to changes in coefficients estimated in other equations of a system, has been used by Lucas as the basis of a powerful criticism of much econometric model building and policy evaluation. It is a convenient moment to discuss the so-called Lucas critique, even though it is somewhat tangential to the question of how to test for rational expectations.

6.6 THE LUCAS CRITIQUE OF ECONOMIC POLICY EVALUATION

A common practice adopted by macroeconomists, particularly those advising government policy-makers, is to estimate a model of the economy and then evaluate different policy options by using their model to work out what will be the results of the various different policies. On the basis of this procedure the economist can then offer advice about the desirability of the different policy options. An assumption that is implicit in this procedure is that the econometrician has successfully estimated the *constant structure* of the economy, and that this estimated structure of the model will not be different under different policies, i.e. that the structure of the model is *policy invariant*. The fundamentally important point made by Lucas (1976) and sometimes referred to as the 'Lucas critique' is that if expectations are rational the type of structure which many econometric models have estimated is *not* the constant structure and will not be policy invariant. On the contrary it will depend amongst other things on the policies the government is pursuing, and as a result the approach to policy evaluation described above is seriously flawed.

To illustrate Lucas's point consider again the Barro model we discussed in the previous sections. We showed there that the model could be written as a two-equation system which for convenience we rewrite as

$$DM_t = \delta_1 X_{t-1} + \delta_2 Z_{t-1} + u_t$$
$$Y_t = \alpha W_t + \beta u_t + v_t. \tag{6.36}$$

But we also showed that from the definition of u_t the output equation could be written in an alternative form as

$$Y_t = \alpha W_t + \beta DM_t - \beta \delta_1 X_{t-1} - \beta \delta_2 Z_{t-1} + v_t. \tag{6.37}$$

Imagine now an econometric model builder who is unaware of the structure from which equation (6.37) comes but finds that when he regresses Y_t on W_t, DM_t, X_{t-1} and Z_{t-1} he obtains a very good explanation of the behaviour of Y_t. Of course, unlike us, he is unaware that the coefficient of DM_t is really β, that the coefficient on X_{t-1} is really $-\beta\delta_1$ and that the co-efficient on Z_{t-1} is really $-\beta\delta_2$. To him these coefficients are numbers which are unrelated to one another. He has just estimated the following regression

$$Y_t = \pi_1 W_t + \pi_2 DM_t + \pi_3 X_{t-1} + \pi_4 Z_{t-1} + v_t \tag{6.38}$$

where the π_i's are estimated coefficients, and found that it works well.

The estimate of equation (6.38) is then this model builder's estimated model of the behaviour of real output in the economy. (Of course in reality a full-scale model of the economy involves many more equations than one but we do not need to allow for more equations to make the point.) He interprets the coefficients π_1, π_2 etc. as good estimates of the constant structure of the economy. Notice that if the economy is actually behaving according to the system described in equations (6.36) there is no reason why the econometric model builder should not find what appears to be a non-rational expectation model of real output such as equation (6.38) working well. But once this model is used to persuade a government to change its policies the non-rational expectation model of Y_t will collapse whereas the rational expectation model will not.

Imagine that on the basis of his model, equation (6.38), the econometrician advises the government to redesign its monetary policy, perhaps with the aim of achieving a consistently higher value for Y_t. Assume that the advice is to change the size of the coefficient linking DM_t and X_{t-1}, that is to change δ_1 to δ_5. What will happen? One thing that will happen is that the econometric model builder will find that his estimated model (6.38) has changed. For, as we know but he does not, the estimated coefficient π_3 is really the negative product of β and the coefficient linking DM_t to X_{t-1}. Since this latter coefficient has now changed then so will the value of π_3. In other words the estimated 'structure' of the economy has not remained invariant to the policies the government is pursuing.

Since the policy advice was based on the idea that the supposed structure of the economy *would* remain unchanged in the face of different policies it is not surprising that the policy advice will not achieve its aim. To see that it will not, consider the system represented by equation (6.36) again. The change in the coefficient on X_{t-1} from δ_1 to δ_5 will imply a change in the money-growth equation, that is in the process determining monetary growth, and hence, given rational expectations, a change in the precise way expectations of monetary growth are formed. This latter change will of course be such that the unexpected component of monetary growth each period will still equal whatever the value of u happens to be in that period. And since the random component of monetary growth is the only monetary influence on real output and has not been affected by the policy change, it follows that the policy change will not have exerted any influence on the behaviour of Y_t: the policy will have failed, and the output equation in (6.36) will be stable.

We have used the Barro model to illustrate the point raised by Lucas, but since the Lucas point is a very important one with wide applications it is worth stating it more generally. The essence of it is that if expectations of a variable are rational they will be determined by the process governing that variable. Thus expectations about policy will be determined by the process governing that policy, the 'policy regime'; and changes in policy regime will alter the precise way in which people form their expectations about policy. Estimated models of the economy which do not allow for changes in expectations when policy regimes change are therefore likely to be seriously flawed in that they will begin to predict the behaviour of the economy badly whenever a policy regime change occurs. By implication these models should not be used as they often are used to evaluate different policy regimes since it is precisely when a different policy regime is adopted that they become unreliable.

To put that another way, there are reasons for thinking that what an econometric model builder might believe is a good estimate of the constant structure of the economy is in fact no such thing, but rather an estimate of a relationship or relationships which are dependent upon a particular policy regime. If the policy regime changes then so will what was thought to be the constant structure. Economists should therefore be cautious in making recommendations about policy changes. Such changes may well alter what appeared to be the constant structure of the economy itself, and these changes too have to be allowed for when evaluating different policies. More fundamentally the Lucas point can be seen as suggesting that the constant structure of the economy which it is a major aim of the macroeconomist to reveal is much more deeply hidden than econometric model builders might have previously thought.

SUMMARY

The aim of this chapter has been to outline some important econometric principles involved in testing theories which include rational expectations. We noted at the outset that *direct* tests of rationality, conducted by the use of survey data on actual expectations, are not in general favourable to rational expectations. We outlined a number of problems with these tests (e.g. the survey data may be subject to important 'errors in variables' problems) which suggest caution in drawing conclusions from these tests. Moreover *market behaviour* may appear to be quite consistent with rational expectations when only a small number of agents actually possess rational expectations, and the majority do not.

We suggest that a more fruitful approach would be the testing of economic models which include rational expectations, for the latter imposes restrictions which can, in principle, be tested. The chapter outlined some statistical methods for testing restrictions, notably the likelihood ratio test. Unfortunately the restrictions implied by rational expectations are all conditional on the economic model being considered. If the underlying economic model is invalid, so might be the tests of rationality.

Finally we showed that rational expectations highlights the need for econometricians to identify the underlying *structure* of the economy if their models are to be used for policy evaluation. The simulation of the behaviour of the economy under alternative policies may be very misleading if the parameters of the econometric model depend in some fashion on the policy being pursued by the government.

SUGGESTIONS FOR FURTHER READING

Reviews of some of the literature on tests of the rational expectations model using direct survey data can be found in chapter 1 of Sheffrin (1983) and chapter 3 of Hudson (1982). Methods of incorporating rational expectations assumptions into economic models and estimating and testing the models are discussed in Wallis (1980), Revankar (1980) and Hoffman and Schmidt (1981). Further discussions of the observational equivalence problem can be found in McCallum (1979), chapters 4 and 5 of Begg (1982), chapter 10 of Minford and Peel (1983) and in Abel and Mishkin (1983). The Lucas critique of policy evaluation is discussed in chapters 4 and 5 of Begg (1982) and in chapter 5 of Minford and Peel (1983).

7

Rational Expectations and Macroeconomic Models: Some Influential Empirical Results

Now that we have explained some of the general principles involved in testing rational expectations models we begin in this chapter the task of examining in detail the results of some of the more important tests of the theory of rational expectations within macroeconomics. In fact the chapter concentrates on two of the most influential empirical studies in this area and some of the work that they have inspired. The first study is by Lucas (1973) and the second is a series of papers by Barro (1977a, 1978a) and Barro and Rush (1980). Both can be seen as attempts to test the major predictions of the rational expectations macroeconomic model developed in chapter 3. The Lucas paper concentrates on testing the prediction that the more unpredictable aggregate demand is, the less the effect on real output of any given unpredictable movement in aggregate demand. The Barro papers test the other major prediction of the model in chapter 3 – that only the unpredictable component of aggregate demand affects real variables such as output and unemployment. The other papers we consider in this chapter can be seen as extensions of the Lucas and/or Barro studies.

7.1 THE LUCAS STUDY: OUTPUT AND INFLATION TRADEOFFS

In chapter 3 we developed a rational expectations model which suggested that only the unpredictable component of aggregate demand would cause output to deviate from its natural rate, and the more unpredictable it was the less effect it would have on the deviation of real output from its natural rate. Formally we could write a simple version of that model as

$$y_t = y_t^n + \beta_1 (\sigma_u^2, \sigma_\varepsilon^2) u_t \qquad (7.1)$$

where 　　　y_t = aggregate real output
　　　　　　y_t^n = the natural level of output
　　　　　　u_t = the unpredictable component of aggregate demand

$$\sigma_u^2 = \text{the variance of } u$$
$$\sigma_\varepsilon^2 = \text{the variance of the relative demand shocks}$$
$$\beta_1 \left(\sigma_u^2, \sigma_\varepsilon^2\right) = \text{a function explained below whose value is positive.}$$

All variables are in logarithms.

This equation states that in the absence of any aggregate demand shock, (i.e. if u_t is zero) output will equal its natural level, y_t^n. If the aggregate demand shock is positive then real output will rise above its natural level; if it is negative it will fall below it. The actual size of the rise or fall, for any given value for u_t, will depend upon the variance of the aggregate demand and relative demand shocks. The higher the variance of the aggregate demand shock the more unpredictable the aggregate demand shock is, and therefore, as explained in chapter 3, the lower will the effect of any given u_t be. In others words the greater the value of σ_u^2 the lower, *ceteris paribus*, the value of $\beta_1 \left(\sigma_u^2, \sigma_\varepsilon^2\right)$. For the reasons explained in chapter 3 the model also predicts that the higher the value of σ_ε^2 the greater, *ceteris paribus*, the value of $\beta_1 \left(\sigma_u^2, \sigma_\varepsilon^2\right)$. The focus of the Lucas (1973) paper is on the first of these predicted relationships – that is between the volatility of aggregate demand and its impact on real output. He tests it using data from a number of different countries over the same time period, reasoning that if equation (7.1) is true, then those countries in which aggregate demand has been highly unpredictable should be those countries in which unpredictable aggregate demand has little effect on real output.

In fact Lucas uses a slightly more complicated version of equation (7.1) in his empirical study. First he rewrites equation (7.1) as

$$y_{cit} = \beta_{1i} \left(\sigma_{ui}^2, \sigma_{\varepsilon i}^2\right) u_{it} \tag{7.2}$$

where y_{cit} is by definition the deviation of aggregate output in the ith country from its natural level, i.e. $y_{it} - y_{it}^n$. The other variables with i subscripts are as before but now refer to the ith country.

Then he allows for the effects of the 'propagation mechanisms' mentioned in chapter 4 by adding the lagged value of y_{cit} to equation (7.2) and attaching a positive coefficient, β_{2i}, to it, giving

$$y_{cit} = \beta_{1i} \left(\sigma_{ui}^2, \sigma_{\varepsilon i}^2\right) u_{it} + \beta_{2i} y_{cit-1} \tag{7.3}$$

The addition of y_{cit-1} implies that any aggregate demand shock will have a drawn out effect on real output: a positive value for u_{it} will, *ceteris paribus*, lead to a positive value for y_{cit}, i.e. output will be above its natural level; next period, even in the absence of a positive value for u_{it+1}, y_{cit+1} will be positive because of the influence of the positive value of $\beta_{2i} y_{cit}$. Provided the value of β_{2i} is less than one the effect of the positive value of u_{it} will gradually become negligible. If β_{2i} was greater than one the effect of a non-zero u_{it} would increase over time, so a value for β_{2i} of less than 1 is a requirement for the model's stability.

Three final assumptions permit Lucas to carry out his test. First he assumes, essentially, that $\sigma_{\varepsilon i}^2$ is constant and roughly the same for all countries and can therefore be ignored. Secondly he assumes that the natural level of output grows at a rate which for any individual country is a constant over time but which may differ between countries. This assumption allows Lucas to measure y_{cit} as the deviation of actual real output, y_{it}, from the value predicted from a regression of y_{it} on a constant and time (where time might take on a value of 1 in the first year of the data period, 2 in the second and so on). Using this as his measure of y_{cit} Lucas can carry out a separate regression of y_{cit} on y_{cit-1} and u_{it} for each of the countries for which he has data once he has solved the problem of how for each country to measure u_{it}. The method employed by Lucas to measure u appears now to be rather simplistic as we shall see when we discuss the Barro studies. He measures each country's aggregate demand at any time by its total nominal spending. He then assumes that for each country the rate of growth of aggregate demand or nominal spending has followed a very simple process, that is

$$DX_{it} = \varkappa_{0i} + u_{it} \tag{7.4}$$

where DX_{it} = the rate of growth of the ith country's nominal spending
       $\varkappa_{0i}$ = the mean value of DX_i over the whole period
       u_{it} = the deviation of DX_{it} from its mean.

Rationality of expectations implies that if equation (7.4) adequately describes the process determining DX_{it} then for each country the anticipated rate of growth of aggregate demand will be $\varkappa_{0i}$ and the unanticipated rate of growth will in any period t be u_{it}. Thus Lucas can and does measure the unanticipated rate of growth of aggregate demand in the ith country in any period t by u_{it}, the deviation of the actual rate of growth of nominal spending from its mean value over the whole period. And he measures the unpredictability of aggregate demand in the ith country by the variance of u_{it}, σ_{ui}^2. Of course this practice is only valid if equation (7.4) does adequately describe the process determining DX_{it} in each country. The extreme simplicity of the process suggests that this is unlikely though Lucas (1973, p. 328 fn. 5) recognizes the problem and argues that the process he has assumed (i.e. equation (7.4)) appears 'roughly accurate for most countries' in his study. The simplicity of the process assumed for aggregate demand is something we shall return to in chapter 8 since it has some bearing on the interpretation of Lucas's results.

If for each country σ_{ui}^2 is a constant over time it follows that $\beta_{1i}\,(\sigma_{ui}^2, \sigma_{\varepsilon i}^2)$ will be a constant, though of course for different countries it will be a different constant. Thus for each country one could use Lucas's measure of unanticipated aggregate demand to estimate the following OLS regression based on equation (7.3)

$$y_{cit} = \beta_{1i}\,u_{it} + \beta_{2i}\,y_{cit-1} + \xi_{it} \qquad (7.5)$$

where β_{1i} is a coefficient ξ_{it} is a random error which is assumed to be serially uncorrelated with mean zero. In fact Lucas actually substitutes for u_{it} from equation (7.4) and estimates the following regression for each country

$$y_{cit} = -\;\beta_{1i}\,\varkappa_{0i} + \beta_{1i}\,DX_{it} + \beta_{2i}\,y_{cit-1} + \xi_{it} \qquad (7.6)$$

Strictly equations (7.5) and (7.6) are equivalent only if in estimating equation (7.6) the restriction is imposed that the coefficient estimated on DX_{it} is equal to the negative of the constant term divided by the mean of DX_{it}, $\varkappa_{0i}$. It appears that Lucas did not in fact impose this restriction, but estimated equation (7.6) freely. However, in what follows we shall assume Lucas estimated the equivalent of equation (7.5).

Thus Lucas can be seen as carrying out a regression for each country in his study in which that country's deviation of real output from its natural level is regressed on its own lagged value and Lucas's measure of the unpredictable and therefore unanticipated component of aggregate demand.

Lucas's study used data from eighteen countries and the regression equation (7.5) was estimated for each of them using annual data over the period 1952 to 1967. If the rational expectations macroeconomic model summarized in equation (7.3) has any validity one would expect, first of all, that the estimate of β_1 for each of the eighteen countries is positive, and that the estimated value of β_2 is between zero and one. In general these predictions of the theory are confirmed by Lucas's results. However, in a number of cases the variables on the right-hand side of equation (7.5) account for rather a small proportion of the variance of the left-hand side variable, y_{cit}, suggesting that some important influences on y_{cit} have been omitted from the estimating equation.

The second and crucial prediction of equation (7.3) is that those countries in which aggregate demand is volatile should be those countries in which β_1 is estimated to be low. Countries with volatile aggregate demand are identified by Lucas as those countries for which the variance of unanticipated aggregate demand, u, is high. To test this prediction rigorously Lucas should estimate equation (7.6) for his eighteen countries jointly, imposing the restriction implied by his model that the β_1 coefficients are negatively related to the estimated variances of u. The Lucas model could then be tested along the lines suggested in chapter 6 by testing for the validity of this restriction. In fact Lucas adopts a much less rigorous approach. He tabulates for each country the estimated variance of the unanticipated aggregate demand, u, and that country's estimated value for β_1. If the prediction is correct then a negative relationship should be observed. Lucas claims that such a relationship can be discerned from his data. As an illustration of this negative relationship Lucas notes that for the USA his estimate of the variance of aggregate demand is 0.00064, whilst for Argentina it is more than twenty times higher at 0.01555; the estimate of β_1 for the USA is 0.910; for Argentina it is much lower at 0.011.

One problem with the Lucas study, recognized by Lucas (1973, p. 331), is that his eighteen countries fall into two distinct groups. The first group consists of sixteen countries in which aggregate demand has been reasonably stable; the second consists of two countries – Argentina and Paraguay – in which aggregate demand has been highly expansive and volatile. The apparent negative relationship between Lucas's estimate of aggregate demand volatility for any country and his estimate of β_1 for the country is heavily dependent upon these two highly volatile countries. To base conclusions on such a small sample is unsatisfactory. However, a number of other authors (e.g. Alberro, (1981); Kormendi and Meguire, (1984)) have employed something like the Lucas approach using data from more countries and have generally found much the same result as that reported in Lucas.

Despite the slightly unsatisfactory nature of the data used by Lucas, and although the tests he applied were hardly rigorous, his paper was influential in that it was one of the first to show that certain of the predictions made by the rational expectations hypotheses were not entirely inconsistent with the data. We shall consider in chapter 8 a more fundamental econometric problem with the Lucas study which casts doubt on the interpretation which Lucas puts on his results. But in the next section of this chapter we shall consider another group of highly influential papers which apply the rational expectations hypothesis to a simple macroeconomic model.

7.2 THE BARRO MODEL

The second influential study, or in this case series of studies, is by Barro (1977a, 1978a) and Barro and Rush (1980) who attempt to test the other major prediction of the rational expectations macroeconomic model developed in chapter 3 and summarized in equation (7.1) – that only unpredictable movements in aggregate demand will affect real variables such as real output or unemployment. We have already referred to these studies and used them to illustrate some of the econometric issues involved in testing the rational expectations hypothesis. In this section we shall consider Barro's model, test procedure and findings in more detail.

(a) *Unanticipated Money and Unemployment/Output: the Barro Procedure*

The starting point of Barro's model is the assumption that the rate of growth of the quantity of money in an economy is the prime determinant of the rate of growth of aggregate demand in that economy. The distinction drawn in chapter 3 between the predictable and unpredictable components of aggregate demand can be easily translated into a distinction between the predictable and unpredictable components of monetary growth. In particular if the quantity of money is the prime determinant of aggregate demand it follows from the analysis in chapter 3 that the predictable component of the rate of growth of the quantity of money will have no effect on any real variable such as the level of output or the level of unemployment; only the unpredictable or random component of monetary growth will affect real variables.

In accordance with the theory of rational expectations Barro identifies the predictable component of monetary growth as that part of the process determining monetary growth which could have been predicted on the basis of the information available at the time. His initial task then is to identify this process. In his original paper Barro (1977a) used annual data for the USA covering the period from 1941 to 1973 and in contrast to Lucas (1973), who after all was considering a much larger number of countries, Barro investigated the process determining monetary growth in some detail. In accordance with certain theoretical considerations and after some empirical experimentation Barro obtained the following fairly complex equation as his best estimate of the process which the annual rate of growth of the quantity of money was following over the period 1941 to 1973.

$$D\hat{M}_t = 0.087 + 0.24\, DM_{t-1} + 0.35\, DM_{t-2} + 0.082\, FEDV_t$$
$$+ 0.027\, UN_{t-1} \tag{7.7}$$

where $D\hat{M}_t$ = the rate of growth of the quantity of money predicted by the process shown in equation (7.7) to occur in period t;

   DM_{t-i} = the actual rate of growth of the quantity of money in period $t-i$. The rate of growth is defined logarithmically i.e. $DM_t = \ln M_t - \ln M_{t-1}$ where M_t is the annual average of the $M1$ definition of the USA money stock;

$FEDV_t$ = a measure of federal government expenditure relative to 'normal';

UN_t = the unemployment rate defined as $\ln[U/(1-U)]_t$ where U is the annual average unemployment in the total labour force.

a '$\char94$' over a variable denotes an estimate of that variable.

So, according to Barro's estimate the predictable component of money growth, $D\hat{M}_t$ depends upon:

1 *FEDV*, a measure of the deviation of government expenditure from its normal level. Barro's argument for the inclusion of this variable is that if government expenditure is equal to its normal level it will tend to be financed by othodox taxation, but if it is, say, abnormally high it is more likely to be financed by measures which increase the rate of monetary growth. The exact method by which Barro measures normal government expenditure is not vital for our purposes – essentially it is through a regression of actual expenditure on its own lagged values.

2 UN_{t-1}, the lagged unemployment rate. Barro argues that the presence of this variable reflects the counter-cyclical response of money to the level of economic activity. When unemployment is high the USA monetary authority has tended to respond by allowing monetary growth to accelerate.

3 Two lagged money growth terms to pick up any elements of serial dependence or lagged adjustment not captured by the other explanatory variables.

Equation (7.7) it should be emphasized is the result obtained from an ordinary least squares (OLS) regression of actual monetary growth, DM_t on the variables on the right-hand side. It amounts to the 'best' statistical description of the process determining DM_t which Barro could find for the period covered by his data. Because of this Barro treats $D\hat{M}_t$ as the best prediction that could be made by rational economic agents of the value of DM_t, thus $D\hat{M}_t$ is identified by Barro as his estimate of the rationally anticipated component of $D\hat{M}_t$, $E_{t-1} DM_t$. In other words Barro assumes that rational agents over the period were aware that the rate of growth of the quantity of money was being determined by the process described in equation (7.7) and were using their knowledge of that process and the coefficients involved in it to predict future monetary growth.

For this assumption to be consistent with rational expectations equation (7.7) must exhibit three key characteristics: first, the variables on the right-hand side of equation (7.7) should not omit any variables which appear to exert an important impact on monetary growth. In fact the right-hand side variables in equation (7.7) account for about 90 per cent of the movements in *DM*, so this criterion seems likely to be satisfied. Second, the component of *DM* which this equation does not account for should not exhibit any pattern for, if it did, then rational agents would exploit that pattern to improve their forecasts. Barro presents some evidence that no such pattern exists: this evidence is from the Durbin–Watson statistic (see Johnston, 1972, pp. 307–313) which tests the null hypothesis that the error in predicting *DM* in any period *t* made by equation (7.7) is unrelated to the error made in the previous period. From the Durbin–Watson statistic which Barro reports one cannot reject the null hypothesis (though strictly speaking the Durbin–Watson test is not applicable because of the presence of the lagged dependent variable). The third key characteristic is that the actual value of all the variables which according to equation (7.7) determine $D\hat{M}_t$ should be known at the end of period $t-1$, or else they cannot be used to predict DM_t. In all cases except *FEDV* this criterion is clearly satisfied since all the other variables are dated $t-1$. But *FEDV* is a currently dated variable and so strictly should not be included in equation (7.7). Barro (1977a, fn. 9) acknowledges this criticism but argues that the principal movements in *FEDV*, which are dominated by changes in wartime activity, would be perceived sufficiently rapidly to influence $D\hat{M}$ without a lag. The role of *FEDV* is explored critically by Pesaran (1982) whose study is considered in more detail in chapter 8.

Having obtained a measure of anticipated monetary growth Barro computes the unanticipated component of monetary growth in each period as the difference between actual monetary growth in the period and the anticipated component of monetary growth in that period, that is $D\hat{M}R = DM - D\hat{M}$. To put this another way $D\hat{M}R$ is the estimated residual from the ordinary least squares regression whose coefficients are shown in equation (7.7), and whose dependent variable is actual monetary growth DM_t.

To test the prediction that the unpredictable component of monetary growth affects real variables Barro first regresses the level of unemployment on the current and lagged values of his $D\hat{M}R$ variable and on two other variables which are seen as influencing the natural rate of unemployment. (The presence of the lagged $D\hat{M}R$'s is taken to reflect the presence of some 'propagation mechanism' such as those described in chapter 4.) Thus Barro carries out an OLS regression of the following form,

$$UN_t = \beta_0 + \beta_1 D\hat{M}R_t + \beta_2 D\hat{M}R_{t-1} + \beta_3 D\hat{M}R_{t-2} + \beta_4 MIL_t + \beta_5 MINW_t + v_t \tag{7.8}$$

where v_t is the equation error term.

The variable *MIL* = (Military Personnel)/(Male population aged 15 to 44) for years in which a selective military draft law was in effect and

$MIL=0$ for the non-selective draft-law years. The rationale for including this variable is that conscription works towards reducing the unemployment rate if individuals are more likely to be drafted into the services if they are unemployed. The variable $MINW$ measures the impact of the minimum wage on the unemployment rate. The number of lagged $D\hat{M}R$ terms that enter into equation (7.8) are determined empirically by Barro. That is, he only retains lagged $D\hat{M}R$ terms whose coefficients are significantly different from zero. One would expect that if the unpredictable growth in the money stock were positive, then output would rise and unemployment fall. Thus one would expect to observe negative coefficients on the current and lagged $D\hat{M}R$'s.

The results of carrying out an OLS regression of equation (7.8) using annual USA data from 1946 to 1973 were

$$U\hat{N}_t = -\,3.07 - 5.8D\hat{M}R_t - 12.1D\hat{M}R_{t-1} - 4.2D\hat{M}R_{t-2}$$
$$\quad\;\;(0.15)\quad(2.1)\qquad\quad(1.9)\qquad\qquad(1.9) \qquad\qquad\qquad (7.9)$$

$$-\,4.7MIL_t + 0.95MINW_t \qquad R^2 = 0.78,\ DW = 1.96.$$
$$\;(0.08)\qquad\;\;(0.46)$$

Estimated standard errors are in parentheses.

Notice that as the theory suggests the unpredictable monetary growth variables have significant negative effects on the level of unemployment. The values of the student's t test statistics for a test of the null hypothesis that the coefficients on the $D\hat{M}R$ variables are zero are 2.8 for $D\hat{M}R_t$, 6.4 for $D\hat{M}R_{t-1}$ and 2.2 for $D\hat{M}R_{t-2}$. These values are to be compared with 2.07 which is the critical value at the 5 percent significance level under the t distribution with 22 degrees of freedom. So we can reject the hypothesis that each of the coefficients on the DMR variables are zero and conclude that current $D\hat{M}R$ and $D\hat{M}R$ lagged two periods have a significant impact on the unemployment rate. Thus the first part of the prediction which Barro set out to test appears to be confirmed by these results – unpredictable monetary growth does affect a real variable in the way suggested. Notice also that the coefficients on the $D\hat{M}R$ variables imply that the lag pattern has a triangular shape with the strongest effect, -12.1, occurring after a 1-year lag and then dying away.

Next, Barro tests the proposition that it is *only* the unpredictable part of money growth that influences the rate of unemployment. He does this by including total money growth, DM, in the unemployment equation as well as the unanticipated component, $D\hat{M}R$. That is, equation (7.8) becomes

$$UN_t = \beta_0 + \beta_1 D\hat{M}R_t + \beta_2 D\hat{M}R_{t-1} + \beta_3 D\hat{M}R_{t-2} + \beta_4 MIL_t +$$
$$\beta_5 MINW_t + \gamma_1 DM_t + \gamma_2 DM_{t-1} + \gamma_3 DM_{t-2} + w_t \qquad (7.10)$$

where w_t is the equation error term.

The null hypothesis that $\gamma_1 = \gamma_2 = \gamma_3 = 0$ can then be tested by using the F distribution as explained in chapter 6. Barro obtains a value of 1.4 for his test statistic which is less than the critical value under the F distribution with 3 and 19 degrees of freedom at the 5 percent significance level. So, the null hypothesis that the γ coefficients are all zero cannot be rejected and therefore neither the current nor the lagged DM's appear to have any influence on the rate of unemployment. Notice that this test is equivalent to testing whether the *anticipated* component of monetary growth has an additional effect on unemployment over and above the effect of the $D\hat{M}R$'s. To see this substitute $DM_t = D\hat{M}_t + D\hat{M}R_t$ into equation (7.10) to give

$$
\begin{aligned}
UN_t = \beta_0 &+ (\beta_1 + \gamma_1)D\hat{M}R_t + (\beta_2 + \gamma_2)D\hat{M}R_{t-1} \\
&+ (\beta_3 + \gamma_3)D\hat{M}R_{t-2} + \beta_4 MIL_t + \beta_5 MINW_t \qquad (7.11) \\
&+ \gamma_1 D\hat{M}_t + \gamma_2 D\hat{M}_{t-1} + \gamma_3 D\hat{M}_{t-2} + w_t.
\end{aligned}
$$

So, including current and lagged total money growth in the output equation and testing the null hypothesis that the coefficients on these variables are all zero is exactly equivalent to including current and lagged predictable components of money growth in the output equation and testing for zero coefficients on these variables. That is, constraining the γ coefficients to zero in equation (7.11) will produce exactly the same sum of square residuals as in equation (7.10) when the γ coefficients are constrained to zero.

Barro's statistical tests all seemed to support one of the main predictions made by the simple rational expectations model developed in chapter 3: that it is unpredictable monetary growth that is important in the determination of the level of unemployment and that predictable monetary growth is irrelevant.

In subsequent papers Barro ((1978a), Barro and Rush (1980)) extended his analysis in two directions. First he examined the influence of predictable and unpredictable monetary growth on real output rather than unemployment: he found evidence here too that only the unpredictable component of monetary growth affected real output, a positive monetary surprise leading to a rise in output above its natural level. Secondly he introduced a third equation – a price equation – and found that as the rational expectations theory predicts an anticipated rise in monetary growth, of say, x percent leads to an immediate x percent rise in the price level, whereas a similar unpredictable rise in monetary growth leads initially to a less than x percent rise in the price level.

In general then Barro's results appear to represent a small but significant body of evidence in support of the sort of rational expectations macroeconomic model developed in chapter 3.

(b) Joint Estimation of the Money Growth and Unemployment/Output Equations

One criticism of Barro's approach to the estimation and testing of the rational expectations model is that he employs a two-step estimation procedure and this is not fully efficient. That is, he first carries out an OLS regression of monetary growth on a number of other variables – the *DM* equation – obtains the residuals from this equation and then, in the second separate stage, uses these residuals, the *DM̂R*'s, in an OLS regression in which unemployment or output is the dependent variable. Such a procedure is not fully efficient in that it does not use all the information contained in the model, in particular it fails to take account of its cross equation restrictions. It therefore bypasses one of the main methods of testing the rational expectations hypothesis, i.e. as explained in chapter 6, testing the restrictions it imposes. An (asymptotically) efficient and more fruitful estimation procedure would estimate all coefficients jointly, imposing the cross equation restrictions. To explain this point (which Barro (1977a), p. 107, fn 15 recognizes) and also to demonstrate that Barro's results appear to hold true for countries other than the USA we shall outline a model similar to Barro's which Attfield *et al.* (1981a) (ADD) applied to UK annual data for the period 1946 to 1977. Their model consists of the following equations

$$DM_t = \alpha_0 + \alpha_1 DM_{t-1} + \alpha_2 DM_{t-2} + \alpha_3 B_t + \alpha_4 S_{t-1} + DMR_t$$

$$y_t = \beta_0 + \beta_1 DMR_t + \beta_2 DMR_{t-1} + \beta_3 DMR_{t-2} \qquad (7.12)$$
$$+ \beta_4 DMR_{t-3} + \beta_5 t + \beta_6 VP_t + v_t.$$

where *DM* is the rate of growth of the money stock, *B* is the real value of the government borrowing requirement and *S* is the real current account balance of payments surplus. In the output equation *y* is the log of real GDP, *t* is a time trend and *VP* is a measure of the variability of the inflation rate. DMR_t and v_t are equation errors.

The first equation in this model is an estimate of the process that monetary growth followed over the period considered. The second is an output equation in which the variables *t* and *VP* determine the natural rate of output. The rationale for the inclusion of *B* in the money equation is that governments may finance expenditures which they are reluctant to pay for through taxes by methods which expand the money stock. Since a given nominal value for the borrowing requirement implies a progressively lower value for *DM* the appropriate 'fiscal' influence on monetary growth is the real value of the borrowing requirement (*B*). Attfield *et al.* argue that their method of dealing with the relationship between fiscal and monetary policy is simpler than that used by Barro (1977a) where the equivalent fiscal variable is government expenditure relative to its normal level. The use of B avoids the problem of estimating the normal level of government expenditure which, ADD argue, Barro handles inconsistently since he assumes an adaptive expectations mechanism for this relationship whilst assuming that agents form their expectations rationally elsewhere in the system. The justification for the inclusion of the lagged real current account balance of payments surplus, S_{t-1}, is that it reflects the UK governments concern with the external balance, a large surplus encourages (or at least allows) a more expansionary monetary policy; a large deficit tends to bring about a contractionary one.

The structure of the output equation reflects the assumption that the natural level of output is a function of two variables: time (t) and a measure of the variability of the inflation rate (VP). The time trend accounts for the effects of a constant natural rate of growth of output whilst VP allows for the possibility that the efficiency of the economy and hence the natural level of output is reduced by a variable inflation rate. Attfield *et al.* suggest that the reasons efficiency might be impaired in periods of variable inflation rates are that the price system fails to transmit as efficiently the information on relative prices needed to co-ordinate economic plans, that the optimum wage and price contract length shortens, making existing arrangements inappropriate, and that government interference in markets is likely to be increased.

From the money growth equation in (7.12) we have

$$DMR_{t-i} = DM_{t-i} - \alpha_0 - \alpha_1 DM_{t-i-1} - \alpha_2 DM_{t-i-2} - \alpha_3 B_{t-i} - \alpha_4 S_{t-i-1}. \tag{7.13}$$

Substituting the expressions for DMR_{t-1}, DMR_{t-2} and DMR_{t-3} into the output equation in (7.12) gives the two equation model

$$DM_t = \alpha_0 + \alpha_1 DM_{t-1} + \alpha_2 DM_{t-2} + \alpha_3 B_t + \alpha_4 S_{t-1} + DMR_t \tag{7.14}$$

$$\begin{aligned} y_t = \beta_0 \\ & + \beta_2 (DM_{t-1} - \alpha_0 - \alpha_1 DM_{t-2} - \alpha_2 DM_{t-3} - \alpha_3 B_{t-1} - \alpha_4 S_{t-2}) \\ & + \beta_3 (DM_{t-2} - \alpha_0 - \alpha_1 DM_{t-3} - \alpha_2 DM_{t-4} - \alpha_3 B_{t-2} - \alpha_4 S_{t-3}) \\ & + \beta_4 (DM_{t-3} - \alpha_0 - \alpha_1 DM_{t-4} - \alpha_2 DM_{t-5} - \alpha_3 B_{t-3} + \alpha_4 S_{t-4}) \\ & + \beta_5 t + \beta_6 VP_t + \beta_1 DMR_t + v_t. \end{aligned}$$

From the model in (7.14) it is possible to illustrate what is meant by cross equation restrictions. Take for example the coefficient estimated on B_t in the DM_t equation: this is an estimate of α_3. But the coefficients estimated on B_{t-1}, B_{t-2} and B_{t-3} in the output equation are estimates respectively of $-\beta_2\alpha_3$, $-\beta_3\alpha_3$, and $-\beta_4\alpha_3$, and so we can deduce from these four estimated coefficients estimates of β_2, β_3 and β_4. Similarly by taking the coefficient estimated on S_{t-1} in the DM_t equation, α_4, and the coefficients estimated on S_{t-2}, S_{t-3} and S_{t-4} in the output equation, which are estimates of $-\beta_2\alpha_4$, $-\beta_3\alpha_4$, and $-\beta_4\alpha_4$, we can deduce other estimates of β_2, β_3 and β_4. The two sets of estimates of β_2, β_3, and β_4 should, in large samples, be approximately the same. This restriction – that the two ways of obtaining estimates of β_2, β_3 and β_4 should give the same results – is an example of the cross equation restrictions implied by the model (7.14). Barro's procedure ignores such restrictions entirely because he estimates the monetary growth and real output equations separately and does not impose the restrictions. There is therefore no guarantee that the restrictions which are implied by his model will be satisfied. As we have said an (asymptotically) efficient procedure would estimate the coefficients in both equations jointly imposing all the cross equation restrictions.

Attfield *et al.* (1981a) employ such a procedure – full information maximum likelihood – to estimate the model (7.14) where the current monetary shock DMR_t times its coefficient β_1 are relegated to the error term in the output equation. That is, if they let the whole error term in the output equation be η, then $\eta_t = v_t + \beta_1 DMR_t$. The variance–covariance matrix of equation errors is then

$$E \begin{bmatrix} DMR_t \\ \eta_t \end{bmatrix} [DMR_t, \eta_t] = \Sigma = \begin{bmatrix} \sigma_{DMR}^2 & \beta_1\sigma_{DMR}^2 \\ \beta_1\sigma_{DMR}^2 & \beta_1^2\sigma_{DMR}^2 + \sigma_v^2 \end{bmatrix}.$$

where σ_{DMR}^2 is the variance of DMR_t and σ_v^2 is the variance of v_t and, to ensure that structural parameters in the model are identified, it is assumed that the covariance between DMR_t and v_t is zero. Attfield *et al.* obtain maximum likelihood estimates by maximizing the criterion

$$-(n/2)\ln[\det(\hat{\Sigma})] = -(n/2)(\ln \hat{\sigma}_{DMR}^2 + \ln \hat{\sigma}_v^2) \tag{7.15}$$

with respect to the α_i's and β_i's in the structure in (7.14), where n is the sample size. Notice that an estimate of β_1 can be obtained by dividing the top right-hand element of the estimated Σ matrix, that is the estimate of the cov(DMR_t, η_t), by the top left-hand element of the covariance matrix.

Attfield *et al.* obtain the following estimates for their model

$$\hat{DM}_t = 0.56 + 0.46DM_{t-1} + 0.33DM_{t-2} - 0.001B_t$$
$$\phantom{\hat{DM}_t = } (1.0) \quad (0.17) \qquad (0.22) \qquad\quad (0.0004)$$

$$\phantom{\hat{DM}_t = } + 0.0027S_{t-1} \tag{7.16}$$
$$\phantom{\hat{DM}_t = + } (0.0008)$$

$$y_t = 10.68 + 0.002DMR_{t-1} + 0.002DMR_{t-2}$$
$$\;\;\;\;\;(0.016)\;\;\;\;(0.001)\;\;\;\;\;\;\;\;\;\;\;\;(0.001)$$

$$+\;0.003\dot{D}MR_{t-3} + 0.025t - 0.025VP_t$$
$$\;\;\;(0.0009)\;\;\;\;\;\;\;\;\;\;(0.0007)\;\;\;(0.009)$$

$$R^2 = 0.994DW = 2.21,\; \hat{\beta}_1 = 0.0017\; (0.0008)$$

where estimated asymptotic standard errors are given in parentheses and a '^' denotes, as before, an estimate of a variable or a coefficient.

In the money equation ADD did try a number of other variables such as the lagged inflation rate, nominal and real rates of interest and real income (as a deviation from trend) to obtain the most satisfactory explanation of the monetary growth process. The variables in (7.16) proved the most suitable determinants of monetary growth.

In the output equation the unpredictable monetary growth variables do have a significant positive effect on real output although the impact of DMR_{t-1} and DMR_{t-2} are less significant than Barro found for the USA. Notice also that the estimates for the UK do not display the strong triangular pattern found by Barro in the USA.

Attfield *et al.* then tested the hypothesis that it is *only* unpredictable money growth that has an impact on real output by inserting actual money growth into the output equation in (7.14) for the periods t, $t-1$, $t-2$ and $t-3$, and comparing the likelihood from this model with the model in (7.16). The resulting test statistic is 5.49 which has to be compared with 9.49 which is the critical value under the chi-square distribution at the 5 percent significance level with 4 degrees of freedom. So the null hypothesis that it is only unpredictable monetary growth which influences real output cannot be rejected.

The above tests are carried out estimating the system as a whole and not as in Barro (1977a) by estimating separately the money growth equation and the unemployment/output equation. Since all the coefficients are estimated simultaneously the estimated model (7.16) which has all the cross equation restrictions imposed can be compared with another model which has the same variables on the right-hand side of each equation but in which the cross equation restrictions are relaxed, that is the coefficients on each variable are freely estimated as

$$DM_t = \pi_0 + \pi_1 DM_{t-1} + \pi_2 DM_{t-2} + \pi_3 B_t + \pi_4 S_{t-1} + u_{1t}$$
$$y_t = \pi_5 + \pi_6 DM_{t-1} + \pi_7 DM_{t-2} + \pi_8 DM_{t-3} + \pi_9 B_{t-1}$$
$$+\;\pi_{10}S_{t-2} + \pi_{11}DM_{t-4} + \pi_{12}B_{t-2} + \pi_{13}S_{t-3}$$
$$+\;\pi_{14}DM_{t-5} + \pi_{15}B_{t-3} + \pi_{16}S_{t-4} + \pi_{17}t + \pi_{18}VP_t + u_{2t}$$

$$(7.17)$$

where u_{it} are equation errors.

Since in (7.17) we have relaxed the cross equation restrictions implied by the rational expectations model (7.14), we can carry out a likelihood ratio test of the restrictions in (7.14) by comparing it with the system in (7.17) and thereby test the rational expectations model. As explained in chapter 6 if the likelihood ratio test suggests that the cross equation restrictions are not valid, then it suggests that the model which imposes them is invalid. For their UK data ADD carried out such a test and obtained a test statistic of 17.93 which has to be compared with a critical chi-square value of 15.5 at the 5 percent and 20.1 at the 1 percent with 8 degrees of freedom. Given that they are working with a very small sample and that the likelihood ratio test is a large sample test ADD do not consider the evidence strong enough to reject the null hypothesis.

In an extension to the above research, ADD (1981b) estimate a three equation quarterly model of unanticipated monetary growth, output and the price level for the UK for the period 1963 to 1978. Apart from the use of quarterly data the main difference in this study is that the current monetary shock is included in the output equation, rather than being relegated to the error term, in what ADD prove is an (asymptotically) efficient estimation procedure. That is, they show that the coefficients of the model are still identified in this case provided it is assumed that the equation errors in the money growth equation and in the output equation are contemporaneously uncorrelated. Attfield *et al.* reach broadly the same conclusion as in the paper using annual data; that it is *only* unanticipated monetary growth which affects real output and that the cross equation restrictions imposed by the model cannot be rejected. Thus the ADD (1981a), results lend support to the findings of Barro.

7.3 THE LEIDERMAN TEST

Soon after the publication of Barro's studies it was pointed out by Leiderman (1980) that Barro's model embodied two important but separate hypotheses – rational expectations and what is called structural neutrality – and that it was possible to test for rational expectations separately, and then, given rational expectations test for structural neutrality. The structural neutrality hypothesis in the Barro model is, as we mentioned in chapter 6, simply the assumption that any growth in the quantity of money which is anticipated, whether those anticipations are formed rationally or not, will not affect the level of real output or unemployment. To understand his argument clearly consider the following simplified version of the Barro model

$$DM_t = E_{t-1} DM_t + DMR_t$$

$$E_{t-1} DM_t = \alpha_1 DM_{t-1} + \alpha_2 DM_{t-2} + \alpha_3 FEDV_t \tag{7.18}$$

$$UN_t = \beta_1 (DM_t - E_{t-1}DM_t) + v_t.$$

The structural neutrality hypothesis is embodied in this model because the coefficient on $E_{t-1}DM_t$ in the unemployment equation has a coefficient which is equal but opposite in sign to the coefficient on DM_t. Thus a rise in monetary growth which is anticipated will have no effect on the level of unemployment.

If now it is assumed that the coefficients on DM_t and $E_{t-1} DM_t$ in the unemployment equation are different so that we are *not* assuming structural neutrality we can rewrite the unemployment equation as

$$UN_t = \beta_{11} DM_t - \beta_{12} E_{t-1} DM_t + v_t \tag{7.19}$$

A test for structural neutrality therefore reduces to the simple test of the null hypothesis $\beta_{11} = \beta_{12} = \beta_1$. If this equality restriction is not supported by the data we can *reject* the neutrality postulate.

We can therefore test for rational expectations by substituting for $E_{t-1} DM_t$ and DM_t into equation (7.19) to give the system

$$DM_t = \alpha_1 DM_{t-1} + \alpha_2 DM_{t-2} + \alpha_3 FEDV_t + DMR_t \tag{7.20}$$

$$UN_t = (\beta_{11} - \beta_{12}) (\alpha_1 DM_{t-1} + \alpha_2 DM_{t-2} + \alpha_3 FEDV_t) + v_t \\ + \beta_{11} DMR_t$$

where we have allowed the term $\beta_{11} DMR_t$ to accumulate in the equation error in the unemployment equation in (7.20). Notice that this means that the covariance between the equation errors in (7.20) is $\beta_{11} \sigma^2_{DMR}$ which is unlikely to be zero. The equations in (7.20) embody the hypothesis of rational expectations but *not the assumption of structural neutrality*. If we estimate the unrestricted version of (7.20), that is

$$DM_t = \pi_1 DM_{t-1} + \pi_2 DM_{t-2} + \pi_3 FEDV_t + \xi_{1t} \\ UN_t = \pi_4 DM_{t-1} + \pi_5 DM_{t-2} + \pi_6 FEDV_t + \xi_{2t} \tag{7.21}$$

where the π_i's are coefficients and ξ_{it} is an equation error, we see there are six unrestricted coefficients in the model in (7.21). In the system in (7.20), however, there are only five coefficients to be estimated namely α_1, α_2, α_3, β_{11} and β_{12}. A test of the rational expectations hypothesis can therefore be constructed by computing the likelihood from the equations in (7.20) and the likelihood from (7.21) and comparing the likelihood ratio test statistic with the chi-square distribution with, for this example, 1 degree of freedom. The rational expectations hypothesis that is, places one restriction on the reduced form.

If the rational expectations hypothesis is not rejected by this test we can test the structural neutrality hypothesis by comparing the likelihood from the system in (7.20) with the likelihood from the same system with the restriction that β_{11} equals β_{12} imposed. Leiderman carries out this test using similar data to that used by Barro (1977a) on Barro's money growth and unemployment model. He uses a full information maximum likelihood technique and concludes that 'the restrictions implied by the constituent hypotheses of rational expectations and "structural neutrality", as well as by the joint neutrality hypothesis, are not rejected by the sample information at the usual significance levels of five and one percent' (Leiderman, 1980, p. 80)

7.4 THE LUCAS AND BARRO APPROACHES COMBINED

The Lucas (1973) paper tests one of the major predictions of the rational expectations model developed in chapter 3 and summarized in equation (7.1) by using cross-country data; the Barro studies test the other major prediction of that model using data from a single country. A natural extension of the two approaches is to combine them and test both predictions at the same time. This has been done in a number of recent papers – here we shall briefly explain and report the results of the study by Attfield and Duck (1983) (A–D). Their model, in simplified form, consists of the following three equations

$$DM_{it} = \alpha_i Z_{it} + DMR_{it} \tag{7.22}$$

$$y_{cit} = \beta_i (DM_{it} - \alpha_i Z_{it}) + v_{it} \tag{7.23}$$

$$\beta_i = \Phi/(\Phi + \sigma_{DMR_i}^2) \tag{7.24}$$

where DM_{it} = the rate of growth of the money stock, in country i
$\quad Z_{it}$ = a variable whose value is known at the end of the previous period and which influences monetary growth
$\quad \alpha_i$ and β_i = coefficients in country i
DMR_{it} and v_{it} = normally and independently distributed random errors with zero mean and variances σ_{DMRi}^2 and σ_{vi}^2, respectively
$\quad y_{cit}$ = the deviation of the log of aggregate real output in country i from its natural rate
$\quad \Phi$ = a constant.

The first of these equations merely states that for any country the quantity of money grows in accordance with an identifiable but stochastic process. This process may differ from country to country, that is why the coefficient α_i is indexed on i – it may be different whichever country i refers to. The second equation embodies the structural neutrality and rational expectations hypothesis – for each country only the unpredictable component of monetary growth causes output to deviate from its natural rate. These two equations then are essentially the Barro model applied to a number of different countries.

Equation (7.24) is a particular form of the relationship derived in chapter 3 and tested in Lucas (1973). The derivation of the specific form need not concern us, its essential implication is that the coefficient linking the deviation of output from its natural rate to the unpredictable component of aggregate demand, or in this case the unpredictable component of monetary growth, depends *negatively* on the variance of unpredictable monetary growth.

The three equations taken together embody both the major predictions outlined in the rational expectations macroeconomic model developed in chapter 3. To test the two predictions A–D test the restrictions implied in equations (7.22) to (7.24). To see what these are first rewrite equations (7.22) to (7.24) as a two-equation model,

$$DM_{it} = \alpha_i Z_{it} + DMR_{it} \tag{7.25}$$

$$y_{cit} = \Phi (\Phi + \sigma^2_{DMR_i})^{-1} (DM_{it} - \alpha_i Z_{it}) + v_{it}.$$

For any single country there are no restrictions imposed on (7.25) by equation (7.24). To see this imagine estimating the DM equation in (7.25) by OLS to obtain an estimate of α_i, $\hat{\alpha}_i$, and using the sum of squared residuals from this equation to construct an estimate of $\sigma^2_{DMR_i}$. The estimate of α_i could then be substituted into the output equation in (7.25) and, from the regression of y_{cit} on $DM_{it} - \hat{\alpha}_i Z_{it}$, a unique estimate of Φ obtained by using the estimate of $\sigma^2_{DMR_i}$. But if there are two countries used in the sample then since Φ is a constant across countries, i.e. it is not indexed on i, there will be a restriction on the model. To see this imagine repeating for a second country the process just described for the first. Since Φ is a constant across countries you should obtain the same estimate of it in this second case. Thus when estimating the model (7.25) using data from two countries the restriction that in each case the estimate of Φ must be the same should be imposed. As the number of countries in the sample increases so does the complexity of the restrictions imposed by (7.25). In fact within the full A–D model there are restrictions across equations within countries, between variances and coefficients within countries, and between coefficients across all countries.

To test the restrictions on the model A–D use annual data for the period 1951 to 1978 from eleven different countries namely the USA, Netherlands, Canada, Denmark, Australia, the UK, Philippines, Columbia, El Salvador, Guatemala and Argentina. The particular countries were selected because an adequate explanation of monetary growth was possible on the basis of a simple and common process. The process consisted of lagged government real expenditure and, for some countries, the lagged rate of monetary growth. For the output equation A–D assume that real output is a function of time, its own lagged value and current or one period lagged unanticipated monetary growth (A–D, 1983, p. 448). They estimate the model using maximum likelihood techniques and find that unantici-pated monetary growth does generally have a positive effect on real output. Eight of the eleven countries have estimates of β that are significantly positive. In addition a likelihood ratio test of the cross equation restrictions does not reject the restrictions at the 1 percent significance level for any of the countries. These results support the prediction that the unpredictable component of monetary growth exerts a significant influence on real output.

Attfield and Duck then test the prediction that it is *only* the unpredict-able component of *DM* that has an impact on real output in the way described in section 7.2(b). They find that the null hypotheses that the anticipated component of monetary growth exerts no influence on real output cannot be rejected for any country at the 1 percent level.

As a preliminary test of the prediction that the larger the variance of *DMR*, the smaller the coefficient β, A–D present a figure which we reproduce in figure 7.1 which is a plot of the eleven estimates of the coefficient on unanticipated monetary growth in output equation, the β_i's, against the corresponding estimates of $\sigma^2_{DMR_i}$, the unpredictability of monetary growth as measured by the sum of square residuals in the money growth equations.

From the points plotted in figure 7.1 the relationship between β and the variability of the unanticipated component of monetary growth is a downward sloping one. Such a figure gives the same sort of support to the prediction that the volatility of aggregate demand and its impact on real output are negatively related as was found by Lucas (1973). Attfield and Duck develop a much more formal likelihood ratio test of this relationship by estimating the model across all countries with the β_i's unrestricted and then with β_i's restricted according to the formula given in equation (7.24). For details of the derivation of the test statistic interested readers are referred to A–D (1983, p. 446). The result of the test was that the restrictions imposed by the rational expectations hypothesis on the β_i coefficients could not be rejected.

The overall conclusion of the A–D paper is that there is some support for the propositions that monetary growth affects real output only if it is unpredictable and that the impact on output of unpredictable monetary growth declines the more unpredictable monetary growth becomes. In a

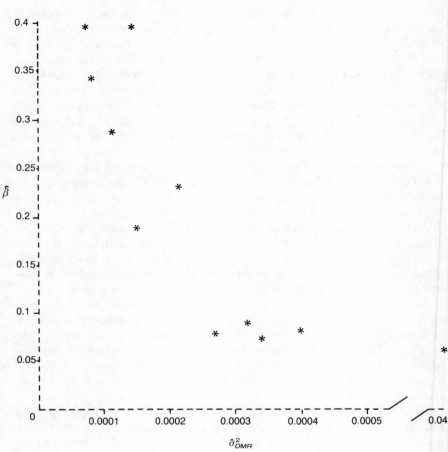

FIGURE 7.1   The influence of monetary shocks and their volatility

recent paper Kormendi and Meguire (1984) reach broadly the same conclusion using a similar model but with a much larger sample of forty-seven countries.

SUMMARY

This chapter has explained and reported the results of two of the most influential studies of the rational expectations hypothesis within a simple macroeconomic model. It has also explained some other work which has been based on those two studies. In general the results of all these studies have been favourable to the rational expectations hypothesis, suggesting at the very least that the usefulness of that hypothesis in one area of macroeconomics cannot lightly be dismissed. But these studies have had their critics and it is to some of the key criticisms of them that we now turn.

SUGGESTIONS FOR FURTHER READING

Hanson (1980), Koskela and Viren (1980) and Lawrence (1983) are all attempts to apply something like the Lucas (1973) test to different data sets. Wogin (1980) and Demery *et al.* (1984) are applications of the Barro model to two other countries, Canada and West Germany respectively. McCallum (1976) and Sargent (1976) are other attempts to test for rational expectations within a simple macro-model of the economy. Alogoskoufis and Pissarides (1983) and Demery *et al.* (1983) concentrate on the price equation in Barro's model, in particular whether there is evidence in the UK that it is 'sticky'. Tests of policy neutrality exploiting regime-switching for identification are a feature of Bean (1983).

8

Criticisms and Reappraisals of
Lucas and Barro Models

In this chapter we shall examine a number of criticisms and extensions of the Lucas and Barro models. The chapter is in two main parts. In the first we examine a problem with the Barro and Lucas tests, one which, in the Lucas model particularly, may considerably weaken the force of the results. Secondly, we shall examine some extensions to the Lucas and Barro tests which are generally unfavourable to the rational expectations hypothesis. We show how, in more recent research, anticipated changes in both nominal income growth and monetary growth have been shown to have significant output and unemployment effects, contrary to the central features of both the Barro and Lucas models. We outline the results of the more important recent contributions, with the caveat stressed here that empirical research in this area is both controversial and very much in its 'infancy'.

8.1 THE EFFECT OF MEASUREMENT ERROR AND MODEL MISSPECIFICATION

In this section we shall examine two related objections to the Lucas and Barro results. The first concerns the possibility that the aggregate demand variable is measured with error. We shall show that the results obtained by Lucas in particular may be due to the fact that nominal income growth is measured with error – an error which varies from country to country. Secondly – and more importantly – we shall investigate the implications of choosing the wrong process determining the behaviour of the aggregate demand variable.

One of the most serious defects in Lucas (1973) paper is that a simple 'errors in variables' model can produce the same apparent results. If nominal income growth (DX) contains a measurement error, the Lucas result may have little or nothing to do with the prediction of the economic model he was seeking to test. To see the point clearly consider Lucas's output equation in (7.6). For simplicity we will drop the term y_{cit-1} and drop for convenience the country subscripts so that the equation to be estimated becomes

$$y_{ct} = -\beta_1 \varkappa_0 + \beta_1 DX_t + \zeta_t \tag{8.1}$$

where ζ_t is a random error term. Suppose, however, that the 'true' change in nominal income is DX_t^* and the relationship between the truth and the variable actually measured is

$$DX_t = DX_t^* + v_t \tag{8.2}$$

with $DX_t^* = \varkappa_0 + u_t^*$; where v_t is a measurement error with zero mean and which is uncorrelated with DX_t and u_t^* is the 'true' unanticipated nominal income growth. Note that the expected mean of both DX and DX^* is $\varkappa_0$.

Let the true relationship be

$$y_{ct} = -\beta_1 \varkappa_0 + \beta_1 DX_t^* + w_t \tag{8.3}$$

with w_t assumed uncorrelated with DX_t^* and with v_t, or equivalently

$$y_{ct} = \beta_1 u_t^* + w_t.$$

If we substitute $DX_t^* = DX_t - v_t$ from equation (8.2) into equation (8.3) we obtain

$$y_{ct} = -\beta_1 \varkappa_0 + \beta_1 DX_t - \beta_1 v_t + w_t \tag{8.4}$$

So, we can interpret the equation to be estimated in (8.1) as (8.4) with $\zeta_t = w_t - \beta_1 v_t$. The problem is then that the ordinary least squares estimator of β_1 is (assuming now that all variables are measured as deviations from sample means to simplify notation):

$$\beta_1 = \Sigma DX_t y_{ct} / \Sigma (DX_t)^2 \tag{8.5}$$

and since the numerator $\Sigma DX_t\, y_{ct} = \Sigma\, (DX_t^* + v_t)\, (\beta_1\, DX_t^* + w_t)$, taking expectations of this expression we obtain

$$E\, (\Sigma DX_t\, y_{ct}) = n\beta_1\, \sigma_*^2$$

where n is the sample size and σ_*^2 is the variance of DX_t^*. We obtain this expression because the components v_t, DX_t^* and w_t all have zero covariances. The expectation of the denominator in (8.5) is of course $n\sigma_{DX}^2$ (where σ_{DX}^2 is the variance of DX) so, in large samples, the ordinary least squares estimator of β_1 in (8.5) tends to the ratio

$$\beta_1 \frac{\sigma_*^2}{\sigma_{DX}^2}\,. \tag{8.6}$$

That is, because DX_t in equation (8.4) is correlated with the measurement error term v_t, the estimator of β_1 is *biased towards zero* because σ_*^2/σ_{DX}^2 is greater than zero but less than 1. The reason that $0 < \sigma_*^2/\sigma_{DX}^2 < 1$ is that σ_*^2/σ_{DX}^2 is the ratio of two positive numbers, variances, and because $\sigma_{DX}^2 = \sigma_*^2 + \sigma_v^2$, where σ_v^2 is the variance of v_t.

The conclusion from the expression (8.6) is that if DX_t is measured with error then we would observe that countries with a value of σ_{DX}^2 which is large relative to σ_*^2 could have a relatively small estimated β_1 not because of Lucas's argument but because the estimator β_1 is biased towards zero. On the other hand those countries in which σ_{DX}^2 and σ_*^2 are approximately the same will have little or no downward bias in the estimator of β_1. That is, Lucas's result could have been obtained because 'unstable price countries' like Argentina have a larger measurement error component in the data on nominal output than in stable price countries like the USA.

This interpretation of Lucas's result is important for it suggests that even where there is no relationship between the true variance of aggregate demand and β_1, an observed relationship may be found between the measured variance in aggregate demand and the estimated coefficient β_1. However, there is an even more important but related problem with Lucas's test. Some may argue that measurement errors are likely to be relatively small compared with the total variance of the true change in aggregate demand. Even if the measurement error did not arise, Lucas's test may still be misleading. This is because he specifies a very simple process determining nominal income growth (see equation (7.4)) – one where aggregate demand change is a constant plus a random error, and therefore unpredictable, term. Reverting now to levels (rather than deviations from means), the rational forecast for DX_t, given information dated $t-1$ is simply the constant $\varkappa_0$. The unanticipated component can therefore be written as

$$u_t = DX_t - \varkappa_0 \tag{8.7}$$

Note that the variance of the unanticipated component is the same as the variance of DX as the variance of the mean must be zero. Suppose that for each country examined, Lucas omitted a variable which influenced DX and which was known to agents at the time they formed an expectation of DX. This would imply that the true process determining DX is given by

$$DX_t = \varkappa_0 + \varkappa_1 Z_{t-1} + u_t^* \tag{8.8}$$

where Z_{t-1} is the variable omitted by Lucas and where u_t^* is the true unanticipated change in aggregate demand. Again for simplicity we will assume that Z_{t-1} is a random variable with zero mean – so that $\varkappa_0$ in equation (8.8) is the same as that given in equation (7.4). The important point to note is that Z_{t-1} is known to agents when they are forecasting DX_t. Solving equation (8.8) for u_t^* we obtain

$$u_t^* = DX_t - \varkappa_0 - \varkappa_1 Z_{t-1}$$

or

$$u_t^* = u_t - \varkappa_1 Z_{t-1}. \tag{8.9}$$

The 'true' equation is

$$y_{ct} = -\beta_1 \varkappa_0 + \beta_1 DX_t - \beta_1 \varkappa_1 Z_{t-1} + w_t \tag{8.10}$$

whereas Lucas estimated

$$y_{ct} = -\beta_1 \varkappa_0 + \beta_1 DX_t + \zeta_t. \tag{8.11}$$

Note that equation (8.10) is equivalent to equation (8.4) with $\varkappa_1 Z_{t-1}$ equal to v_t. Since higher values of Z_{t-1} will be associated with higher values of DX_t (by equation (8.8)) the results we derived from the 'errors in variable' case will 'carry over' to the case of a wrongly specified nominal income growth process. Countries with high variance in Z_{t-1} and hence DX_t will tend to have estimated values for β_1 which are lower simply because Lucas failed to account for the influence of Z_{t-1} on DX_t. In this case an omitted variable from equation (8.11) is negatively correlated with the included one (DX_t) leading to incorrect estimates of β_1. By adopting such a simple process for nominal income growth, Lucas's test may be very open to this weakness, and his results must be interpreted cautiously.

The 'errors in variables' problem carries over to the models of Barro and of Attfield and Duck and again in these cases we can treat the problem from the point of view of a misspecification of the monetary growth equation – i.e. biases may arise when a variable is omitted from the money growth equations. We write a simplified version of the Barro model as:

$$\begin{aligned} DM &= \alpha X + \delta Z + DMR \\ y &= \beta DMR + v \end{aligned} \tag{8.12}$$

where we have dropped the t subscript. We will assume in what follows that the value of the parameter 'α' is known, this simplifies the algebra considerably without much loss in generality.

The relationship in equations (8.12) are assumed to be the 'truth', that is the true processes which generate monetary growth and output. Now, suppose that when equations (8.12) are estimated the term δZ is omitted so that the output equation actually estimated is

$$y = \beta(DM - \alpha X) + w \tag{8.13}$$

where w is an error term. Since the true output equation from equation (8.12) is

$$y = \beta(DM - \alpha X - \delta Z) + v$$

we must have in equation (8.13) that $w = v - \beta\delta Z$. So, we can see why a misspecification of the money growth equation – in the sense that a variable is omitted – is the equivalent of an errors in variables problem. It is because the true equation error, DMR, in equation (8.12) is measured incorrectly in equation (8.13) and the measurement error, δZ, enters into a term in the output equation error in equation (8.13). It follows that since the explanatory variable in equation (8.13) is $DM - \alpha X$ which is equal to $\delta Z + DMR$, from equation (8.12), then the explanatory variable and the equation error in equation (8.13) are correlated as they both contain δZ. So, if we use ordinary least squares to estimate the relationship in equation (8.13) we obtain, with variables now measured as deviations from means:

$$\begin{aligned}
\beta &= \Sigma(\delta Z + DMR)y/\Sigma(\delta Z + DMR)^2 \\
&= \Sigma(\delta Z + DMR)(\beta DMR + v)/\Sigma(\delta Z + DMR)^2.
\end{aligned} \qquad (8.14)$$

In large samples therefore the estimator of β will tend to:

$$\frac{\beta\sigma_{DMR}^2}{(\delta^2\sigma_z^2 + \sigma_{DMR}^2)} \qquad (8.15)$$

where σ_z^2 and σ_{DMR}^2 are the variances of Z and DMR respectively.

So, we have the same result as in expression (8.6) that the estimator of β is 'biased' towards zero by the ratio $\sigma_{DMR}^2/(\delta^2\sigma_z^2 + \sigma_{DMR}^2)$, the term $\delta^2\sigma_z^2$ being of course the variance of the measurement error in DMR. Attfield and Duck (1983, p. 447) derive a similar result under the much more general conditions that 'α' is a vector which has to be estimated, that there are other exogenous variables in both the money and output equations and that the coefficients in both equations are estimated jointly using the maximum likelihood procedure.

In the context of the Attfield and Duck model the importance of the expression in (8.15) is that the larger is $\delta^2\sigma_z^2$ relative to σ_{DMR}^2 the closer the expression in equation (8.15) is to zero. Therefore, even though there is no relationship between β and σ_{DMR}^2 in the true model in equation (8.12) if variables are omitted from the money equation we might observe an *apparent* relationship between the estimated β and the estimated error variance obtained from the money growth equation, $\delta^2\sigma_z^2 + \sigma_{DMR}^2$, in a survey across countries.

Attfield and Duck argue, however, that the 'bias' could work in the *opposite* direction. First, suppose that in equation (8.15) the variance due to the omitted variable, $\delta^2\sigma_z^2$, is constant across countries, then, with β constant, any differences in estimates of β are due solely to variations in σ_{DMR}^2. But, an increase in σ_{DMR}^2 in equation (8.15) leads to an *increase* in the estimator of β. If then β really does decline as σ_{DMR}^2 rises according to the formula we developed i.e. $\beta = \Phi/(\sigma_{DMR}^2 + \Phi)$ then, in equation (8.15), the estimator of β will tend to:

$$\Phi\sigma_{DMR}^2/(\Phi + \sigma_{DMR}^2)(\delta^2\sigma_z^2 + \sigma_{DMR}^2) \qquad (8.16)$$

and so as σ_{DMR}^2 rises if $\delta^2\sigma_z^2$ is constant the apparent relationship between σ_{DMR}^2 and the estimator of β will *understate* the true relationship.

Second, suppose the proportion of the variance of the true unanticipated money growth component, σ_{DMR}^2, to the total variance in the denominator of equation (8.15) is approximately the same from country to country, i.e. $\sigma_{DMR}^2/(\delta^2\sigma_z^2 + \sigma_{DMR}^2) = g$ where g is a constant across countries. In this case observed differences in the estimator of β for different countries must be due to differences in β because β tends to βg and, since $0 < g < 1$, the relationship between the estimator of β and the estimated error variance from the money growth equation may underestimate the relationship between the true parameter β and σ_{DMR}^2.

In the context of the Barro model we discussed in chapter 7 it can be seen from equation (8.14) that the estimator of the coefficient on the current monetary shock in the output equation will be biased toward zero. Attfield (1983) extends the above result to the case where a current money shock and a number of lagged shocks are included in the output equation and shows that all the coefficients on the monetary shock variables are biased toward zero by the same factor. Attfield also shows in this paper that tests can still be carried out on the significance of anticipated money growth even where the money growth equation is misspecified in the sense described in this chapter.

8.2   EXTENSIONS OF THE LUCAS MODEL

The Lucas model can be criticized along two related lines. First Lucas did not test for 'structural neutrality' – i.e. he did not test whether anticipated changes in aggregate demand had real output effects. Examination of equation (7.6) will indicate how such a test could have been carried out (we repeat the equation here for convenience):

$$y_{ct} = -\beta_1\varkappa_0 + \beta_1 DX_t + \beta_2 y_{ct-1} + \zeta_t \qquad (7.6)$$

where, to repeat, $\varkappa_0$ is the mean of DX_t. Since $\varkappa_0$ can be estimated from the sample of observations on DX_t, the constant term in a regression of output on nominal income growth and lagged output should be the negative of the mean of DX times the coefficient on DX_t itself. This restriction could have been imposed (by taking $\varkappa_0$ from DX_t and estimating the restricted equation without an intercept term) and tested but Lucas failed to do so. Imagine that such a test were performed and the restriction rejected. This would imply that an additional constant term would be significant in equation (7.6), and this could be the effect on output of the anticipated component of nominal income growth (i.e. $\varkappa_0$). An alternative interpretation is possible however: y_{ct} could be measured with a constant error, so that one might expect a constant term to appear in equation (7.6) which is different from $-\beta_1\varkappa_0$. In this case it would not be possible to test for structural neutrality: since anticipated nominal income growth is a constant, and since there is a legitimate constant in the output equation, it is impossible to disentangle their separate effects. In formal terms the coefficient on anticipated nominal income growth is not identified.

The second weakness of the Lucas test concerns his failure to allow for other influences on changes in aggregate demand, influences that rational agents could incorporate into their forecasts of DX_t. An obvious extension of the Lucas test would involve an investigation of other influences on DX_t in much the same way as Barro and others did for the money supply. Tests of structural neutrality can be performed once variables which influence DX_t are identified, providing of course that those variables do not also have an independent influence on y_{ct}. This extension to the Lucas test was the main feature of an empirical paper by Gordon (1982), to which we now turn.

To begin, Gordon examined the behaviour of nominal income growth net of the natural growth of output (which we call DX_t^T) over the period 1890 to 1980 in the USA. He fitted a 'first stage' regression of DX_t^T against its principal determinants. These were mainly lagged DX^T, lagged money growth, lagged inflation and y_{ct-1}. We write this first stage regression as:

$$DX_t^T = \alpha'Z_{t-1} + u_t \qquad (8.17)$$

where Z_{t-1} is a vector of variables known to agents at $t-1$ which influence DX^T; α is a vector of coefficients and u_t is an equation error term. u_t is considered to be unanticipated nominal income growth (net of the natural growth of output). According to the Lucas model, only the unanticipated component of DX^T will affect real output: its anticipated component will have no measurable output effect. For this reason Gordon sets up the following equation to estimate:

$$y_{ct} = \beta_0\,(\alpha'Z_{t-1}) + \beta_1 u_t + \beta_2 y_{ct-1} - \Sigma\beta_{2+i}\dot{P}_{t-i} + w_t \qquad (8.18)$$

where $\alpha'Z_{t-1}$ (from equation (8.17)) represents anticipated nominal income growth, $\dot{P}_{t-i}$ is a measure of lagged inflation for period $t-i$ and w_t is the equation error. The inflation terms are included because Gordon wanted to test for possible effects of lagged inflation on current output – a feature of an alternative model he wished to compare with that of Lucas. The Lucas model implies that $\beta_0 = \beta_{2+i} = 0$ (for all i), but β_1 and β_2 would be positive constants. Without going into needless detail here, Gordon's alternative model predicts that β_0 and β_{2+i} should also be positive.

TABLE 8.1   Gordon's extension to the Lucas test

Estimate of	1929.4–1953.4 ($n=10$)	1954.1–1980.4 ($n=20$)
β_0	0.88*	0.91*
β_1	0.83*	0.75*
β_2	0.99*	0.94*
$\sum_{i=1}^{n}\beta_{2+i}$	−0.60*	−1.06*

*Indicates significance at 1 per cent level.

Gordon estimated equations (8.17) and (8.18) using quarterly US data. His estimates of equation (8.18) are reported in Table 8.1. It is immediately obvious that his results constitute a clear-cut rejection of the Lucas model. First lagged inflation exerted a significant negative effect on output (in both inter-war and post-war years). Gordon claims that lagged inflation terms of up to 5 years have measurable effects on current output. Secondly – and perhaps more importantly – the coefficient on anticipated nominal income growth (β_0) was significantly positive in all periods. The results reported in Table 8.1 show that anticipated changes in aggregate demand had real effects in the US economy, contrary to the central feature of Lucas's model.

These findings directly contradict the evidence put forward by Barro and Attfield, Demery and Duck, presented in chapter 7, for in these studies anticipated money growth was found to have no real output effect in either the US or the UK. Gordon suggested a reconciliation of these contradictory findings. Since anticipated aggregate demand (as measured by anticipated nominal income growth) does influence output but anticipated money does not, it follows that anticipated money growth does not influence aggregate demand. This interpretation is very reminiscent of traditional Keynesian views on the impotence of monetary policy. Gordon summarizes this interpretation as follows:

To the extent that output was insulated from the impact of anticipated monetary changes . . . this occurred more because of a restricted impact of money on spending than because of any independence of real output from anticipated changes in spending. In other words, policy ineffectiveness . . . is more related to factors set forth in early postwar Keynesian models than those advanced by Lucas. (Gordon, 1982, p. 1197)

The test performed by Lucas was not a particularly powerful one in the sense that it was not possible to test for the effects of anticipated changes in aggregate demand. Gordon provides a more powerful test and rejects the main feature of the Lucas model – that only unanticipated changes in aggregate demand affect output. Similar results were obtained for the UK by Demery (1984).

8.3 EXTENSIONS OF THE BARRO MODEL

(a) Mishkin's Test

In the previous section we accepted the view that anticipated money growth has not had any measurable output effect – a conclusion drawn from a number of empirical studies from the US and UK. But the conclusions of these papers have been challenged in two important papers by Mishkin (1982a, b). The main feature of Mishkin's tests that distinguishes it from others is the length of the lag on anticipated and unanticipated money growth. In Barro and Rush's quarterly model of the US for example, lag lengths of seven or eight quarters were most common and similarly Attfield, Demery and Duck found a lag length of six quarters using UK data. In Mishkin's test, lagged terms in anticipated and unanticipated money growth up to twenty quarters were included in the output equation.

Following Leiderman, Mishkin estimated aggregate demand and output equations simultaneously, imposing the relevant cross-equation restrictions in a manner similar to that described in chapter 7. This permitted him to test separately for rational expectations and structural neutrality (see chapter 7, section 7.3). He adopted three alternative aggregate demand variables, inflation, nominal income growth and money growth ($\dot{P}$, DX and DM respectively). According to structural neutrality, only unanticipated values of each of these should influence output. The likelihood ratio tests of the 'rational expectations' and 'structural neutrality' restrictions are set out in Table 8.2.

Mishkin's equations were estimated using quarterly US data over the period 1954 to 1976. When adopting money growth as the aggregate demand variable, his results constitute an emphatic reversal of the Barro result. The tests of rationality and neutrality both imply rejection of the null hypothesis at the 1 per cent level of significance – the reverse of the findings of Leiderman, reported in chapter 7. Interestingly, when Mishkin performed the same tests on a model restricted to only seven lags in unanticipated money, his results were similar to those of Leiderman. The likelihood ratio test statistics for rationality, neutrality and the joint hypotheses were 19.44, 3.36 and 22.69 respectively, neither of which constitutes a rejection of the null hypothesis at the 5 per cent level. In this way Mishkin stresses the importance for his results of lengthening the lag to twenty quarters. (Similar results were obtained by Mishkin when unemployment rather than output was used as the dependent variable.)

It follows from these tests that anticipated money growth had significant output effects in the US economy, though as we shall see, the neutrality results are conditional on the identification of anticipated and unanticipated money growth. The pattern of the lagged effects of anticipated money on output is also of some interest. The coefficients attached to the first ten quarter lagged terms in anticipated monetary growth were found to be significantly positive; the remaining ten terms were found to have a negative and significant effect on output. It is clear from Mishkin's results that the relationship between monetary growth and output is both drawn out and complex. Similar patterns were observed when nominal income growth was the aggregate demand variable (the first seven lagged terms in anticipated nominal income growth carried positive coefficients and the last thirteen terms carried negative terms).

TABLE 8.2 Mishkin's extension to the Barro test
(likelihood ratio statistics: output equation)

	Aggregate demand variable		
Test	*DM*	*DX*	$\dot{P}$
Rationality	29.17*	12.86	10.23
Neutrality	15.45*	30.22*	18.52*
Joint test	43.83*	43.19*	28.45**

*Indicates a rejection of the null hypothesis at 1 per cent level.
**Indicates a rejection of the null hypothesis at 5 per cent level.

There is another feature of these results that is worthy of comment. The rationality restrictions are rejected when money growth is adopted as the aggregate demand variable. This invalidates the neutrality test as this is conditional on rational expectations being true. It follows that strictly speaking nothing can be said about the effects of anticipated money, as Mishkin has failed to model satisfactorily the manner in which expectations are formed.

However, when Mishkin adopts nominal income growth and inflation as the aggregate demand variables, the rationality restrictions are not rejected (at the 5 percent level) so the neutrality tests in this case are valid. As can be seen from Table 8.2 neutrality is rejected for models in which nominal income growth (DX) and inflation ($\dot{P}$) are the aggregate demand variables. Again similar results were obtained from estimates of the unemployment (rather than output) equation (although rationality was rejected at the 5 percent level when inflation was included as the aggregate demand variable in the unemployment equation). Mishkin concludes:

> Rejections of the joint hypotheses of rationality and neutrality are thus seen to occur primarily because of the rejections of neutrality rather than rationality. This result might give some encouragement to those who are willing to assume rationality of expectations in constructing their macro models, yet are unwilling to assume the short-run neutrality of policy. (Mishkin, 1982b, p. 799)

Mishkin and Gordon adopt very different ways of modelling persistence of the deviation of output from its 'natural' or normal level. Gordon includes the lagged dependent variable, as Lucas had done in the original paper. Mishkin formally allows for persistence by extending the lagged influence of money for a period of 5 years, so that money growth 5 years previously has measurable contemporary output effects. Yet despite the very different approaches both papers come to the same conclusion: anticipated changes in aggregate demand have significant output effects. Their results offer encouragement to those who wish to maintain a role for government stabilization policy, though it is clear from Mishkin's results that policy design will have to take into account the drawn-out effects of aggregate demand changes on output and economic activity.

(b) Pesaran's Test

The final critique of the Barro model illustrates an important methodological point. Pesaran (1982) argued that the tests conducted by Barro (and others) are inadequate in one important respect. It is quite possible for Barro's model to be quite 'comformable' to the data and yet be rejected when compared with an alternative model which is also 'conformable' to the data. 'A "proper test" of a hypothesis', argues Pesaran, 'invariably requires consideration of at least one genuine alternative' (p. 535). Pesaran attempted to do this by comparing the Barro model with a 'Keynesian' alternative.

Pesaran first modified the Barro model to remove what he considered an unsatisfactory feature of Barro's original formulation. You will recall from chapter 7 that Barro included a variable *FEDV* as a major determinant of money growth. This is the deviation of federal government expenditures from their normal levels. Pesaran's concern with this variable is simply that its value is not known to agents at time $t-1$ when they are attempting to forecast money growth. To avoid this problem, Pesaran developed a forecasting model for *FEDV* and re-estimated the money growth equation (presented in equation (7.7) in chapter 7). The point estimates he obtained from this procedure were almost identical to those obtained by Barro and reported in equation (7.7) above. Naturally because the forecasted *FEDV* will differ from the actual *FEDV*, Pesaran's computed values for *DMR* will differ from those used by Barro.

Pesaran then set up alternative Keynesian models, in which unemployment is a linear function of current and lagged money growth (with no distinction between anticipated and unanticipated), current government expenditure and other variables which affect output. The two models – Barro-type and Keynesian-type – are not nested, which means that one cannot be expressed as a restricted version of the other. For this reason Pesaran used non-nested hypothesis testing procedures. These procedures essentially test each hypothesis on the assumption that the alternative hypothesis is true. Pesaran was able to reject the Barro model on the assumption that the Keynesian model is true; however, he was not able to reject the Keynesian model under the assumption that the Barro model was true. By performing what he calls a 'proper' test, Pesaran was able to reject the Barro model in favour of a Keynesian alternative, even when in some sense the Barro model 'conformed' to the data. Pesaran's point is that the Keynesian model 'conformed' even more closely.

SUMMARY

In this chapter we have discussed some notable criticisms and extensions of the Lucas and Barro tests. In the first place, biases may arise in estimated coefficients if the process determining aggregate demand is not correctly specified in the sense that important influences on aggregate demand are omitted (influences that rational agents will be aware of). This problem is particularly serious for the tests performed by Lucas, in which he sought to show that countries experiencing a high variation in unanticipated aggregate demand will be characterized by lower coefficients linking unanticipated aggregate demand and output. If Lucas omitted important influences on nominal income growth – and it is very likely that he did – then we would expect to find an observed relationship between the variance of unanticipated aggregate demand and the influence of aggregate demand on output even when one does not exist in fact.

The Lucas and Barro models have been extended and criticized by a number of researchers, the most important of which are reviewed in this chapter. Gordon specified a more complete forecasting model for nominal income growth, and demonstrated that anticipated changes in aggregate demand had significant and important output effects. Mishkin lengthened the lag on unanticipated money, nominal income and inflation and also found that anticipated changes in aggregate demand had important output and employment effects in the US economy. Lastly, Pesaran tested the Barro model against an alternative Keynesian model and found he could reject the former but not the latter. Many of the empirical studies which have followed the influential papers of Lucas and Barro have rejected the main findings of these papers.

9

Rational Expectations in Macroeconomics: Some Case Studies

The applications of rational expectations to macroeconomics we have been considering have mostly concerned expectations of aggregate demand and its determinants. This is hardly surprising in the light of the emphasis given to aggregate demand in the theory of the business cycle, but as we illustrated in chapter 1, expectations play a prominent role in many other areas of macroeconomic analysis. Our main aim in this chapter is to illustrate the implications of rational expectations in some of these other areas by taking three case studies. The case studies are chosen to illustrate what Robert Hall has referred to as the 'general assimilation of rational expectations into macroeconomic research' (Hall, 1981, p. 193).

In chapter 5 the role of exchange-rate expectations was shown to be central in explaining the amount that domestic interest rates may depart from world rates. In our first example, we examine a number of studies which test whether these expectations are rational. We have mentioned on several occasions the role of income expectations in determining the level of consumption expenditure – a principle feature of the permanent income hypothesis. Our second case study examines the implications of making such expectations rational and evaluates the relevant empirical evidence. Our final example of the application of rational expectations considers the relationship between interest rates on assets with varying redemption dates – the term structure of interest rates.

9.1 SPOT AND FORWARD EXCHANGE RATES

The analysis of the open economy in chapter 5 was greatly simplified by the assumption that the expected depreciation of the exchange rate was at all times zero and therefore the domestic and world interest rates were always equal. In the real world when exchange rates are flexible, or when they are fixed but occasionally changed, non-zero expectations of exchange rate movements are common and therefore the shifts in the aggregate demand curve discussed in that chapter will become more complicated to analyse. In this section we shall show how non-zero expectations of exchange-rate movements allow interesting tests of rational expectations when markets exist for forward trading in the currency. It has been argued that because the price of foreign exchange is free to move from day to day (or even hourly) – at least under a regime of 'floating exchange rates' – one would expect to find favourable evidence for the existence of rational expectations, if the hypothesis were true. Tests for rationality in other markets – for example the labour market – may be rendered difficult by the presence of institutional and other barriers to price flexibility. Given that these are generally absent from foreign exchange markets, and given the widespread dissemination of information in these markets, one would expect to find strong evidence of rational expectations if expectations are rational.

The expectation of the future depreciation of currency is, strictly speaking, unobservable. Yet the foreign exchange market (like many other asset markets) has one feature which may provide a good indicator of what agents' expectations are. It is possible to buy and sell foreign exchange in 'futures' markets: i.e. it is possible to conclude a contract now to buy foreign exchange at some specific future date at a price specified now. These markets are known as forward exchange markets. Thus someone who knows that he will want to buy dollars (with pounds) in three months time could either agree a price for that transaction now (i.e. buy in the forward market) or wait three months and buy in the 'spot' market. (The spot market is the market where foreign exchange is bought and sold immediately or 'on the spot'.) Which will the rational agent do? If he expects the price of dollars, the exchange rate, in the spot market in three months' time to be the same as the current forward price, then a rational agent would be indifferent between the transactions under certain conditions.

What are these conditions? The first is that the agent is risk neutral. The advantage of the forward market is that the transaction is risk-free: the price is specified now, with certainty. In contrast the future spot price cannot be known with certainty precisely because it is a future price. A risk-averse individual would only be indifferent between transacting on the forward market and transacting on the future spot market if the terms he expects on the uncertain future spot market were sufficiently more favourable than the forward market to encourage him to take the risk. But the risk-neutral trader in foreign exchange will not need more favourable terms: he will be indifferent between transacting in the forward and future spot markets provided the expected future spot rate is the same as the forward rate offered currently.

There is a second condition required for a rational agent to be indifferent between equal forward and expected future spot rates. Suppose that there are costs associated with transactions in the foreign exchange markets (brokers' fees etc.). If the cost of transactions in forward and spot markets are the same, then risk-neutral traders will again be indifferent between the same forward and expected future spot rates. But imagine that transactions costs are greater in the forward market (and there is some evidence to suggest that they might be) than they are in the spot market. Here again a rational trader will want sufficiently advantageous terms in the forward market to compensate for the extra costs of transacting. The forward rate may not be equal to the expected future spot rate.

There may be other reasons why forward and expected future spot rates may not be equal (e.g. Frenkel and Razin (1980) show that stochastic prices may result in a divergence between the two, but admit that this effect is of little significance in practice). It is therefore important to distinguish two hypotheses. The first is referred to as the efficient markets hypothesis. This says that agents use all available information to forecast the future spot rate – i.e. they form rational expectations of the future exchange rate. The market efficiency hypothesis states that the market behaves as if traders possessed rational expectations. Thus market efficiency implies:

$$S_{t+1} = E_t S_{t+1} + \varepsilon_{t+1} \tag{9.1}$$

where ε_{t+1} is a serially independent forecast error with mean zero and S is the spot rate. The error term is, moreover, uncorrelated with any lagged (and therefore known) variable. Clearly market efficiency on its own is not testable as the expectations term on the right-hand side of equation (9.1) is not observable. The second hypothesis – referred to by Bilson (1981) as the 'speculative efficiency' hypothesis – requires that the forward rate is equal to the expected future spot rate,

$$F_t = E_t S_{t+1} \tag{9.2}$$

Here F_t denotes the forward rate at time t for foreign exchange transactions which will take place at time $t+1$. Equation (9.2) depends for its validity on risk neutrality and identical transactions costs in forward and spot markets. Combining equations (9.1) and (9.2) we obtain the speculative efficiency hypothesis as:

$$S_{t+1} = F_t + \varepsilon_{t+1} \tag{9.3}$$

It is now clear that tests of equation (9.3) are not tests of 'market efficiency' or rational expectations on its own, for equation (9.3) could only be derived with the auxiliary assumptions of risk neutrality and identical transaction costs. For this reason, Bilson's term 'speculative efficiency' helps to emphasize that we have two hypotheses in equation (9.3): rational expectations and the equality of forward and expected future spot rates. Nevertheless, equation (9.3) (or something very like it) has formed the basis of a large number of tests of rational expectations in the foreign exchange market.

Before we look more closely at the tests for the validity of equation (9.3) we must note a problem if that equation is written in the levels of the forward and spot rates. If equation (9.2) is correct, then we could write:

$$\frac{1}{F_t} = \frac{1}{E_t S_{t+1}} \tag{9.4}$$

Equation (9.4) says that the inverse of the forward rate is equal to the inverse of the expected future spot rate. But the inverse of the forward rate is the exchange rate viewed from the 'other side' of the foreign exchange market. An example will make this clear. Suppose that F (and therefore S) are defined as the sterling price of one unit of foreign exchange (say, $1). Imagine that £0.50 will buy $1 in the forward exchange market (so that $F=£0.5$). But the exchange rate may also be thought of as the dollar price of pounds; in this case it will take $2 to buy £1. The dollar price of pounds is the inverse of the pound price of dollars (i.e. it is equal to $1/F$). This means that the left-hand side of equation (9.4) is the same exchange rate, viewed in terms of the other currency. But if agents are risk neutral and if transactions costs are the same in forward and spot markets, it follows that the forward rate $(1/F)$ will equal the expected future spot rate similarly expressed. This means that if equation (9.2) describes the sterling price of foreign exchange, a similar equation could be written describing the foreign price of sterling, thus:

$$\frac{1}{F_t} = E_t\left(\frac{1}{S_{t+1}}\right) \tag{9.5}$$

Equations (9.4) (and therefore (9.2)) and (9.5) can only both be true if $E_t(1/S_{t+1})=1/E_t(S_{t+1})$. But the expectation of an inverse is not equal to the inverse of an expectation. This is easily demonstrated by the use of Figure 9.1.

Suppose that the spot rate in period $t+1$ is known to take on two values with equal probability. There is a 0.5 chance that $S_{t+1}=S_0$ and a 0.5 chance that $S_{t+1}=S_1$. In this case the expected value for S_{t+1} is midway between S_0 and S_1, labelled ES in Figure 9.1. The downward sloping line (labelled $1/S$) in the figure represents the inverse function – so that it represents on the vertical axis the inverse of points on the horizontal axis. Thus the inverse of ES is read off on the vertical axis as $1/ES$. If S_0 and S_1 each occur with probability 0.5, then their inverse will also each occur with probability

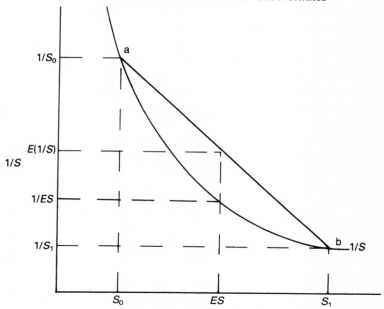

FIGURE 9.1   Siegel's Paradox.

0.5. The expected value of $1/S$ (labelled $E(1/S)$) is midway between $1/S_0$ and $1/S_1$, which is also midway along the line labelled a–b. Because the inverse function is 'convex', $E(1/S)$ is greater than $1/ES$. This is an example of Jensen's inequality which is known as Siegel's paradox (named after Siegel (1972)) in the foreign exchange literature. If the forward rate, expressed in terms of the sterling price of foreign exchange, is exactly equal to the expected future spot rate (similarly defined) then the forward rate, expressed in terms of the dollar price of sterling, cannot be equal to the expected future spot rate (similarly defined).

The most common method of avoiding the implications of Siegel's paradox is to define all exchange rates in logarithms. Suppose that equation (9.1) is not true in levels but is true in logarithms. We therefore rewrite it (using lower-case letters to denote logarithms) as:

$$s_{t+1} = E_t s_{t+1} + \varepsilon_{t+1} \tag{9.6}$$

where for simplicity the notation used for the error is maintained, though clearly it is not the same as that given in equation (9.1). We can similarly rewrite equation (9.2) as

$$f_t = E_t s_{t+1} \tag{9.7}$$

Equations (9.6) and (9.7) imply:

$$s_{t+1} = f_t + \varepsilon_{t+1} \qquad (9.8)$$

Equation (9.6) represents 'market efficiency' and equation (9.8) represents 'speculative efficiency'. If f and s refer to the logarithms of (respectively) the forward and spot rates for the sterling price of dollars, then $-f$ and $-s$ are the forward and spot rates for the dollar price of sterling (this is because $\log(1/x)$ is equal to $-\log(x)$).

It is now clear that Siegel's paradox will not apply to the logarithms of the exchange rates. The negative of equation (9.6) is the appropriate equation describing market efficiency with the exchange rate defined as the dollar price of sterling and the negative of equation (9.7) incorporates 'speculative efficiency' with the exchange rates similarly defined. The negatives of equations (9.6) and (9.7) imply that the negative of equation (9.8) is also true. Siegel's paradox does not arise when the exchange rates are logged. As a result most of the empirical studies of exchange-rate behaviour work in logarithms.

Under speculative efficiency equation (9.8) should be true in periods when the exchange rate is strictly fixed and in periods when it is flexible. In the former, if agents do not anticipate a devaluation (or a revaluation) of the currency by the monetary authorities, then the expected spot rate and the forward rate should both equal the current rate. However, if there is a slight chance of a devaluation (for example), the forward rate may persist at a different level from the spot rate over a period of time. If the rumours of the devaluation disperse, then the forward rate will fall back in line. This is sometimes referred to as the 'peso effect'; the Mexican peso sold at a discount on the forward market over a lengthy period over which the spot rate did not change. Equation (9.8) would not have been satisfied for the peso over this period even though the market may have been rationally anticipating the 50 per cent devaluation which in fact occurred in 1976. Rational agents found the timing of the devaluation in this case difficult to forecast. Moreover in periods of fixed exchange rates there is little or no variability of f and s so that estimation of equations like (9.8) may prove impossible in practice. Fortunately we have experienced long enough periods of flexible exchange rates to allow empirical examination of equation (9.8). It is to such tests of market efficiency and speculative efficiency that we now turn.

(a) Weak Tests

A weak test of speculative efficiency involves estimation of the following:

$$s_{t+1} = \alpha + \beta f_t + u_{t+1} \tag{9.9}$$

where α and β are parameters and u_{t+1} is an error term.

If speculative efficiency is valid in the foreign exchange market, then we would expect to find the null hypothesis H_0: $\alpha=0$ and $\beta=1$ to be true. Estimation of equation (9.9) may give parameter estimates such that α is not zero and β is not one. If such tests have been correctly carried out (statistically speaking) market efficiency (as opposed to speculative efficiency) may still be valid.

Suppose, for example, that *risk-averse traders* will only trade in the future spot market if the terms being offered there are sufficiently attractive to compensate for the extra risks incurred in delay. A trader seeking to buy dollars (for example) in the forward market will buy at a forward rate which is less advantageous to him (i.e. if the exchange rate is defined as the sterling price of a dollar, f_t may be greater than $E_t s_{t+1}$). On the other hand traders buying sterling with dollars will be prepared to trade in the forward market at a rate that is also less attractive to them when compared with the expected future spot rate (in this case f_t will be less than $E_t s_{t+1}$). If the number of British traders buying dollars and the number of American traders buying sterling are roughly equal, dealers in the foreign exchange market will be able to balance their books at a forward rate that is equal to the expected future spot rate. British and American traders will happily buy in the forward market at a rate that is equal to the expected future spot rate but without the latter's uncertainty. However, if the forward market is 'unbalanced' in some way – for example if there are far more British traders seeking to buy dollars forward than there are Americans buying sterling – then the market forward rate may depart from the expected future spot rate. It follows then that the sign of the risk premium cannot be decided *a priori*.

Suppose that risk considerations mean that $f_t = \alpha + E_t s_{t+1}$, where α is a constant. This would be true if there are more risk-averse buyers of dollars in the forward market than sellers. Market efficiency now implies:

$$s_{t+1} = E_t s_{t+1} + \varepsilon_{t+1} = -\alpha + f_t + \varepsilon_{t+1} \tag{9.10}$$

In this case estimation of equation (9.9) will lead to a non-zero intercept. Note that the market is still efficient and is using all current information in its forecast of the exchange rate. Speculative efficiency does not hold because of the presence of a risk premium.

It still appears possible to test for market efficiency for equation (9.10) predicts that the coefficient of f_t will be 1. If equation (9.9) were estimated by ordinary least squares techniques (which assume that the error term, u_{t+1}, is uncorrelated with f_t) then an estimator of the coefficient β may still be biased downwards. Why may this arise? The answer lies in the fact that the risk premium may not be a simple constant (α in the example) but is likely to fluctuate from period to period. Thus we may write $f_t = \alpha + E_t s_{t+1} + v_t$, where v_t is a random, serially independent variable designed to pickup random movements in the risk premium. The forward rate is now a 'noisy' predictor of the future spot rate. Cosset (1984) provides evidence that the risk premium is highly volatile and random and Cornell (1977) has shown that the risk premium changes sign over time but has a mean of zero. The spot rate equation is now:

$$s_{t+1} = -\alpha + f_t + \varepsilon_{t+1} - v_t \tag{9.11}$$

If equation (9.11) were the true model, it may now be clear why ordinary least squares estimates of equation (9.9) will lead to biased estimates of equation (9.11). In particular the estimate of β may be less than 1. This is because f_t and v_t are positively correlated so that f_t and u_{t+1} will be negatively correlated. This will lead to a downward bias in the estimator of β (see the discussion of this point in chapter 6). It is possible to employ statistical techniques that take into account the correlation of f_t and the error (instrumental variable estimation for example) but some of these methods are not statistically efficient, so that the standard errors of the estimates may be inflated. This further complicates our task, which is to discover whether β is statistically different from 1. The discussion in this section would suggest that one would be surprised if the joint hypothesis that $\alpha = 0$ and $\beta = 1$ were satisfied in the ordinary least squares of equation (9.9) even when market efficiency is true.

Many weak tests – i.e. estimates of the coefficients in equation (9.9) – have failed to reject the speculative efficiency hypothesis. The results of some recent studies are set out in Table 9.1. The three studies reported in the table adopt different estimation methods. Edwards (1983) uses seemingly unrelated regression, a method which accounts for the fact that the errors in each of the four equations may be correlated with one another. This arises from the fact that all four exchange rates involve the dollar: an unexpected shock which affects the dollar – an unexpected change in the US money supply for example – will affect all four currencies simultaneously. Frenkel (1981) uses instrumental variable estimation and Baillie *et al.* (1983) use ordinary least squares. Despite the use of very different techniques, the results of each study are remarkably similar. For the pound–dollar, the mark–dollar and the lira–dollar the hypothesis that

$\alpha=0$ and $\beta=1$ cannot be rejected at the 5 per cent level. The speculative efficiency hypothesis cannot be rejected for these currencies. In each of the three studies, speculative efficiency can be rejected for the French franc–dollar rate, both because the constant is non-zero and the coefficient on the forward rate is less than one. These results are typical of others – the speculative efficiency hypothesis is rejected for some but not for other exchange rates. The weak tests are inconclusive.

A further implication of speculative efficiency is that the error term in equation (9.9) should be serially independent, because under this hypothesis it represents the forecast errors of rational agents. The Durbin–Watson statistic (DW in Table 9.1) is a test of first-order serial correlation. Given the nature of the data – monthly in each case – this is a fairly weak test of the serial independence of the error since one might reasonably expect to find higher-order serial correlation in the residuals. The results reported by Baillie *et al.* indicate that the residuals in the pound–dollar case are subject to first-order serial correlation though Frenkel's estimates suggest otherwise.

Of course where we fail to reject H_0: $\alpha=0$ and $\beta=1$, it does not follow that speculative efficiency is true, only that these weak tests have failed to reject it. The tests reported in Table 9.1 may be insufficiently powerful to allow rejection. One possible reason for this is that both forward and spot rates may be strongly time-trended. If s and f are both on a strong upward (or downward) trend, it may be difficult to obtain true estimates of the parameters α and β. For this reason Bilson (1981) wrote the speculative efficiency hypothesis as

TABLE 9.1   Weak tests of speculative efficiency ($s_{t+1} = \alpha + \beta f_t + u_{t+1}$)

	Edwards (1983)		Frenkel (1981)			Baillie *et al.* (1983)		
Data	Monthly		Monthly			Four-weekly		
Time period	1973–1979		1973–1979			1973–1980		
Estimation by	SURE		INV			OLS		
Estimates of	α	β	α	β	DW	α	β	DW
Pound–dollar	−0.033	0.957	0.030	0.961	1.74	0.033	0.956	1.33
	(0.018)	(0.025)	(0.018)	(0.025)		(0.016)	(0.022)	
Franc–dollar	−0.568	0.816	−0.236	0.844	2.24	−0.174	0.884	1.85
	(0.179)	(0.058)	(0.080)	(0.053)		(0.060)	(0.040)	
DM–dollar	0.026	0.967	−0.021	0.973	2.10	−0.024	0.968	1.98
	(0.027)	(0.032)	(0.027)	(0.032)		(0.020)	(0.024)	
Lire–dollar	0.246	0.962	—	—	—	−0.235	0.964	1.67
	(0.155)	(0.023)				(0.120)	(0.018)	

Terms in parentheses are estimated standard errors. SURE are seemingly unrelated regression estimates; INV are instrumental variable estimates; OLS are ordinary least squares estimates.

$$s_{t+1} - s_t = \alpha_0 + \beta_0(f_t - s_t) + u_{t+1} \qquad (9.12)$$

where the right-hand side is the rate of change of the exchange rate and $f_t - s_t$ is called the 'forward premium'. Again speculative efficiency implies that $\alpha_0 = 0$ and $\beta_0 = 1$. Using ordinary least squares to estimate equation (9.12), Bilson obtains mixed results. For the pound–dollar and mark–dollar rates the speculative efficiency hypothesis is not rejected (though the Durbin–Watson statistic indicated the presence of serial correlation in the error for the pound–dollar). In the case of the franc–dollar and lira–dollar the speculative efficiency hypothesis was rejected both because the estimate of β_0 was different from 1 and because the errors showed signs of serial correlation (in the case of the lira–dollar).

(b)   Sources of forecast error

A number of studies have extended the weak test by investigating the source of the forecast error ε_{t+1}. Under speculative efficiency the error in equation (9.9) must be uncorrelated with any part of the agents' information set and this includes all lagged variables (which rational agents are assumed to know and therefore use in their forecast of the future spot rate). However, unanticipated changes in the determinants of the exchange rate will be correlated with the forecast error.

From chapter 5 the reader will recall that the difference between the domestic and foreign interest rates is equal (under uncovered interest parity) to the expected rate of depreciation of the currency. (In the case of covered interest parity, the difference between domestic and world interest rates is equal to the forward premium, $f_t - s_t$.) This condition requires perfect mobility in international capital movements. It can be written as:

$$di_t = i_t - i_t^f = E_t s_{t+1} - s_t \qquad (9.13)$$

where i_t and i_t^f are respectively the domestic and foreign interest rates. Relaxing the assumption of perfect capital mobility, equation (9.13) could be written

$$di_t = \frac{E_t s_{t+1} - s_t}{\gamma} \qquad (9.14)$$

where γ is a positive constant which reflects the degree of capital mobility ($\gamma = 1$ indicates perfect mobility, $\gamma > 1$ implies less than perfect mobility). Leading equation (9.14) by one period and solving for the spot rate gives

$$s_{t+1} = E_{t+1} s_{t+2} - \gamma di_{t+1} \qquad (9.15)$$

Taking expectations of equation (9.15) conditional on information dated t, and subtracting from equation (9.15) we derive the forecast error:

$$s_{t+1} - E_t s_{t+1} = -\gamma(di_{t+1} - E_t di_{t+1}) + v_{t+1} \tag{9.16}$$

where $v_{t+1} = E_{t+1}s_{t+2} - E_t s_{t+2}$ and is defined as the revision in the forecast of the spot rate two periods on as more information becomes available between period t and $t+1$. Under rational expectations the revision in the forecast will be random and uncorrelated with any information known to agents at time t. Thus v_{t+1} can be treated as a random variable which is serially independent. Using equation (9.6) it follows that

$$\varepsilon_{t+1} = -\gamma(di_{t+1} - E_t di_{t+1}) + v_{t+1}$$

i.e. the forecast error depends negatively upon the unexpected interest rate differential (defined as the domestic rate minus the foreign rate). In this case the speculative efficiency hypothesis may be written

$$s_{t+1} = \alpha + \beta f_t - \gamma(di_{t+1} - E_t di_{t+1}) + v_{t+1} \tag{9.17}$$

where once again $\alpha = 0$ and $\beta = 1$. The unanticipated interest differential should enter with a negative coefficient. However, when Frenkel (1981) estimated equation (9.17) he found a positive and significant coefficient on the interest differential 'surprise' or 'innovation'. The following estimates for the dollar–pound rate (using monthly data for the period 1973 to 1979) are typical of his findings:

$$\hat{s}_{t+1} = \begin{array}{ccc} 0.021 & + \ 0.965 f_t & + \ 0.152 di_{t+1} \ DW = 1.69 \\ (0.02) & (0.026) & (0.118) \end{array}$$

$$\hat{s}_{t+1} = \begin{array}{ccc} 0.031 & + \ 0.959 f_t & + \ 0.432(di_{t+1} - E_t di_{t+1}) \ DW = 1.78 \\ (0.017) & (0.024) & (0.181) \end{array}$$

(The terms in parentheses here and throughout the chapter are estimated standard errors.)

The interest rate differential on its own has no significant effect on the spot rate, but its unanticipated value does (Frenkel derived the anticipated interest rate differential by regressing di on a number of variables known to rational agents and taking residuals of this equation as the unanticipated differential). However, the sign of the unanticipated differential is not that predicted by the assumption of uncovered interest parity (it is expected to be negative but turns out to be positive). Frenkel explains this result by arguing that his data period covered a time of unusually high inflation. In such times the nominal interest rates at home and abroad will be dominated by inflationary expectations. Assuming that the domestic and foreign *real* interest rates are equal, the difference between domestic and foreign *nominal* interest rates will simply reflect different expected rates of inflation. This may be written:

$$di_t = (E_t p_{t+1} - p_t) - (E_t p^f_{t+1} - p^f_t) \tag{9.18}$$

where p and p^f are the logarithms of domestic and foreign price levels respectively. If the domestic inflation rate is expected to be far higher than that abroad, domestic nominal interest rates will exceed foreign ones. Thus a rise in the interest rate differential will be associated with a widening of the expected inflation rates.

Since a higher domestic rate of inflation will cause the currency to devalue (i.e. s will rise), a higher value for the unexpected component of di will be associated with a higher s. In this way Frenkel explains the positive sign to the interest differential surprise in the spot-rate equation. The assumption of speculative efficiency (i.e. $\alpha=0$ and $\beta=1$) is again not rejected by the estimates reported above.

Edwards (1983) develops a richer model of exchange-rate determination and investigates the impact of unanticipated domestic and foreign real income, real interest rates and money supplies on $s_{t+1}-f_t$. His results were again favourable to the speculative efficiency hypothesis, though only one-third of the 'surprise' or 'news' variables had the expected signs.

(c)   Semi-strong Tests

According to speculative efficiency, the forward rate is all that is required to predict the future spot rate. All other information (like lagged spot and forward rates) will already have been incorporated into the expectation of s_{t+1} and will be captured by the presence of f_t. If other variables were added to equation (9.9), they should (under speculative efficiency) enter with zero coefficients. Frenkel (1980) added a time trend and lagged spot rates to equation (9.9) and found them jointly non-significant. Frenkel (1981) added the lagged forward rate to equation (9.9). Typical of his results is the following for the dollar–pound rate (again using monthly data over the period 1973 to 1979):

$$\hat{s}_{t+1} = \underset{(0.018)}{0.031} + \underset{(0.116)}{1.047f_t} - \underset{(0.113)}{0.088f_{t-1}} \qquad DW=1.94$$

The current forward rate enters with a coefficient of 1 and the lagged forward rate carries an insignificant coefficient. Rather different results were obtained by Hansen and Hodrick (1980). Using weekly data with a 13-week forward rate, they write the speculative efficiency hypothesis as

$$s_{t+13} = \alpha + \beta f_t + u_{t+13}$$

with $\alpha=0$, $\beta=1$ and u_{t+13} is the equation error term. $s_{t+13}-f_t$ is the exchange forecast error which should again be independent of all information dated $t-1$ and before (as all this information is included in f_t). To test this they estimate the following:

$$s_{t+13} - f_t = \alpha_0 + \beta_0(s_t - f_{t-13}) + \beta_1(s_{t-1} - f_{t-14}) + u_{t+13}$$

where the first two variables on the right-hand side of the equation are lagged forecast errors. Under rational expectations and risk neutrality one would expect $\alpha_0 = \beta_0 = \beta_1 = 0$. In general these restrictions were found to be valid except for the mark–dollar rate (over the period 1973 to 1979). If the lagged forecast errors are included for other exchange rates the results change significantly. The lagged forecast errors for the own and other exchange rates were found to have significant effects on the current forecast error in the case of three rates (Canadian dollar–dollar, mark–dollar and Swiss franc–dollar). They had no effect on the current forecast error in the case of two rates (pound–dollar and French franc–dollar). Like the weak tests of speculative efficiency, the semi-strong tests have met with mixed success but unsurprisingly the more powerful tests tend to reject speculative efficiency with greater frequency.

(d) An Alternative Approach

In a rather different approach the assumption of speculative efficiency may be tested by exploiting the cross-equation restrictions that it implies. This approach has been adopted by Baillie *et al.* (1983) and Hakkio (1981). In order to see how speculative efficiency imposes restrictions of this sort we shall present a simplified version of the Baillie *et al.* and Hakkio models. Suppose that s_t and f_t follow a simple first-order autoregressive process of the following form:

$$s_t = \gamma_1 s_{t-1} + \gamma_2 f_{t-1} + \omega_{1t}$$
$$f_t = \beta_1 s_{t-1} + \beta_2 f_{t-1} + \omega_{2t} \tag{9.19}$$

where γ_i and β_i are coefficients and ω_{it} is a random error which is serially uncorrelated with mean zero. We note that speculative efficiency implies that $s_{t+1} - f_t = \varepsilon_{t+1}$ (see equation (9.8)). Taking expectations of this expression conditional on information dated $t-1$, we can write

$$E_{t-1}s_{t+1} - E_{t-1}f_t = 0$$

since $E_{t-1}\varepsilon_{t+1} = 0$.

Leading the first equation in (9.19) by one period and taking expectations of both equations in (9.19) conditional on information dated $t-1$, we can write:

$$E_{t-1}s_{t+1} = \gamma_1 E_{t-1}s_t + \gamma_2 E_{t-1}f_t$$
$$E_{t-1}f_t = \beta_1 s_{t-1} + \beta_2 f_{t-1}$$

Since speculative efficiency implies that the difference between $E_{t-1}s_{t+1}$

and $E_{t-1}f_t$ is zero, and noting that $E_{t-1}s_t = \gamma_1 s_{t-1} + \gamma_2 f_{t-1}$, we must have the following restrictions on the model in equations (9.19):

$$(\gamma_1^2 + \gamma_2\beta_1 - \beta_1)s_{t-1} + (\gamma_1\gamma_2 + \gamma_2\beta_2 - \beta_2)f_{t-1} = 0 \tag{9.20}$$

This restriction is satisfied when

$$\gamma_1^2 + \gamma_2\beta_1 - \beta_1 = 0$$

and

$$\gamma_1\gamma_2 + \gamma_2\beta_2 - \beta_2 = 0$$

These conditions can be rearranged to give

$$\beta_1 = \frac{\gamma_1^2}{1-\gamma_2}.$$

and

$$\beta_2 = \frac{\gamma_1\gamma_2}{1-\gamma_2}.$$

Imposing these restrictions, we can write equations (9.19) as

$$
\begin{aligned}
s_t &= \gamma_1 s_{t-1} + \gamma_2 f_{t-1} + \omega_{1t} \\
f_t &= \left(\frac{\gamma_1^2}{1-\gamma_2}\right)s_{t-1} + \left(\frac{\gamma_1\gamma_2}{1-\gamma_2}\right)f_{t-1} + \omega_{2t}.
\end{aligned}
\tag{9.21}
$$

These two equations can be estimated imposing the non-linear restrictions between the coefficients that are implied by speculative efficiency. The likelihood of the model given by equations (9.21) may be compared with the likelihood of an unrestricted model which is given by:

$$
\begin{aligned}
s_t &= \pi_1 s_{t-1} + \pi_2 f_{t-1} + \xi_{1t} \\
f_t &= \pi_3 s_{t-1} + \pi_4 f_{t-1} + \xi_{2t}
\end{aligned}
$$

where ξ_{it} is a random error which is serially uncorrelated with mean zero.

If speculative efficiency is true, we would expect the likelihood from the unrestricted model to differ insignificantly from that of the restricted model. This example illustrates the general point made in chapter 6 – namely that rational expectations introduces restrictions across equations which may be tested using the likelihood ratio test (or something similar).

In practice the processes for s and f described in equations (9.19) are unlikely to be this simple. Even if we restrict the process to include only lagged values of s and f, it is highly likely that longer lags in s and f will have an effect on their current values. A lengthening of the lags in equations

(9.19) will not change the type of restrictions imposed, but it will greatly complicate them. Indeed the cross-equation restrictions may become so complicated as to make computation of the restricted model difficult or impossible in practice. For this reason, Hakkio was obliged to limit himself to four lagged terms in equations (9.19) even when there was firm evidence of longer lags. The likelihood ratio tests of the restrictions conducted by Hakkio rejected the speculative efficiency hypothesis for five exchange rates (gilder–dollar, mark–dollar, Canadian dollar–dollar, Swiss franc–dollar and pound–dollar).

Using similar methods, Baillie *et al.* (1983) investigated the speculative efficiency hypothesis using weekly data for six dollar-exchange rates (pound, mark, lira, French franc, Canadian dollar and Swiss franc). They avoided the necessity of computing the restricted model by estimating the unrestricted model and testing the restrictions using the Wald test. This test examines the validity of the restrictions without the need to estimate the restricted model. The Wald test is equivalent to the likelihood ratio test in large samples. Baillie *et al.* reject the speculative efficiency hypothesis in all cases.

The tests carried out by Hakkio and Baillie *et al.* are more powerful than the weak tests described at the beginning of this section. But there may be reasons to think that they may reject the null hypothesis of speculative efficiency even when the latter is in fact true. The tests they use are large sample tests and the distributions of the test-statistics they use (like the likelihood ratio) are not known for small samples. The application of these tests may increase the probability of rejection of the null hypothesis when it is in fact true. There is no way as yet of evaluating the quantitative importance of this problem.

(e) Summary

In this section we have examined the application of rational expectations to the forward and spot foreign exchange markets. The joint assumptions of rational expectations (or market efficiency) and (*inter alia*) risk neutrality – called speculative efficiency by Bilson (1981) – imply that the forward rate is an unbiased and efficient predictor of the future spot rate. Weak tests of this hypothesis are often favourable though there are cases when even weak tests of speculative efficiency are unfavourable to the hypothesis. In general as the tests become more powerful, the speculative efficiency hypothesis is rejected. It is not possible to attribute the rejection of speculative efficiency to the failure of either of the joint assumptions of efficiency and risk neutrality. The evidence does indicate that profits lie unexploited in many foreign exchange markets, but as Bilson argues 'these profits may be eliminated by transactions costs or they may provide an adequate compensation for risk and hence it is not possible to make inferences about the efficiency of the foreign exchange market on the basis of these results' (Bilson, 1981, p. 449). This example illustrates the difficulty of testing rational expectations without also testing the specific economic model with which it is combined.

9.2   THE CONSUMPTION FUNCTION

In this second case study, we shall examine the implications of rational expectations for the theory and associated empirical tests of aggregate consumption behaviour. Again it will become clear that rational expectations cannot be tested on its own. At best we shall be able to test the joint hypothesis of rational expectations and the economic model with which it is combined.

(a)   The Rational Expectations – Life Cycle Hypothesis

We begin with models first introduced by Ando and Modigliani (1963) and Friedman (1957) which we shall call, for convenience, the life-cycle/ permanent income hypothesis. According to this theory, households generally seek to even out their consumption from period to period over their life-cycle. The reasons for this may be stated simply: utility gains from higher consumption in good times (when income is above normal) do not offset utility losses from lower consumption in bad times. This is because households' utility functions are often assumed to be subject to diminishing marginal utility. For this reason, risk-averse households will prefer a constant consumption stream to one with the same mean but which is more variable through time.

The life-cycle model takes the planning horizon of the household to be its remaining life span. According to the theory, the household will calculate its lifetime wealth and then fix a consumption trajectory to exhaust that wealth. Clearly the household will not know with certainty or precision what its future income will be (or for that matter, what its planning horizon is precisely). It will instead form an expectation of the future stream of income it will receive. The introduction of rational expectations to this theoretical framework will inevitably have important consequences as we shall see.

A simple version of the life-cycle hypothesis suggests that current consumption (C_t) is a given fraction of the sum of non-human wealth (denoted A_t, which is comprised of current household assets) and the present value of future labour income (denoted H_t, which is referred to as human wealth). This is formally expressed as

$$C_t = \varkappa(A_t + H_t) + u_t \tag{9.22}$$

where $\varkappa$ is a constant and u_t is 'transitory' consumption which is assumed to be independent of A_t and H_t. By its very nature, transitory consumption is random and can be assumed to be serially independent. Whilst A_t is directly observable, H_t is not, as it depends on expectations of future labour income. To make the analysis of the problem easier, we shall assume that the household's planning horizon is infinite. Whilst this assumption may seem extraordinary, its use is only to simplify the analysis. One way of interpreting the assumption of an infinite planning horizon is to imagine that the current and all future households seek to leave bequests to the next generation. With this assumption we may write the household's human wealth as:

$$H_t = \sum_{i=0}^{\infty} (1+\delta)^{-i} Y^e_{t+i} \tag{9.23}$$

where δ is the (constant) rate at which households discount the future and Y^e_{t+i} is the expected labour income (i.e. excluding the income arising as a return on assets) in period $t+i$. Early studies of the life-cycle hypothesis made *ad hoc* assumptions in solving for expectations of future labour income – like the adaptive expectations hypothesis. Under rational expectations, however:

$$Y^e_{t+i} = E_t Y_{t+i} = E(Y_{t+i}|I_t)$$

so that:

$$H_t = \sum_{i=0}^{\infty} (1+\delta)^{-i} E_t Y_{t+i} \tag{9.24}$$

where I_t is the information set of the household at time t. Imposing rational expectations on (9.23) gives us – in combination with equation (9.22) – the rational-expectations/life-cycle hypothesis, which we shall refer to as RE-LCH in what follows. How are equations (9.22) and (9.24) to be estimated? One method would involve the following sequence: investigate the process determining labour income, solve for H_t and substitute the resulting expression into equation (9.22). Suppose, for example, that we know that labour income follows a simple first-order autoregressive process of the form:

$$Y_t = \alpha Y_{t-1} + v_t \tag{9.25}$$

where α is a constant such that $0 < \alpha < 1$ and v_t is a serially independent random variable with zero mean. It follows that

$$E_t Y_{t+1} = \alpha Y_t,$$

$$E_t Y_{t+2} = \alpha \ E_t Y_{t+1} = \alpha^2 Y_t,$$

$$E_t Y_{t+3} = \alpha E_t Y_{t+2} \doteq \alpha^3 Y_t, \text{ etc.}$$

Substituting these and further terms into equation (9.24), we obtain

$$H_t = \sum_{i=0}^{\infty} (1+\delta)^{-i} \alpha^i Y_t. \tag{9.26}$$

Since $\Sigma[\alpha/(1+\delta)]^i = (1+\delta)/(1+\delta-\alpha)$, we can write equation (9.26) as

$$C_t = \varkappa A_t + \left(\frac{\varkappa \ (1+\delta)}{1+\delta-\alpha} \right) Y_t + u_t$$

or in terms of lagged income

$$C_t = \varkappa A_t + \left(\frac{\varkappa \alpha (1+\delta)}{1+\delta-\alpha} \right) Y_{t-1} + u_t + \left(\frac{\varkappa \ (1+\delta)}{1+\delta-\alpha} \right) v_t \tag{9.27}$$

It is clear that equations (9.25) and (9.27) could be estimated jointly. The interested reader can check that the model is just identified, so that estimates of the parameters (α, $\varkappa$ and δ) may be obtained. Simple labour income processes like that set out in equation (9.25) are unlikely in practice. The introduction of other variables (like higher order lags in Y) to equation (9.25) will only complicate the solution and thus complicate the non-linear, cross-equation restrictions that rationality implies. These complications may even make the computation of the restrictions difficult or impossible to achieve in practice.

To avoid such problems, a simpler solution is available. In order to help follow the steps of the argument, we write equation (9.24) more fully as:

$$H_t = Y_t + (1+\delta)^{-1} E_t Y_{t+1} + (1+\delta)^{-2} E_t Y_{t+2} + \ldots \tag{9.24}$$

Lagging equation (9.24) by one period and multiplying both sides by $(1+\delta)$ we obtain:

$$(1+\delta) H_{t-1} = (1+\delta) Y_{t-1} + E_{t-1} Y_t + (1+\delta)^{-1} E_{t-1} Y_{t+1}$$
$$+ (1+\delta)^{-2} E_{t-1} Y_{t+2} + \ldots \tag{9.28}$$

Subtracting equation (9.28) from (9.24) and rearranging gives

$$H_t = (1+\delta)(H_{t-1} - Y_{t-1}) + \sum_{i=0}^{\infty} (1+\delta)^{-i} (E_t Y_{t+i} - E_{t-1} Y_{t+i}) \tag{9.29}$$

where the last term describes the forecast revisions for future labour income as more information becomes available between periods $t-1$ and t. What can be said about the way in which these forecasts are revised from one period to the next? Clearly if agents are rational, in period $t-1$ they will use all information currently available to them. Their forecast in period t will include information dated $t-1$ but it will also include information agents could not have forecasted in $t-1$ (i.e. it will include 'news', 'innovations' or 'surprises').

The first term in the forecast revision is $E_tY_t-E_{t-1}Y_t$ or equivalently $Y_t-E_{t-1}Y_t$. This is the unanticipated component of current labour income. Note that as the anticipated component of income ($E_{t-1}Y_t$) is fully known in both t *and* $t-1$, it does not affect the forecast revision. We would therefore expect the labour income innovation to appear in the human-wealth equation. But the household may make other adjustments to expectations of future labour income (i.e. income dated $t+1$ and onwards) because it has some extra information (including the income innovation). Consequently the forecast revision term on the right-hand side of equation (9.29) will depend on the current labour income innovation and all other 'news' or unpredictable pieces of information that could not be anticipated in period $t-1$. With these considerations in mind, we rewrite equation (9.29) as

$$H_t = (1+\delta)(H_{t-1}-Y_{t-1}) + \beta(Y_t-E_{t-1}Y_t) + \xi_t \qquad (9.30)$$

where ξ_t is the sum of all other information surprises in period t which cause the household to revise its forecast of future labour income.

Noting that $H_{t-1} = (1/\varkappa)C_{t-1}-A_{t-1}-(1/\varkappa)u_{t-1}$ (from equation (9.22) lagged one period), we can substitute equation (9.30) back into equation (9.22) to give

$$C_t = (1+\delta)C_{t-1} + \varkappa[A_t-(1+\delta)(A_{t-1}+Y_{t-1})] + \varkappa\beta(Y_t-E_{t-1}Y_t) + v_t \qquad (9.31)$$

where $v_t = u_t-(1+\delta)u_{t-1} + \varkappa\xi_t$.

The right-hand side of equation (9.31) includes A_t, the current stock of real non-human wealth. This can be defined as the previous period's non-human wealth plus any savings from the previous period (or minus any dissaving), together with the interest earned; current non-human wealth is given by

$$A_t = (1+r)[A_{t-1} + Y_{t-1} - C_{t-1}] \qquad (9.32)$$

where r is the average real rate of return on holdings of non-human wealth. We shall assume that r is expected to remain constant throughout the household's lifetime. Substitution of equation (9.32) into equation (9.31) gives:

$$C_t = [(1+\delta)-\varkappa(1+r)]C_{t-1} + \varkappa\{[(1+r)-(1+\delta)][A_{t-1}+Y_{t-1}]\}$$
$$+ \varkappa\beta(Y_t-E_{t-1}Y_t) +v_t \tag{9.33}$$

If households discount the future at the same rate as they earn on real assets (i.e. if $\delta = r$), equation (9.33) becomes:

$$C_t = (1+r)(1-\varkappa)C_{t-1} + \varkappa\beta(Y_t-E_{t-1}Y_t) + v_t \tag{9.34}$$

The combination of rational expectations and the life-cycle model has produced a surprisingly simple consumption function – one that explains current consumption by its own lagged value together with random terms which reflect information innovations in period t and the existence of transitory consumption (u_t and u_{t-1}). The presence of transitory consumption in v_t introduces problems for the estimation of equation (9.34), for the error in this equation may be subject to serial correlation if the variance of transitory consumption is relatively large. It will also be correlated with C_{t-1}. To simplify the analysis we shall assume that transitory consumption is zero, so that the error in equation (9.34) will be serially independent under rational expectations.

Equation (9.34) states simply that consumption will follow what is called a 'random walk', i.e. its current level depends only on its lagged value and a random term. If $\varkappa=r/(1+r)$, the coefficient on C_{t-1} will be one: if $\varkappa$ is less than $r/(1+r)$, the coefficient on C_{t-1} will be greater than one and equation (9.34) will exhibit a trend in consumption (i.e. C_t will rise through time). The central proposition of the RE-LCH is that current consumption can be explained (and therefore forecasted) by including only its own lagged value. The intuition behind this result is straightforward enough. In period $t-1$, given the information available, households set consumption at C_{t-1}. This decision took full account of all information dated $t-1$ and earlier. In period t consumption will be adjusted because of the availability of new information, which was not available at $t-1$. This new information will be independent of all previous information; for if it were not, agents would have predicted it, and incorporated it into their consumption decision at time $t-1$. Thus the revision in consumption between periods $t-1$ and t will only reflect innovations in the determinants of life-cycle labour income. This remarkable result was first noted by Robert Hall (1978) who argued that 'no variable apart from current consumption should be of any value in predicting future consumption' (p. 971).

(b)   Testing RE-LCH

One obvious weak test of RE-LCH would involve the estimation of the following:

$$C_t = \alpha + \beta C_{t-1} + w_t \tag{9.35}$$

The theory predicts that w_t is serially independent (providing there is no transitory consumption); the estimate for β may be expected to be close to 1. Examples of weak tests are presented in Table 9.2. The estimate of β is close to 1 in all cases. This test is hardly an exacting one for if β were found to be greater or less than 1, the RE-LCH may still be valid providing $\varkappa$ is not equal to $r/(1+r)$. Moreover, consumption could follow a random walk process under other models of consumption behaviour – i.e. the RE-LCH may be observationally equivalent to some other model in its prediction of consumption as a random walk. This point is made by Davidson and Hendry (1981). Taking an earlier model of consumption first presented in Davidson et al. (1978), they write

$$\Delta c_t = \beta_0 + \beta_1(y_t - y_{t-1}) + \beta_2(y-c)_{t-1} + \varepsilon_{1t}$$
$$y_t = \alpha y_{t-1} + \varepsilon_{2t} \tag{9.36}$$

where ε_{it} is an equation error term. Lower-case notation denotes that the variables are expressed as logarithms. The first equation in (9.36) is referred to as a 'servo-mechanism' model of consumption. Rearranging the equations in (9.36), the consumption function becomes

$$c_t = \beta_0 + (1-\beta_2)c_{t-1} + (\beta_1\alpha-\beta_1+\beta_2)y_{t-1} + \beta_1\varepsilon_{2t} + \varepsilon_{1t}.$$

TABLE 9.2   Weak tests of RE-LCH

	Estimates of β
Hall (1978) Quarterly US data 1948–1977	1.011 (0.003)
Davidson and Hendry (1981) Quarterly UK data 1964–1979	0.72 (0.25)
Daly and Hadjimatheou (1981) Quarterly UK data 1956–1978	1.0041 (0.00001)

Numbers in parenthesis are estimated standard errors.

Now if the Davidson–Hendry model were true, econometricians investigating a random walk in consumption may find strong evidence of it (providing the parameters α, β_1 and β_2 took values such that the coefficient on y_{t-1} were close to zero). Davidson and Hendry (1981) conclude that even if 'the Davidson *et al.* model were actually correct, the Hall model would appear to give a good description of the data and would probably not be rejected' (p. 177). From this it is clear that a more powerful test is required.

There are two (not unrelated) features of equation (9.34) that can be exploited in testing RE-LCH. First only unanticipated current labour income will affect consumption. The effects of anticipated income, $E_{t-1}Y_t$, will already have been 'absorbed' in C_{t-1}. Secondly no variables dated $t-1$ and earlier, other than C_{t-1}, will have any significant influence on current consumption, for these too will have been accounted for in C_{t-1}. One obvious way to proceed would involve adding to equation (9.35) other predetermined variables (like Y_{t-1}, Y_{t-2}, C_{t-2} etc.). If any of these were significant, the RE-LCH (at least in the form set out in equation (9.34)) would be rejected.

Tests of this sort have generally refuted these implications of RE-LCH. Examples of such tests are:

1 Hall (1978) himself found that the market value of corporate stocks (lagged) did have a statistically significant effect on consumption.
2 Davidson and Hendry (1981) found, using UK data, that lagged income and a lagged measure of liquidity were also significant in a consumption function which contains lagged consumption.
3 Daly and Hadjimatheou (1981) noted that higher-order lags in consumption and income significantly contributed to the explanation of consumption.

A related test of RE-LCH exploits the fact that only unanticipated current real labour income will have any influence on consumption. If equation (9.35) were replaced by:

$$C_t = \alpha + \beta C_{t-1} + \lambda(Y_t - E_{t-1}Y_t) + \Phi E_{t-1}Y_t + w_t \qquad (9.37)$$

the RE-LCH would predict that λ is greater than zero and that Φ is equal to zero. Only the real income 'innovation' would affect consumption once the influence of C_{t-1} is allowed for. Bilson (1980) estimated equation (9.37) for three countries. His real disposable income equation (not labour income which is what is strictly implied by the theory) from which $E_{t-1}Y_t$ was generated included lagged income terms only. His results are set out in Table 9.3 (Bilson restricted β to be 1).

The RE-LCH is rejected for Germany (because λ is not significantly different from zero) and for the US (because Φ is significantly different

TABLE 9.3   Consumption effects of anticipated and unanticipated income (all data are quarterly covering 1964 to 1978)

	Germany	UK	US
λ	0.188	0.360	0.231
	(0.57)	(0.06)	(0.06)
Φ	0.078	0.064	0.258
	(0.07)	(0.06)	(0.07)

Numbers in parentheses are estimated standard errors.

from zero), but RE-LCH is not rejected for the UK. However, Bilson also included in his regressions lagged values of both real wage changes and real stock prices. Bilson's results confirm those already reported. Similar results have also been reported by Flavin (1981).

In contrast, Muellbauer (1983) found, using quarterly UK data, that the lagged variables determining $E_{t-1}Y_t$ played no significant role when the consumption function was estimated over the entire data period (1955 to 1979). This result is similar to that reported by Bilson using UK data and reported in Table 9.3. However, when the data period is split into two (before and after 1972, second quarter, when the exchange rate ceased to be strictly fixed), the RE-LCH is firmly rejected in both of the two sub-periods. The rejection arises both because other lagged variables did have significant effects on consumption and because the output surprises or innovations were not significant in the second of the two periods.

In general then, these stronger tests of RE-LCH are unfavourable to the hypothesis. However, the hypothesis is a joint one, so that it is not possible to attribute the failure to the restrictions imposed by rational expectations. Attfield and Browning (1984) develop a RE-LCH in which they test the rational expectations restrictions conditional on the life-cycle model being true. They reject the rational expectations restrictions. However, their test is conditional on the truth of the underlying economic model. Moreover, the failure of the joint test discussed above may be due to the inappropriate nature of some of the assumptions we have used in deriving equation (9.34). We have already noted that the presence of transitory consumption may complicate the dynamic structure of equation (9.34). The tests we have described have generally ignored the problems introduced by the presence of transitory consumption. But other assumptions may also be invalid.

First, the life-cycle model assumes that households may borrow and lend at a given real rate of interest in order to smooth out their consumption plans. If the 'capital market' is imperfect, the household may face liquidity constraints and may therefore fail to achieve its optimal plan in any one year. This point finds support in the results obtained by Davidson and Hendry reported above.

Secondly, as Hayashi (1982) has argued, the rate used by households to discount the future (i.e. δ) may not be equal to the real rate of return on non-human wealth (i.e. r). If δ and r were not equal, estimates of both can only be derived by the joint estimation of equations (9.32) and (9.33). Note that lagged income and lagged assets should be significant in the consumption function even when RE-LCH is true. Hayashi found that, for the US at least, r and δ were significantly different from each other and this may be an important reason for the rejection of RE-LCH in the other studies.

Thirdly, the real rate of return (r) may not be a constant. Wickens and Molana (1984) show that, with variable r, consumption will depend additionally on the expected rate of return and the real interest rate innovation as well as the real income innovation and lagged consumption. Again the significance of other lagged terms in the consumption function may arise from the fact that they help to predict the real rate of return.

(c) Summary

In this section we have applied the notion of rational expectations to an established theory of consumption – the permanent income-life-cycle theory. We found that the joint hypothesis of rational expectations and the life-cycle hypothesis implies, given certain conditions, that consumption should follow a random walk, with the current level of consumption determined only by its value in the previous period together with a random error term. Tests of the joint hypothesis are generally unfavourable to the RE-LCH. The failure of empirical tests may not mean that the rational expectations-life-cycle hypothesis is invalid. It may mean that the 'auxiliary' assumptions used are themselves defective.

9.3   THE TERM STRUCTURE OF INTEREST RATES

In this section we will see how the assumption of rational expectations places certain testable restrictions on the relationship between long-run and short-run interest rates. We will also note a number of similarities between the analysis in this section and that in section 9.1 on the relationship between forward and spot exchange rates.

The bond market at any time t consists of a number of outstanding bonds with differing maturity dates. At one end of the scale there are short-term bonds which are about to be redeemed and at the other end long-term bonds, perpetuities, which will never be redeemed. The term structure of interest rates is the relationship between the rates of return on bonds with different maturity dates. In a world of perfect certainty and perfect foresight the traditional view of the term structure is that long-run interest rates are simply averages of future short-term rates so that:

$$i_{nt} = (1/n)\,(i_{1t} + i_{1t+1} + i_{1t+2} + \ldots + i_{1t+n-1}) \tag{9.38}$$

where i_{1t} denotes the 'one period' rate, that is, the market rate of interest at time t on bonds with one period to maturity; i_{nt} denotes the 'n period' rate, that is, the market interest rate at time t on bonds with n periods to maturity. The expression in equation (9.38) tells us that if short-term rates are constant at time t and for the following $n-1$ periods the n period rate will equal the one-period rate.

In a world of uncertainty it may be assumed that the expression in equation (9.38) becomes

$$i_{nt} = (1/n)\,(i_{1t} + E_t i_{1t+1} + E_t i_{1t+2} + \ldots + E_t i_{1t+n-1}). \tag{9.39}$$

That is, individuals at time t can observe the current market short rate, i_{1t}, and the current market rate on a bond which has maturity date n, i_{nt}. They have to form expectations, however, about future short rates. This is where the theory of rational expectations emerges once again. We will see that if individuals are rational the manner in which they form the expectations in equation (9.39) places certain testable restrictions on the underlying model.

Following the work of Sargent (1979) we will work with a model in first differences so we define

$$i_{nt-1} = (1/n)\,(i_{1t-1} + E_{t-1} i_{1t} + \ldots + E_{t-1} i_{1t+n-2}). \tag{9.40}$$

Then, subtracting equation (9.40) from equation (9.39) gives

$$\begin{aligned} \Delta i_{nt} = i_{nt} - i_{nt-1} &= (1/n)\,(\Delta i_{1t} + E_t i_{1t+1} - E_{t-1} i_{1t} + E_t i_{1t+2} \\ &\quad - E_{t-1} i_{1t+1} + \ldots + E_t i_{1t+n-1} - E_{t-1} i_{1t+n-2}). \end{aligned} \tag{9.41}$$

Now suppose that at time $t-1$ the only information available to individuals is contained in the set I_{t-1}. For example I_{t-1} may consist of just Δi_{1t-1} and Δi_{nt-1}, the most recent changes in the short and long rates. Then, taking expectations of the left-hand side of equation (9.41) conditional on I_{t-1} yields

$$E(\Delta i_{nt}|I_{t-1}) = E_{t-1}\Delta i_{nt}$$

which is in accordance with our definition of rational expectations in chapter 2.

Likewise, taking expectations of the first term on the right-hand side of equation (9.41) gives $E(\Delta i_{1t}|I_{t-1}) = E_{t-1}\Delta i_{1t}$. The expectation of the second term on the right-hand side of equation (9.41) is

$$E(E(i_{1t+1}|I_t)|I_{t-1}) = E(i_{1t+1}|I_{t-1}) = E_{t-1}i_{1t+1}. \tag{9.42}$$

Taking expectation of all the remaining terms in equation (9.41) produces

$$E_{t-1}\Delta i_{nt} = (1/n)(E_{t-1}\Delta i_{1t} + E_{t-1}\Delta i_{1t+1} + \ldots + E_{t-1}\Delta i_{1t+n-1}). \tag{9.43}$$

Assume now that the only information available is Δi_{1t-1} and Δi_{nt-1} and suppose we write the two regression equations

$$\Delta i_{1t} = \alpha\Delta i_{1t-1} + \beta\Delta i_{nt-1} + u_{1t} \tag{9.44a}$$

$$\Delta i_{nt} = \gamma\Delta i_{1t-1} + \delta\Delta i_{nt-1} + u_{2t} \tag{9.44b}$$

where u_{1t} and u_{2t} are random errors with zero means and are uncorrelated with Δi_{1t-1} and Δi_{nt-1}.

Now the important point about the rational expectations assumptions which lead to equation (9.43) is that they impose restrictions on equation (9.44b). To see the form of the restrictions we will work with the very simple case when $n=2$. The relationship in equation (9.43) now becomes

$$E_{t-1}\Delta i_{2t} = (1/2)(E_{t-1}\Delta i_{1t} + E_{t-1}\Delta i_{1t+1}). \tag{9.45}$$

From the equations in (9.44) we can deduce that

$$E_{t-1}\Delta i_{1t} = \alpha\Delta i_{1t-1} + \beta\Delta i_{2t-1} \tag{9.46a}$$

$$E_{t-1}\Delta i_{2t} = \gamma\Delta i_{1t-1} + \delta\Delta i_{2t-1} \tag{9.46b}$$

since $E_{t-1}u_{1t} = 0 = E_{t-1}u_{2t}$. These expressions enable us to obtain the expectations on the right-hand side of equation (9.45). That is $E_{t-1}\Delta i_{1t}$ is obtained directly from equation (9.46a) and $E_{t-1}\Delta i_{1t+1}$ can be obtained by noting that

$$E_{t-1}\Delta i_{1t+1} = E_{t-1}(\alpha\Delta i_{1t} + \beta\Delta i_{2t})$$

then, using equations (9.46) we have

$$E_{t-1}\Delta i_{1t+1} = \alpha(\alpha\Delta i_{1t-1} + \beta\Delta i_{2t-1}) + \beta(\gamma\Delta i_{1t-1} + \delta\Delta i_{2t-1})$$

so

$$E_{t-1}\Delta i_{1t+1} = (\alpha^2 + \beta\gamma)\Delta i_{1t-1} + (\alpha\beta + \beta\delta)\Delta i_{2t-1}.$$

We can now rewrite equation (9.45) as

$$E_{t-1}\Delta i_{2t} = (1/2)[\alpha\Delta i_{1t-1} + \beta\Delta i_{2t-1} + (\alpha^2 + \beta\gamma)\Delta i_{1t-1} + (\alpha\beta + \beta\delta)\Delta i_{2t-1}]$$

$$= (1/2)[(\alpha + \alpha^2 + \beta\gamma)\Delta i_{1t-1} + (\beta + \alpha\beta + \beta\delta)\Delta i_{2t-1}]. \tag{9.47}$$

But, from the unrestricted equations in (9.44) we have that

$$E_{t-1}\Delta i_{2t} = \gamma\Delta i_{1t-1} + \delta\Delta i_{2t-1} \tag{9.48}$$

Comparing equation (9.48) with equation (9.47) we see that rational expectations imposes the restrictions that

$$\gamma = \frac{\alpha + \alpha^2 + \beta\gamma}{2}$$

and

$$\delta = \frac{\beta + \alpha\beta + \beta\delta}{2}$$

or, alternatively

$$\gamma = \frac{\alpha(1+\alpha)}{2-\beta} \tag{9.49a}$$

and

$$\delta = \frac{\beta(1+\alpha)}{2-\beta} \tag{9.49b}$$

In other words, if the assumption of rational expectations is correct we would expect that a regression of the two equations in (9.44), using a large sample of obervations, would produce estimates of γ and δ approximately equal to the expressions on the right-hand sides of equations (9.49a) and (9.49b) evaluated at the estimates of α and β. Moreover, we could test the restrictions by comparing the likelihood for the unrestricted equation in (9.44) with the restricted version where the right-hand side of equations (9.49) replaces γ and δ in the second equation in (9.44). As we saw in chapter 6 the likelihood ratio test statistic could then be compared with a chi-square variate with, in this case, 2 degrees of freedom since there are two restrictions on the model.

Suppose now that we have data on a one-period rate and on a three-period rate so that $n=3$. The term structure in equation (9.39) now becomes

$$i_{3t} = (1/3)(i_{1t} + E_t i_{1t+1} + E_t i_{1t+2})$$

and the unrestricted regressions in (9.44) become

$$\Delta i_{1t} = \alpha \Delta i_{1t-1} + \beta \Delta i_{3t-1} + u_{1t} \tag{9.50a}$$

$$\Delta i_{3t} = \gamma \Delta i_{1t-1} + \delta \Delta i_{3t-1} + u_{2t} \tag{9.50b}$$

Carrying out similar substitutions to the ones that led to equations (9.46) we obtain

$$\gamma = (1/3)(\alpha+\alpha^2+\alpha^3+\beta\gamma+2\alpha\beta\gamma+\beta\gamma\delta) \tag{9.51a}$$

$$\delta = (1/3)(\beta+\alpha\beta+\beta\delta+\alpha^2\beta+\alpha\beta\delta+\beta^2\gamma+\beta\delta^2) \tag{9.51b}$$

Clearly then as n becomes larger the restrictions placed upon the γ and δ coefficients become more complex. Sargent (1979) generalizes the model to the case where:

$$i_{nt} = (1/n)(i_{1t}+E_t i_{1t+1}+E_t i_{1t+2} + \ldots + E_t i_{1t+n-1})$$

with the unrestricted regressions:

$$\Delta i_{1t} = \alpha_1 \Delta i_{1t-1} + \ldots + \alpha_m \Delta i_{1t-m}+\beta_1 \Delta i_{nt-1} + \ldots + \beta_m \Delta i_{nt-m} + u_{1t} \tag{9.52a}$$

$$\Delta i_{nt} = \gamma_1 \Delta i_{1t-1} + \ldots + \gamma_m \Delta i_{1t-m}+\delta_1 \Delta i_{nt-1} + \ldots + \delta_m \Delta i_{nt-m} + u_{2t} \tag{9.52b}$$

In this case the restrictions on the γ_i's and δ_i's in (9.52) are complicated non-linear functions of the α_i's and β_i's.

Sargent's derivation of the restrictions for the general case need not concern us here. What we do need to know, however, is how these complex restrictions can be imposed on the term structure model so that the rational expectations assumptions can be tested. Sargent's suggested solution to this problem can be seen by looking at the simple case where $n=3$ which led to the restrictions of (9.51). He suggests that we first obtain estimates of α and β, $\hat{\alpha}$ and $\hat{\beta}$, from an ordinary least squares regression of equation (9.50a). We then set γ and δ on the right-hand side of equations (9.51) to zero and obtain

$$\gamma^{(1)} = \frac{\hat{\alpha} + \hat{\alpha}^2 + \hat{\alpha}^3}{3}$$

$$\delta^{(1)} = \frac{\hat{\beta} + \hat{\alpha}\hat{\beta} + \hat{\alpha}^2\hat{\beta}}{3}$$

These estimated values of γ and δ, $\gamma^{(1)}$ and $\delta^{(1)}$, are then substituted into the right-hand side of the equations in (9.51) together with the original estimates of α and β to give

$$\gamma^{(2)} = \frac{\hat{\alpha}+\hat{\alpha}^2+\hat{\alpha}^3+\hat{\beta}\gamma^{(1)}+ 2\hat{\alpha}\hat{\beta}\gamma^{(1)}+\hat{\beta}\gamma^{(1)}\delta^{(1)}}{3}$$

$$\delta^{(2)} = \frac{\hat{\beta}+\hat{\alpha}\hat{\beta}+\hat{\beta}\delta^{(1)}+\hat{\alpha}^2\hat{\beta}+\hat{\alpha}\hat{\beta}\delta^{(1)}+\hat{\beta}^2\gamma^{(1)}+\hat{\beta}\delta^{(1)}\delta^{(1)}}{3}.$$

The values of $\gamma^{(2)}$ and $\delta^{(2)}$ are then inserted into the right-hand side of equations (9.51) and so on until the method converges, that is, until the differences between $\gamma^{(k)}$ and $\gamma^{(k-1)}$ and $\delta^{(k)}$ and $\delta^{(k-1)}$ from iteration k to $k-1$ become negligible. At this point we will have found values of γ and δ that satisfy the equations in (9.51). Sargent in fact shows how the restrictions can be incorporated into a maximum likelihood procedure so that the restrictions can be tested using the likelihood ratio.

Sargent applies the above method to the model in equations (9.52) with $m=4$ using quarterly data on the 5-year government bond rate and the 91-day Treasury bill rate for the period 1953(2) to 1971(4) in the US. We reproduce his results in Table 9.4. The unrestricted estimates were obtained by ordinary least squares while the maximum likelihood estimates were obtained with all the restrictions on the γ and δ coefficients imposed. The likelihood ratio test statistic for testing the null hypothesis that the restrictions are correct is 8.58 which has to be compared with a chi-square variate with 8 degrees of freedom. At the 5 per cent significance level the critical value of chi square is 15.5. The rational expectations restrictions, therefore, cannot be rejected.

The above procedure gives a flavour of how the assumption of rational expectations can be used to give a model of the term structure of interest rates which can be tested. It should be pointed out, however, that Sargent's empirical results have not gone unchallenged. Shiller (1980) argues, for example, that Sargent's method of first differencing his data imposes further restrictions on the stochastic properties of his model which he does not test. Attfield and Duck (1982) found they could reject the rational expectations theory of the term structure of interest rates when they applied the above to 3-monthly, 5-yearly and 10-yearly rates of interest in the UK.

TABLE 9.4   Estimates for a 5-year bond rate and 91-day Treasury bill rate

j	1	2	3	4
Unrestricted estimates				
α_j	−0.3663	−0.3235	0.1234	−0.0694
β_j	0.6373	0.4322	−0.3286	0.1703
γ_j	−0.2962	0.0203	0.2480	−0.1047
δ_j	0.2812	0.1200	−0.3934	0.0765
Maximum likelihood estimates				
α_j	−0.0717	−0.3660	−0.1465	0.0433
β_j	0.3700	0.3270	0.0995	0.0900
γ_j	−0.0183	−0.0154	−0.0033	0.0014
δ_j	0.0298	0.0172	0.0063	0.0029

Likelihood ratio test statistic = 8.5816

Summary

In this section we have shown how rational expectations introduces testable restrictions when applied to the term structure of interest rates. Whilst tests of these restrictions (using the likelihood ratio method) were favourable when applied to US data, they were unfavourable when applied to the term structure of UK interest rates. The section completes the chapter. We have seen that the introduction of rational expectations in macroeconomics has had (and can be expected to continue to have) widespread repercussions in macroeconomic models which emphasize the role of expectations.

10

Summary and Conclusions

10.1 THE RATIONAL EXPECTATIONS HYPOTHESIS

The central theme running through this book is the idea that if an economic variable is determined in line with a discernible process, rational people will form their expectation of that variable in accordance with that process, using all the relevant information (concerning the process) available to them at the time they form their expectation. That, in a nutshell, is the rational expectations hypothesis.

At first sight this idea might appear quite reasonable and innocuous. After all, why should people who have information on the process determining a variable not use it to improve their forecast of a variable? Or again why should they, as, for example, the adaptive expectations hypothesis suggests they might, form their expectation of a variable in accordance with a process that is at odds with the discernible process which the variable is following? One of the main achievements of the rational expectations hypothesis has been to raise these questions about alternative ways of modelling expectations and, in so doing, to force economic theorists to examine more closely than they did before the logic or theoretical underpinnings of the method of expectations formation which they assume when building an economic model in which expectations play a part.

The attractiveness of the rational expectations hypothesis lies in the fact that it meets two related criticisms of 'received theories' of expectation formation. First, many common methods of modelling expectations imply that forecast errors will display systematic and therefore predictable patterns. Do such theories of expectation formation explain why an obvious pattern to the forecast error does not alert the forecasting agent to his or her mistakes? Agents forming expectations 'purposefully' will surely use such information in forming new forecasts. Secondly, what reasons are put forward to explain why rational people do not use other relevant information relating to the process determining a variable which would help them make more accurate forecasts of that variable? Whilst this attack may not be fatal to other methods of expectation formation it should at least spur a search for more rigorous, and, one would hope, more fruitful alternatives to these other methods.

But the rational expectations hypothesis has done far more than put other theories of expectations formation on the defensive for, as we have seen, it has been used to generate distinctive and important predictions in many areas of macroeconomics. This is partly because of the pervasive importance of expectations in macroeconomics; partly because of the wide range of variables in macroeconomics which are seen as being determined by processes and to which therefore the rational expectations hypothesis can be applied; and partly because of the type of model with which the hypothesis is often combined. But it is mainly because in most of the areas in which the rational expectations hypothesis has been applied, the amount of information rational people are assumed to possess is sufficient to enable them to predict the predictable component of the process determining a variable. In other words the amount of information people are assumed to have relating to the process a variable is following is sufficient to ensure that the unanticipated component of that process is solely that part of the process which is inherently unpredictable.

This assumption about the amount of information rational agents possess is obviously very strong and, some would say, very unrealistic. It has been justified on a number of grounds. First, a world in which expectations are rationally formed but on the basis of a very restricted information set would be difficult to distinguish from a world in which expectations are not formed rationally. So, in order to make any distinctive, testable predictions, a strong assumption about the available information has to be made. A second reason is that it is difficult to establish general principles about what information to exclude from or include in the information set beyond the obvious principle that the actual future values of variables cannot be part of the current information set. It is therefore difficult to know what information it is reasonable to assume is not available to, or, more accurately, not used by rational people. In the absence of such general principles the exclusion of any information from the information set assumed to be possessed by rational people must be arbitrary. Because of this apparent lack of good theoretical reasons for assuming that rational people do not in fact use certain information which is available and could be helpful in forecasting a variable, economists employing the rational expectations hypothesis have on the whole assumed that none of the information about a process which they themselves are aware of, or their models suggest is important and available, is unused by or unknown to rational agents. The third and related reason for the strong assumption about the information set is that presumably information relevant to a process will tend to become more rather than less well known. Therefore, it is likely to become closer to rather than further from the truth to assume that the process a variable is following is known and that the information available to and used by rational people to forecast that variable is sufficient to allow them to forecast all but the inherently unpredictable component of that process.

This last sentence illustrates the sense in which rational expectations can be viewed as an equilibrium concept whereas other methods of forming expectations cannot be. For if other methods of forming expectations are assumed within an economic model there must be some scope to change and improve that method of forecasting. The whole model is not therefore in full equilibrium, something is likely to be changing. But once expectations are formed rationally this ceases to be the case, the whole model can then be in full equilibrium since there is no scope to improve on rational expectations. Thus by incorporating rational expectations into a model in which expected variables are important one can genuinely analyse the model in equilibrium, and compare the different equilibria that might arise if different assumptions are made about the process followed by, for example, certain policy variables.

With this in mind, some have argued that rational expectations is likely to be more useful when its application is to phenomena well known and understood by economic agents. In the macroeconomic context then, it is hardly surprising that rational expectations was first applied to the problem of the business cycle, as the following quotation from Lucas illustrates:

> In so far as business cycles can be viewed as repeated instances of essentially similar events, it will be reasonable . . . to assume [that economic agents'] expectations are rational, that [economic agents'] have fairly stable arrangements for collecting and processing information, and that they utilise this information in forecasting the future in a stable way, free of systematic and easily correctable biases. (Lucas, 1977, p. 15)

10.2 POLICY CONCLUSIONS

The basic principle of policy-making suggested by the rational expectations hypothesis is that policies are likely to fail if, to be effective, they require that people do not know or cannot discern the process actually determining those policies. The reason is of course that rational people can discern and understand the process determining a policy variable just as they can understand any other process. In accordance with this basic principle a key criterion for assessing a policy is whether it is likely to continue to achieve its aims when the policy has become widely known and predictable, and a key challenge in policy-making is to devise policies which satisfy this criterion. This will almost certainly make policy-making more difficult, indeed it may rule out the achievement of some targets of policy altogether because some targets can only be achieved if people make mistakes. Within any economic model it is generally possible to impose some arbitrary irrationality and thereby allow certain policies or policy processes to 'work'. An obvious example is the assumption of adaptive expectations of the rate of inflation within the natural rate of unemployment model. This assumption of irrationality allows a policy of continuously accelerating the rate of growth of aggregate demand to 'work' in securing a level of unemployment permanently below the natural level of unemployment. Such a policy would not work if expectations were assumed to be rational. The assumption of rationality, therefore, makes policy towards unemployment more difficult in that it rules out certain policies that would work under other assumptions, and indeed may imply that the target (in this case a lower level of unemployment than the natural rate) is not systematically achievable.

As we have stressed and illustrated throughout the book, expectations play an important role in many areas of macroeconomics, and so the general arguments stated in the previous paragraph can be applied to a wide range of macroeconomic policy problems. In fact, however, one macroeconomic policy problem in particular has been at the centre of the debate about rational expectations in macroeconomics and has been used to illustrate the general principles outlined above. This is the major problem of how best to ensure that an economy operates with a minimum of fluctuations around its long-run sustainable level of output and employment – the central problem analysed in Keynes's *General Theory* and still arguably *the* macroeconomic problem. The reason that this problem has been centre stage in the debate about rational expectations and macroeconomics is that in an early application of the rational expectations hypothesis to a familiar macroeconomic model, it was shown that the conventional Keynesian view of government stabilization policy would fail.

This demonstration thus provided what, at the time, appeared to be a startling counter-example to the then prevailing view that governments could best minimize an economy's output fluctuations by systematically varying its own expenditures and monetary policy to offset fluctuations in private sector spending. This counter-example was a jolt to most macroeconomists who saw the problem of stabilization policy primarily in terms of how to estimate macroeconomics models of the economy and from those estimates, derive precisely what systematic government policy variation would best achieve full employment stability. It seemed to suggest that such a view was fundamentally misconceived, and that to estimate models of the economy with the aim of working out precisely what systematic policy changes would stabilize output was a fruitless task. Changes in policy would influence real variables (such as output) only if they were unpredictable. But such changes could not be unpredictable if they were systematic for that characteristic implies that they are the result of a discernible and predictable process. Therefore no possible systematic policy manipulation could stabilize output any more efficiently than any other and hence it was a waste of effort trying to find one that would.

The force of this counter-example has weakened somewhat in recent years. This is partly because, as we have shown, it relies for its full strength on the combination of the rational expectations hypothesis with a particular model of how the economy works, a model which tends to emphasize the speed with which equilibrium is achieved by price movements and which many economists find unrealistic. It has also been weakened by the evidence – reviewed in chapter 8 – which emerged in response to the empirical studies of, for example, Lucas (1973) and Barro (1977a, 1978a) Barro and Rush (1980) and which seems to suggest that the rational expectations equilibrium model on which the counter example relies is a less than adequate explanation of many economies.

A further weakening has probably occurred as a result of the experience of a number of economies in the 1980s, in particular that of the UK. Following the election of Mrs Thatcher in May 1979 the UK Government announced what was called the Medium Term Financial Strategy, (MTFS), which amongst other things announced the rates of growth of the money supply it planned for the years 1979 to 1984, and also the size of the public sector borrowing requirement (PSBR) it planned for the same years. The rate of growth of the money supply was planned to fall gradually from 7 to 11 per cent in 1980/81 to 4 to 8 per cent in 1983/84; the PSBR as a percentage of GDP was planned to fall from 3.75 per cent in 1980/81 to 1.5 per cent in 1983/84. Both sets of plans were aimed to achieve a gradual reduction in the rate of growth of aggregate demand and thereby to reduce inflation. One of the main reasons given for publishing it was to provide a firm basis for expectations. To some economists the subsequent behaviour of the UK economy in response to the Thatcher government's policies amounts to a clear refutation of the rational expectations hypothesis. Their argument is that the policies to be carried out by the Thatcher government were laid bare in the MTFS and were therefore predictable. If people were rational they would use the MTFS to predict that the rate of growth of aggregate demand was set to fall. One would therefore have predicted, on the basis of the model developed in chapter 3, that in the UK there would have been a gradual fall in the rate of inflation but no significant rise in unemployment or drop in real output as a result. But, in actual fact, although the rate of inflation did drop significantly, the level of unemployment rose very sharply indeed. This was the main conclusion of a careful analysis of what has been termed the 'Thatcher experiment' by Buiter and Miller (1983). They summarize their findings thus:

> There is nothing in the behaviour of inflation, unemployment and output since 1979 to support the view that establishing the credibility of an anti-inflationary policy is by itself sufficient to achieve a desired reduction in inflation without appreciable costs in the form of increased unemployment and lost output. (Buiter and Miller, 1983, pp. 364–365)

However, the mere announcement of a policy does not necessarily imply that rational agents will believe that it will be pursued in fact. It is always possible to argue that the 'Thatcher experiment' was not a credible one. The possibility is raised in the following quote from Minford:

> It is quite wrong to suggest that merely 'announcing intentions' will itself establish a credible strategy. The Rational Expectations view of the economy has never made such a suggestion . . . The Rational Expectations view does however assert that, once fully believed, new policies will immediately condition expectations of inflation, output growth etc. However, assessing the speed at which this credibility will be attained is a highly uncertain matter. (Minford, 1980, p. 131)

The possible lack of credibility of monetary policies announced since 1979 has also figured in an analysis by Sargent (1981). He argued that in its early years the MTFS suffered a lack of credibility partly because a number of members of the government's own party, indeed its own Cabinet, were known to be sceptical of the approach adopted in the MTFS and to be ready to change it; partly because the large public sector deficits envisaged in the MTFS were hardly consistent with the planned reductions in the growth of the money supply; and partly because in the first year of the strategy it appeared to fall apart in that both monetary growth and the PSBR appeared to overshoot their targets quite substantially. All this suggests that rational agents may well not have been using the MTFS to predict the future rate of growth of aggregate demand. Instead they may have been rationally anticipating a continuation of previous policies, and been surprised by the declining rate of growth of aggregate demand that actually occurred.

At the moment it is too early to assess the importance of the behaviour of the UK economy in the early 1980s for testing the validity of the rational expectations hypothesis. All one can say is that that behaviour looks to be highly unfavourable to the hypothesis at least when it is combined with the sort of flexible price macroeconomic model developed in chapter 3. Of course if this judgement is confirmed then it would at most constitute one significant block of evidence against the rational expectations hypothesis. For a full assessment of the usefulness of the hypothesis one would need to consider all the other evidence too.

10.3 TESTS OF THE RATIONAL EXPECTATIONS HYPOTHESIS

Any hypothesis is ultimately judged on its usefulness in explaining data and on its ability to survive attempts to refute it. A vast amount of research in the last 10 years has been directed towards testing the rational expectations hypothesis in different macroeconomics contexts. We have been able to discuss in detail only a comparatively small number of these tests and many more results are likely to be published in the next few years, so any conclusions about the usefulness of the rational expectations hypothesis can, at the moment, be no more than tentative. However, one or two substantial points can be made.

First, the rational expectations hypothesis does appear to impose restrictions on what we should observe in macroeconomic data, and these restrictions are often quite demanding. In principle then one should be able to test the rational expectations hypothesis by testing for the validity of these restrictions. However, one problem dogs the testing of any hypothesis about expectations. It is that one can usually never test a hypothesis about expectations in isolation, one can only test it in combination with a particular model. The restrictions imposed by the rational expectations hypothesis are almost always dependent upon the model with which it is combined. Hence it is almost always possible to 'explain away' the failure of the rational expectations hypothesis to survive an attempt to refute it by arguing that the rest of the model is at fault. Only if one is absolutely certain (and one never really can be) about the model with which the rational expectations hypothesis is combined can one really be sure about whether it is the rational expectations hypothesis itself which is being tested. In practice, if in a variety of contexts, the rational expectations hypothesis is consistently rejected, this will suggest – though not prove – that the rational expectations assumption is itself invalid.

Bearing this important qualification in mind, it would appear at the moment that the evidence in favour of the rational expectations hypothesis within macroeconomics is very mixed. Certain early empirical studies suggested that the hypothesis, when combined with the 'natural rate hypothesis', might be a useful one in macroeconomics (in particular the studies of Lucas and Barro discussed in chapter 7). More recently that evidence has been seriously questioned along the lines explained in chapter 8. As we indicated in that chapter some of the evidence points to the failure of the underlying model – what we termed 'structural neutrality' – rather than to the failure of rational expectations itself. The case studies discussed in chapter 9 also reveal at best only moderate support; in particular the application of the rational expectations hypothesis to the foreign exchange market – a market in which one might expect the assumptions behind the rational expectations hypothesis to hold more firmly than in other markets – has proved only mildly successful. But again we stressed the fact that the rational expectations hypothesis can only be tested conditional on the truth of the underlying model with which it is combined. There can be little doubt that the rational expectations hypothesis will continue to be attractive to those estimating models in which expectations play a prominent role.

10.4 CONCLUSIONS

The rational expectations hypothesis has made a major impact on macro-economics. It has fundamentally changed the way in which expectations are dealt with and has stressed that a requirement for a successful macro-economic policy is that it does not rely on consistently being unpredicted. However, it has not yet established itself as an empirically sound hypothesis. If it does not do so then its major contribution will probably be to force economic theorists to put forward alternatives to it which are theoretically sounder than existing alternatives and empirically sounder than the rational expectations hypothesis itself.

Bibliography

Abel, A.B. and Mishkin, F.S. (1983) An integrated view of tests of rationality, market efficiency and the short run neutrality of monetary policy, *Journal of Monetary Economics*, **11**, pp. 3–23.

Alberro, J. (1981) The Lucas hypothesis on the Phillips curve: Further international evidence, *Journal of Monetary Economics*, **7**, pp. 239–50.

Alogoskoufis, G. and Pissarides, C.A. (1983) A test of price sluggishness in the simple rational expectations model: UK 1950–1980, *Economic Journal*, **93**, pp. 616–628.

Ando, A. and Modigliani, F. (1963) The 'life cycle' hypothesis of saving: Aggregate implications and tests, *American Economic Review*, **53**, pp. 53–84.

Attfield, C.L.F. (1983) An analysis of the implications of omitting variables from the monetary growth equation in a model of real output and unanticipated money growth, *European Economic Review*, **23**, pp. 281–90.

Attfield, C.L.F. and Browning, M.J. (1984) A differential demand system, rational expectations, and the life cycle hypothesis, *Econometrica* (forthcoming).

Attfield, C.L.F., Demery, D. and Duck, N.W. (1981a) Unanticipated monetary growth, output and the price level: UK 1946–1977, *European Economic Review*, **16**, pp. 367–85.

Attfield, C.L.F., Demery, D. and Duck, N.W. (1981b) A quarterly model of unanticipated monetary growth, output and the price level in the UK 1963–1978, *Journal of Monetary Economics*, **8**, pp. 331–50.

Attfield, C.L.F. and Duck, N.W. (1982) Tests of the rational expectations model of the term structure of UK interest rates, *Economics Letters*, **10**, pp. 115–121.

Attfield, C.L.F. and Duck, N.W. (1983) The influence of unanticipated money growth on real output: Some cross country estimates, *Journal of Money, Credit and Banking*, **15**, pp. 442–454.

Azariadis, C. (1975) Implicit contracts and underemployment equilibria, *Journal of Political Economy*, **83**, pp. 1183–1202.

Baillie, R.T., Lippens, R.E. and McMahon, P.C. (1983) Testing rational expectations and efficiency in the foreign exchange market, *Econometrica*, **51**, pp. 553–564.

Baily, M.N. (1974) Wages and employment under uncertain demand, *Review of Economic Studies*, **41**, pp. 37–50.

Barro, R.J. (1976) Rational expectations and the role of monetary policy, *Journal of Monetary Economics*, **2**, pp. 1–33.

Barro, R.J. (1977a) Unanticipated money growth and unemployment in the United States, *American Economic Review*, **67**, pp. 101–15.

Barro, R.J. (1977b) Long term contracting, sticky prices, and monetary policy, *Journal of Monetary Economics*, **3**, pp. 305–316.

Barro, R.J. (1978a) Unanticipated money, output and the price level in the United States, *Journal of Political Economy*, **86**, pp. 549–80.

Barro, R.J. (1978b) A stochastic equilibrium model of an open economy under flexible exchange rates, *Quarterly Journal of Economics*, **92**, pp. 149–164.

Barro, R.J. and Grossman, H.I. (1971) A general disequilibrium model of income and employment, *American Economic Review*, **61**, pp. 82–93.

Barro, R.J. and Rush, M. (1980) Unanticipated money and economic activity, in *Rational Expectations and Economic Policy* (Ed. S. Fischer), University of Chicago Press for National Bureau of Economic Research, Chicago.

Bean, C. (1983) A little bit more evidence on the natural rate hypothesis from the UK, *Centre for Labour Economics*; London School of Economics Discussion Paper, no. 149.

Begg, D.K.H. (1982) *The Rational Expectations Revolution in Macroeconomics*, Philip Allan, Oxford.

Bilson, J.F.O. (1980) The rational expectations approach to the consumption function, *European Economic Review*, **13**, pp. 273–299.

Bilson, J.F.O. (1981) The 'Speculative Efficiency' Hypothesis, *Journal of Business*, **54**, pp. 435–451.

Blinder, A.S. and Fischer, S. (1981) Inventories, rational expectations and the business cycle, *Journal of Monetary Economics*, **8**, pp. 277–304.

Buiter, W.H. (1980) The macroeconomics of Dr. Pangloss, *Economic Journal*, **90**, pp. 34–50.

Buiter, W.H. (1983) Real effects of anticipated money: Some problems of estimation and hypothesis testing, *Journal of Monetary Economics*, **11**, pp. 207–24.

Buiter, W.H. and Miller, M. (1981a) The Thatcher experiment: the first two years, *Brookings Papers in Economic Activity*, pp. 315–80.

Buiter, W.H. and Miller, M. (1981b) Monetary policy and international competitiveness: The problems of adjustment, in W.A. Eltis and P.J.N. Sinclair (eds), *The Money Supply and The Exchange Rate*, Clarendon Press: Oxford.

Buiter, W.H. and Miller, H.M. (1983) Changing the rules: Economic consequences of the Thatcher regime, *Brookings Papers on Economic Activity*, **2**, pp. 305–365.

Cagan, P. (1956) The monetary dynamics of hyperinflation, in M. Friedman (ed.) *Studies in the Quantity Theory of Money*, Chicago, University of Chicago Press.

Calvo, G. and Rodriguez, C. (1977) A model of exchange rate determination under currency substitution and rational expectations, *Journal of Political Economy*, **84**, pp. 617–625.

Carlson, J.A. (1977) A study of price forecasts, *Annals of Economic and Social Measurement*, **6**, pp. 27–56.

Cornell, B. (1977) Spot rates, Forward rates and exchange market efficiency, *Journal of Financial Economics*, **5**, pp. 55–66.

Cosset, J.C. (1984) On the presence of risk premiums in foreign exchange markets, *Journal of International Economics*, **16**, pp. 139–154.

Cox, W.M. (1980) Unanticipated money, output and prices in the small open economy, *Journal of Monetary Economics*, **6**, pp. 359–384.

Daly, V. and Hadjimatheou, G. (1981) Stochastic implications of the life cycle – permanent income hypothesis: Evidence for the UK economy, *Journal of Political Economy*, **89**, pp. 596–599.

Davidson, J.E.H. and Hendry, D.F. (1981) Interpreting econometric evidence: The behaviour of consumers' expenditure in the UK, *European Economic Review*, **16**, pp. 177–192.

Davidson, J.E.H., Hendry, D.F., Srba, F. and Yeo, S. (1978) Econometric modelling of the aggregate time series relationship between consumers' expenditure and income in the UK, *The Economic Journal*, **88**, pp. 661–692.

Demery, D. (1984) Aggregate demand rational expectations and real output: Some new evidence for the UK 1963.2 – 1982.2, *Economic Journal* (forthcoming).

Demery, D., and Duck, N.W. (1984) Inventories and monetary growth in the business cycle: Some theoretical considerations and empirical results for the UK, *The Manchester School* (forthcoming).

Demery, D., Duck, N.W., and Musgrave, S.W. (1983) Price Sluggishness in the UK: an alternative view, *University of Bristol Discussion Paper*.

Demery, D., Duck, N.W. and Musgrave, S.W. (1984) Unanticipated money growth, output and unemployment in West Germany 1964–1981, *Weltwirtschaftliches Archiv* (forthcoming).

Dornbusch, R. (1976) Expectations and Exchange Rate Dynamics, *Journal of Political Economy*, **84**, pp. 1161–1176.

Dornbusch, R. (1980a) *Open Economy Macroeconomics*, Basic Books, New York.

Dornbusch, R. (1980b) Exchange rate economics: Where do we stand? *Brookings Papers on Economic Activity*, **1**, pp. 143–185.

Driskill, R. (1981) Exchange rate overshooting, The trade balance and rational expectations, *Journal of International Economics*, **11**, pp. 361–377.

Duck, N.W. (1983) The effects of uncertainty about the money supply process in a rational expectations macroeconomic model, *Scottish Journal of Political Economy*, **30**, pp. 142–152.

Duck, N.W. (1984) Prices, Output and the balance of payments in an open economy with rational expectations, *Journal of International Economics*, **16**, pp. 59–78.

Edwards, S. (1983) Floating exchange rates, expectations and new information, *Journal of Monetary Economics*, **11**, pp. 321–336.

Fellner, W. (1980) The valid core of rationality hypotheses in the theory of expectations, *Journal of Money, Credit and Banking*, **12**, pp. 763–87

Figlewski, S. and Wachtel, P. (1981) The formation of inflationary expectations, *Review of Economics and Statistics*, **58**, pp. 1–10.

Fischer, S. (1977) Long-term contracts, rational expectations and the optimal money supply rule, *Journal of Political Economy*, **85**, pp. 191–205.

Flavin, M. (1981) The adjustment of consumption to changing expectations about future income, *Journal of Political Economy*, **89**, pp. 974–1009.

Flemming, J.S. (1976) *Inflation*, Oxford, Oxford University Press.

Frenkel, J.A. (1980) The forward exchange rate, expectations and the demand for money – The German hyperinflation: Reply, *American Economic Review*, **70**, pp. 771–775.

Frenkel, J.A. (1981) Flexible exchange rates, prices and the role of 'News': Lessons from the 1970's *Journal of Political Economy*, **89**, pp. 665–705.

Frenkel, J.A. and Razin, A. (1980) Stochastic prices and tests of efficiency of foreign exchange markets, *Economics Letters*, **6**, pp. 165–170.

Friedman, B.M. (1980) Survey evidence on the 'Rationality' of interest rate expectations, *Journal of Monetary Economics*, **6**, pp. 453–65.

Friedman, B.M. (1979) Optimal expectations and the extreme information assumptions of rational expectations macromodels, *Journal of Monetary Economics*, **5**, pp. 23–41.

Friedman, M. (1957) *A Theory of the Consumption Function*, Princeton, Princeton University Press for National Bureau of Economic Research, Princeton.

Friedman, M. (1959) *A Program for Monetary Stability*, New York, Fordham University Press.

Friedman, M. (1968) The role of monetary policy, *American Economic Review*, **58**, pp. 1–17.

Friedman, M. and Schwartz, A.J. (1982) *Monetary Trends in the United States and the United Kingdom*, Chicago, University of Chicago Press.

Gordon, D.F. (1974) A neoclassical theory of Keynesian unemployment, *Economic Inquiry*, **12**, pp. 431–59.

Gordon, R.J. (1982) Price inertia and policy ineffectiveness in the United States, 1890–1980, *Journal of Political Economy*, **90**, pp. 1087–1117.

Gray, J.A. (1976) Wage indexation: a macroeconomic approach, *Journal of Monetary Economics* **2**, pp. 221–235.

Hakkio, C.S. (1981) Expectations and the forward exchange rate, *International Economic Review*, **22**, pp. 663–678.

Hall, R.E. (1978) Stochastic implications of the life cycle – permanent income hypothesis: Theory and evidence, *Journal of Political Economy*, **86**, pp. 971–987.

Hall, R.E. (1981) Comments: 'Interpreting Economic Evidence' by Davidson and Hendry, *European Economic Review*, **16**, pp. 193–194.

Hansen, L.P. and Hodrick, R.J. (1980) Forward exchange rates as optimal predictors of future spot rates: An economic analysis, *Journal of Political Economy*, **88**, pp. 829–853.

Hanson, J.A. (1980) The short-run relations between growth and inflation in Latin America, *American Economic Review*, **70**, pp. 972–89.

Hayashi, F. (1982) The permanent income hypothesis: Estimation and testing by instrumental variables, *Journal of Political Economy*, **90**, pp. 895–916.

Hoffman, D.L. and Schmidt, P. (1981) Testing the restrictions implied by the rational expectations hypothesis, *Journal of Econometrics* **15**, pp. 265–87.

Hudson, J. (1982) *Inflation: A Theoretical Survey and Synthesis*, London, George Allen & Unwin.

Johnston, J. (1972) *Econometric Methods*, New York (2nd edition) McGraw-Hill.

Keynes, J.M. (1936) *The General Theory of Employment, Interest and Money*, London, Macmillan.

Kormendi, R.C. and Meguire, P.G. (1984) The real output effects of monetary shocks: cross country tests of rational expectations propositions, *Journal of Political Economy* (forthcoming).

Koskela, E. and Viren, M. (1980) New international evidence on output inflation trade-offs: A note, *Economics Letters*, **6**, pp. 233–39.

Krueger, A.O. (1983) *Exchange Rate Determination*, Cambridge University Press: Cambridge.

Kydland, F.E. and Prescott, E.C. (1977) Rules rather than discretion: the inconsistency of optimal plans, *Journal of Political Economy*, **85**, pp. 473–91.

Lawrence, C. (1983) Rational Expectations, supply shocks and the stability of the inflation output trade-off. Some time series evidence for the United Kingdom 1956–1977, *Journal of Monetary Economics*, **11**, pp. 225–46.

Leiderman, L. (1980) Macroeconometric testing of the rational expectations and structural neutrality hypothesis for the United States, *Journal of Monetary Economics*, **6**, pp. 69–82.

Lucas, R.E. Jr. (1972) Expectations and the neutrality of money, *Journal of Economic Theory*, **4**, pp. 103–24.

Lucas, R.E. Jr. (1973) Some international evidence on output–inflation trade offs, *American Economic Review*, **63**, pp. 326–34.

Lucas, R.E. Jr. (1975) An equilibrium model of the business cycle, *Journal of Political Economy*, **83**, pp. 1113–44.

Lucas, R.E. Jr. (1976) Econometric policy evaluation: A critique, in K. Brunner and A.H. Meltzer (eds) The Phillips Curve and Labour Markets, *Supplement to the Journal of Monetary Economics*.

Lucas R.E. Jr. (1977) Understanding business cycles, in K. Brunner and A.H. Meltzer (ed) *Stabilisation of the Domestic and International Economy*, Amsterdam, North Holland.

Lucas, R.E. Jr. and Sargent, T.J. (1978) After Keynesian macroeconomics, in *After the Phillips Curve: Persistence of High Inflation and High Unemployment*, Federal Reserve Bank of Boston, Conference Series No. 19.

McCallum, B.T. (1976) Rational expectations and the natural rate hypothesis: Some consistent estimates, *Econometrica*, **44**, pp. 43–52.

McCallum, B.T. (1977) Price level stickiness and the feasibility of monetary stabilisation policy under rational expectations, *Journal of Political Economy*, **85**, pp. 627–34.

McCallum, B.T. (1978) Price level adjustments and the rational expectations approach to macroeconomic stabilisation policy, *Journal of Money, Credit and Banking*, **10**, pp. 418–36.

McCallum, B.T. (1979) On the observational inequivalence of classical and Keynesian models, *Journal of Political Economy*, **87**, pp. 395–402.

McCallum, B.T. (1980) Rational expectations and macroeconomic stabilisation policy, *Journal of Money, Credit and Banking*, **12**, pp. 716–46.

Maddala, G.S. (1977) *Econometrics*, New York, McGraw-Hill.

Malinvaud, E. (1977) *The Theory of Unemployment Reconsidered*, Oxford, Blackwell.

Marini, G. (1985) Intertemporal substitution and the role of monetary policy, *Economic Journal* (forthcoming).

Minford, P. (1980) Memorandum in House of Commons, Treasury and Civil Service Committee, *Memorandum on Monetary Policy* (No. 720).

Minford, P. and Peel, D. (1983) *Rational Expectations and the New Macro-economics*, Oxford, Martin Robertson.

Mishkin, F. (1982a) Does anticipated monetary policy matter? An econometric investigation, *Journal of Political Economy*, **90**, pp. 22–50.

Mishkin, F. (1982b) Does anticipated aggregate demand policy matter? *American Economic Review*, **72**, pp. 788–802.

Muellbauer, J. (1983) Surprises in the consumption function, *Economic Journal*, **93**, Supplement, pp. 34–50.

Muellbauer, J. and Portes, R. (1978) Macroeconomic models with quantity rationing, *Economic Journal*, **88**, pp. 788–821.

Muth, J.F. (1960) Optimal properties of exponentially weighted forecasts, *Journal of the American Statistical Association*, **55**, pp. 299–306.

Muth, J.F. (1961) Rational expectations and the theory of price movements, *Econometrica*, **29**, pp. 315–35.

Neary, J.P. and Stiglitz J.E. (1983) Toward a reconstruction of Keynesian economics: Expectations and constrained equilibria, *Quarterly Journal of Economics*, **98**, Supplement, pp. 199–228.

Parkin, M. and Bade, R. (1982) *Modern Macroeconomics*, Oxford, Phillip Allan.

Pearce, D.K. (1979) Comparing survey and rational measures of expected inflation, *Journal of Money, Credit and Banking*, **11**, pp. 447–56.

Pesando, J.E. (1975) A note on the rationality of the Livingston price expectations, *Journal of Political Economy*, **83**, pp. 849–58.

Pesaran, M.H. (1982) A critique of the proposed tests of the natural rate–rational expectations hypothesis, *Economic Journal*, **92**, pp. 529–554.

Phelps, E.S. (1967) Phillips Curves, Expectations of inflation and optimal unemployment over time, *Economica*, **34**, pp. 254–281.

Phelps, E.S. (1970) The New Microeconomics in Employment and Inflation Theory, in E. S. Phelps et al. (eds) *Microeconomic Foundations of Employment and Inflation Theory*, New York, Norton, pp. 1–27.

Phelps, E.S. and Taylor, J.B. (1977) The stabilising powers of monetary policy under rational expectations, *Journal of Political Economy*, **85**, pp. 165–90.

Revankar, N.S. (1980) Testing of the rational expectations hypothesis, *Econometrica*, **48**, pp. 1347–64.

Sargent, T.J. (1976a) The observational equivalence of natural and unnatural rate theories of macroeconomics, *Journal of Political Economy*, **84**, pp. 631–640.

Sargent, T.J. (1976b) A classical macroeconometric model of the United States, *Journal of Political Economy*, **84**, pp. 207–38.

Sargent, T.J. (1979) A note on maximum likelihood estimation of the rational expectations model of the term structure, *Journal of Monetary Economics*, **5**, pp. 133–143.

Sargent, T.J. (1981) Stopping moderate inflation: the methods of Poincare and Thatcher, *University of Minnesota Discussion Paper*.

Sargent, T.J. and Wallace, N. (1975) Rational expectations, the optimal monetary instrument and the optimal money supply rule, *Journal of Political Economy*, **83**, pp. 241–54.

Sargent, T.J. and Wallace, N. (1981) Some unpleasant monetarist arithmetic, *Quarterly Review, Fall,* Federal Reserve Bank of Minneapolis, pp. 1–17.

Shackle, G.L.S. (1958) *Time in Economics*, Amsterdam, North Holland.

Sheffrin, S.M. (1983) *Rational Expectations*, Cambridge, Cambridge University Press.

Shiller, R.J. (1978) Rational expectations and the dynamic structure of macro-economic models, *Journal of Monetary Economics*, **4**, pp. 1–44.

Shiller, R.J. (1980) Alternative tests of rational expectations models: The case of the term structure, (Working Paper No. 563: National Bureau of Economic Research).

Siegel, J.J. (1972) Risk, interest rates and the forward exchange, *Quarterly Journal of Economics*, **86**, pp. 303–309.

Solow, R.M. and Stiglitz, J.E. (1968) Output, employment and wages in the short run, *Quarterly Journal of Economics*, **82**, pp. 537–60.

Taylor, J.B. (1979) Staggered wage setting in macroeconomic model, *American Economic Review Papers and Proceedings*, **69**, pp. 108–13.

Tobin, J. (1961) Money, capital and other stores of value, *American Economic Review Papers and Proceedings*, **51**, pp. 26–37.

Turnovsky, S.J. (1970) Some empirical evidence on the formation of price expectations, *Journal of the American Statistical Association*, **65**, pp. 1441–54.

Turnovsky, S.J. (1980) The choice of monetary instruments under alternative forms of price expectations, *The Manchester School*, **45**, pp. 39–63.

Wallis, K.F. (1980) Econometric implications of the rational expectations hypothesis, *Econometrica*, **48**, pp. 49–73.

Walters, A.A. (1971) Consistent expectations, distributed lags and the quantity theory, *Economic Journal*, **81**, pp. 273–281.

Weber, W. (1981) Output variability under monetary policy and exchange rate rules, *Journal of Political Economy*, **89**, pp. 733–751.

Weiss, L. (1980) The role for active monetary policy in a rational expectations model, *Journal of Political Economy*, **88**, pp. 221–33.

Wickens, M.R. (1982), The efficient estimation of econometric models with rational expectations, *Review of Economic Studies*, **49**, pp. 55–67.

Wickens, M.R. and Molana, H. (1984) Stochastic life cycle theory with varying interest rates and prices, *The Economic Journal*, **94**, Supplement, pp. 133–147.

Wogin, G. (1980) Unemployment and monetary policy under rational expectations: Some Canadian evidence, *Journal of Monetary Economics*, **6**, pp. 59–68.

Author Index

Subject Index